Piccadilly

Also by Midge Gillies

Army Wives: From Crimea to Afghanistan: The Real Lives of the Women Behind the Men in Uniform

Literary Non-Fiction: A Writers & Artists' Companion

The Barbed-Wire University: The Real Lives of Allied Prisoners of War in the Second World War

Writing Lives: Literary Biography

Waiting for Hitler: Britain on the Brink of Invasion

Amy Johnson: Queen of the Air

Marie Lloyd: The One and Only

Piccadilly

The Circus at the Heart of London

Midge Gillies

TWO ROADS

First published in Great Britain in 2022 by Two Roads
An Imprint of John Murray Press
An Hachette UK company

1

Map by Barking Dog Art

A CIP catalogue record for this title is available from the British Library

Hardback ISBN 978 1 529 33971 0
eBook ISBN 978 1 529 33974 1

Typeset in Sabon MT Std by Palimpsest Book Production Ltd, Falkirk, Stirlingshire

Printed and bound in Great Britain by Clays Ltd, Elcograf S.p.A.

John Murray policy is to use papers that are natural, renewable and
recyclable products and made from wood grown in sustainable forests.
The logging and manufacturing processes are expected to conform
to the environmental regulations of the country of origin.

Two Roads
Carmelite House
50 Victoria Embankment
London EC4Y 0DZ

www.tworoadsbooks.com

To Dr Clare Makepeace (1979-2019)
An irreplaceable friend and a fine historian.

Contents

Part Four: Lights, Camera, Action!

Part Five: The Blackout

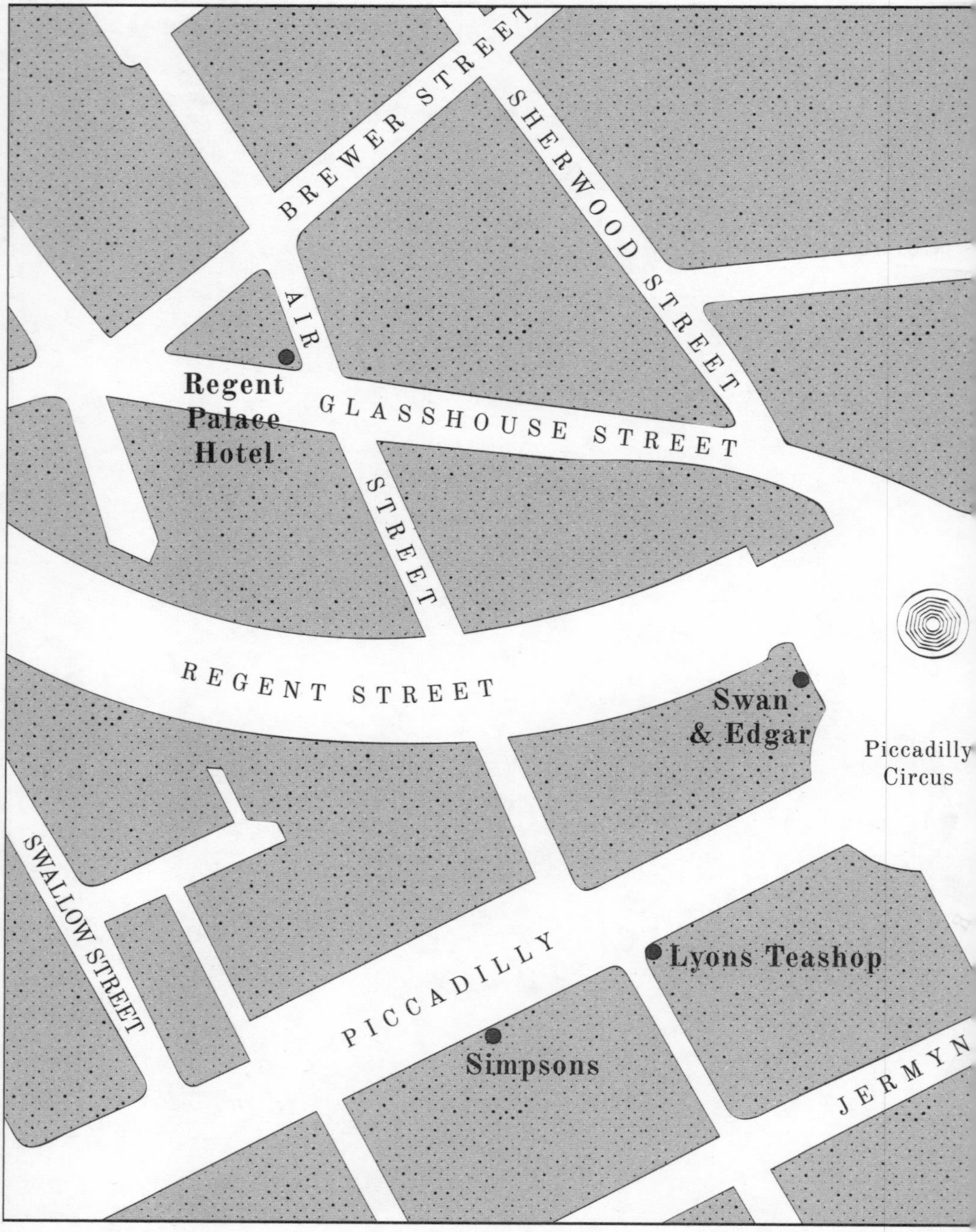
BREWER STREET
SHERWOOD STREET
AIR STREET
Regent Palace Hotel
GLASSHOUSE STREET
REGENT STREET
Swan & Edgar
Piccadilly Circus
SWALLOW STREET
PICCADILLY
Lyons Teashop
Simpsons
JERMYN

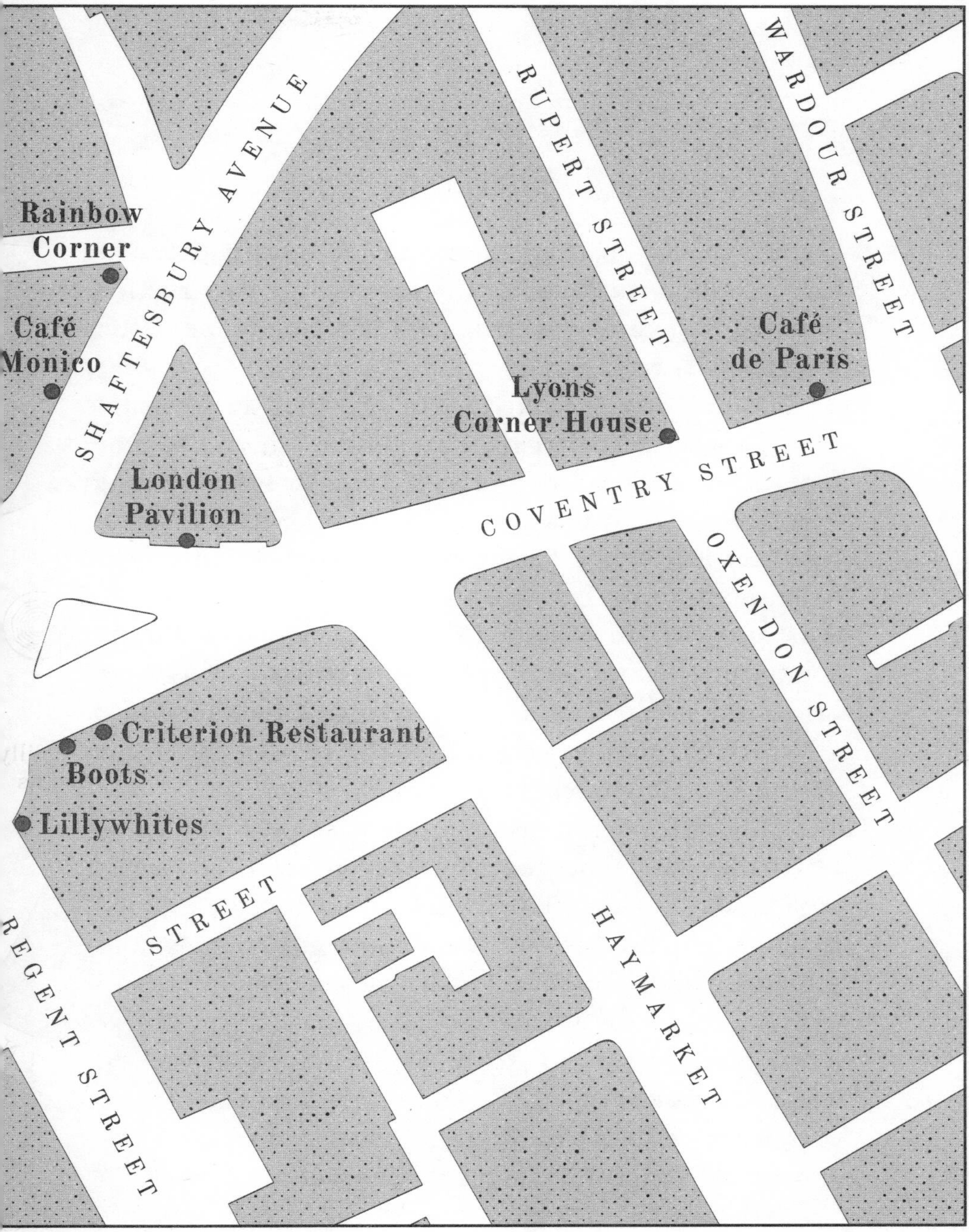

SHAFTESBURY AVENUE
RUPERT STREET
WARDOUR STREET
Rainbow Corner
Café Monico
Café de Paris
Lyons Corner House
London Pavilion
COVENTRY STREET
OXENDON STREET
Criterion Restaurant
Boots
Lillywhites
STREET
REGENT STREET
HAYMARKET

Key Buildings of Piccadilly Circus

Boots, the chemist, opened 'Store 1000' in 1925, opposite its current position in Piccadilly Circus, as part of the Criterion Building. It became the company's first twenty-four-hour, seven-days-a-week shop.

The **Café de Paris,** a subterranean nightclub in Coventry Street, opened just after the First World War and became famous for daring acts and as a place to see promising new performers. It was also well known for its glamorous customers, including Bright Young Things and members of European royal families.

The ornate **Criterion restaurant**'s central position and discreet comfort made it the ideal venue for meetings such as those held by the suffragettes, or for courting couples who needed a respectable place to take tea. Its theatre was one of the first to be built entirely underground.

James Lillywhite opened his first shop in 1863 at number 31 Haymarket and concentrated on selling items connected with cricket. In 1925 **Lillywhites** moved to the Criterion Building and became well known for outfitting famous sportsmen and women and pilots such as Amy Johnson.

The **London Pavilion** started as a song-and-supper annexe to the Black Horse Inn and became a music hall in 1861. The building was replaced in 1885 with a theatre of varieties where stars such as Marie Lloyd and Vesta Tilley appeared. In 1918 it became a theatre and was famous for spectacular reviews. In 1934 it was converted to a cinema, which closed in 1982. Its façade still stands.

The first **Lyons Teashop** opened in 1894 at 213 Piccadilly and offered affordable food in a clean and respectable setting, served by Nippy waitresses.

Lyons Corner House in Coventry Street was built in 1907 and became part of a chain of restaurants in London offering a wide range of food at reasonable prices. The Piccadilly restaurant could seat 4,500 diners and provided a safe meeting place for groups such as young women and gay men in a room known as the Lilypond.

The **Regent Palace Hotel**, part of the Lyons catering empire, offered affordable accommodation in a glamorous, art deco setting squeezed between Brewer, Sherwood, Glasshouse and Air streets. When it opened in 1915 it was the largest hotel in Europe and had 1,028 bedrooms; at its height it employed over 1,000 staff.

Rainbow Corner, the Red Cross Club at 23 Shaftesbury Avenue, on the corner of Denman Street, provided a 'home from home' of entertainment, food, friendship and advice for American servicemen in London during the Second World War.

Simpsons, originally a menswear's department store, opened in 1936 at 203 Piccadilly and became famous for its modernist frontage and avant-garde window displays. It closed in 1998 and is now the Waterstones flagship bookstore.

Swan & Edgar began life in the early nineteenth century as a haberdashery stall run by William Edgar, the son of a farmer, who was reported to sleep under his stall. He joined forces with fellow stallholder George Swan to create a shop that eventually expanded into a department store specialising in supplying actors, music hall stars and dancers with copies of the latest Paris fashions. Its customer base grew with the advent of the underground and the revolution in department stores. Its frontage was rebuilt between 1910 and 1920 and its café became a favourite meeting place for courting couples.

Introduction: 'Meet Me under the Guinness Clock'

There's nowhere quite like Piccadilly Circus.

Its cat's cradle of streets and alleyways creates an intoxicating thoroughfare with the power to propel an individual onwards to adventure, romance, or something more sinister. Arriving can feel like stepping onto a giant roulette wheel. A visit can lead to an illicit kiss, an act of rebellion or protest, a shady hotel suite, a comforting cup of tea, a mind-expanding, drug-fuelled 'trip', or a comfy pair of new slacks. It's a place of bright lights that make it difficult to hide.

Shoppers from Oxford Circus stagger, laden with bags, down Regent Street. Shaftesbury Avenue offers a starry pathway to Theatreland, Soho and Chinatown. Monopoly's very own Coventry Street links Piccadilly Circus to the cinemas of nearby Leicester Square, while Haymarket and Lower Regent Street take the visitor to Trafalgar Square's art galleries and, eventually, Parliament. The great thoroughfare of Piccadilly itself goes west, ushering us to refined shopping arcades, exclusive clubs and hushed restaurants.

Piccadilly Circus exists at different levels. Climbing the Tube steps encourages you to look up and, if you do, you can't fail to notice the on-high grandeur of the place: the green dome of the former County Fire Office with Britannia looking down on passers-by, the classical opulence of the London Pavilion and the Victorian fussiness of the Criterion Building. No other tourist destination in the capital straddles the hub of such sharply contrasting thoroughfares or is studded with such an array of different buildings.

I remember the first time I visited Piccadilly Circus. It was the 1970s and my mother and I took the train from Suffolk to buy the hockey boots I needed as I made the transition to secondary school. For my mother, the only possible shop to buy them from was Lillywhites. It wasn't that sports shops didn't exist in East Anglia; rather, going to that particular store represented a rite of passage for her. She spoke wistfully of Lyons Teashop and Corner House and told me how she used to visit them in her Sunday best with her beloved only sister, after whom I was named. Here they would exchange wartime confidences behind steamed-up windows or assess a new boyfriend while a better class of waitress hovered nearby, always on the move and careful not to show that she had heard everything that had been said.

Once I started to go to the capital alone, and eventually to live there, I collected my own Piccadilly memories. It was the obvious place to meet friends before we went to see a film or ventured into Soho's alleyways to find somewhere to eat or drink. As I emerged from the depths of the Tube station, with its elegant columns and shiny floors, to the brilliance of Piccadilly Circus's shop windows and glowing adverts, I had to make a conscious effort to compose my face, to resist the impulse to 'ooh' and 'ahh'. I've never lost that feeling of wonder.

Piccadilly Circus is the ideal meeting place because it has turned gatherings into an art form. The constant comings and goings offer rich pickings for anyone who enjoys people-watching and its position at the confluence of so many distinct areas means you're just as likely to rub shoulders with an actor as you are with a sex worker, that you'll be in a sea of tourists but also in the midst of people who view themselves as quintessential Londoners, you'll pass chambermaids on their way to turn back the covers on luxury beds and guests ready to dive into them, shop assistants on their lunch break and shoppers hell-bent on spending.

The area was a '24/7' sort of place long before that term existed. Decades ahead of round-the-clock news, it was thrilling to know that you could buy the next day's paper from a vendor who would cut the string holding the bundle of newspapers together with a knife used solely for that purpose before he handed you tomorrow's headlines. I always found it reassuring, too, that if the bright lights had given you a headache, Boots the Chemists was there for out-of-hours pain relief. Even the birds, who continue to chirrup as you approach Leicester Square after dark from Coventry Street, recognise that they have entered a world where normal rules don't apply.

When I worked in a magazine office in nearby Soho, Piccadilly Circus acted as a bridge between that sleazy part of London and the Mayfair that I knew was out of my league socially. It was a liminal space where anything went and where, for a night at least, you could be someone else. I remember eating in a new restaurant near Piccadilly Circus with a friend from work. There was something different about the venue, but we couldn't quite put our finger on it. It wasn't until the main course arrived that we realised that we were the only diners not in drag. We were underdressed, but welcomed. It didn't seem at all surprising that, when we searched for the restaurant a few weeks later, it had vanished into thin air.

Piccadilly Circus's success as a meeting place for people from different backgrounds, classes, sexualities and ethnicities has put it at the forefront of social change. Its hotels, restaurants and cafés have long proved safe havens for women, for people new to the capital and for same-sex couples, among others, and in doing so it has changed attitudes and helped to initiate legislation. The rich and privileged have encountered people outside their social milieu on the stage or the Tube, or in a shop or café, and those encounters have slimmed down the yawning gaps in our social hierarchies. Likewise, the less privileged, from sales assistants to shoppers visiting from outside London, have got to know a world they might otherwise not have come across.

From the very start of its history, Piccadilly Circus quickly became an important meeting place, and as its popularity grew during the early decades of the twentieth century it became *the* meeting place for different groups of people. The arches of the County Fire Office on the north-west side provided the first spark of romance for many gay couples, and Lyons Corner House in Coventry Street welcomed both gay men and young women who were starting to earn an independent living for the first time in the early twentieth century. Here, and at the first Lyons Teashop, at 213 Piccadilly, female friends swapped confidences over a scalding hot drink and a slice of Swiss roll in a setting that was both affordable and respectable. The Criterion restaurant and the fifth-floor tearooms at Swan & Edgar created a similar haven for young women, although tea came with a higher price tag. The Regent Palace Hotel, another part of the Lyons empire, turned a blind eye to illicit meetings of all kinds and, during the Second World War, GIs found a 'home from home' in Rainbow Corner, in a club that threw away its key to make the point that it never closed.

Within Piccadilly itself there is no more famous meeting

place than the unassuming steps of Eros – the god who presides over the area – where, at first, flower girls, shoe-shiners and newspaper-sellers gathered to sell their wares and where, later, courting couples and early tourists came to watch the world go by. Over the years Eros has been moved about the Circus to accommodate traffic and underground work,[1] but has never lost his allure. For over a hundred years, his steps have provided a unique view of London – for visitors taking in the capital for the first time, immigrants sizing up their new home, or hippies just 'hanging out'.

It is still a place to meet friends and to gather with kindred spirits. While writing this book I've watched Scottish football fans tentatively climb Eros wrapped in their team's flag to touch, with reverence, the god's foot before retreating to the safety of ground level. I've made my own pilgrimage to the Criterion Theatre and emerged after the show to what appeared to be a spontaneous flash mob but which, in reality, was probably a carefully planned advertising stunt. It was an early outing for my daughter's new bubblegum-pink hair and, when a young woman bounced up to us, we assumed she was about to ask for money. Instead, she beamed, 'I *love* your hair!' before fading into the crowds. It was the sort of fleeting encounter that Piccadilly Circus does so well and which leaves you feeling that the world is full of opportunities. For me, it reinforced the idea of Piccadilly Circus as *the* meeting place and a location that belongs to everyone – no matter their background.

This coming together of such a variety of different people is at its most startling when they gather to witnesses celebration or protest. Campaigners and revellers make their way to Piccadilly Circus to lean into the weight of past gatherings, from the Relief of Mafeking in 1900 to the end of two world wars, and because of an intimacy and spontaneity that is lacking in other places of protest or celebration. Nearby Trafalgar Square is too sprawling and its art galleries and embassies too formal; Parliament Square is a heavily policed outcrop of government and Speakers' Corner in Hyde Park is beholden to individual egos and less spontaneous in its protests.

Piccadilly Circus is certainly not the most beautiful part of London, but its bright lights have always made it one of the most exciting. From the moment you emerge, blinking, from the underground station, you face a sensory assault. As a very young girl Petula Clark cheered up GIs and British troops by singing in concerts held at the Criterion Theatre and Rainbow Corner club in Piccadilly Circus. Twenty years later she was still urging her audience to forget about their troubles by going Downtown, and for many listeners it seemed obvious that the neon lights and traffic noise she was singing about were waiting for them at Piccadilly Circus. In the 1930s, the writer Thomas Burke spoke of 'homing exiles'[2] returning to Piccadilly Circus, and it is remarkable the hold it exerts over people who may only have visited it once and may not even be from London.

My mother's emotions were part of a long-standing nostalgia for a place that represents home, but also the thrill of encounters. Since the First World War Piccadilly Circus has encapsulated for thousands of servicemen a longing for Blighty and memories of the good times to be had there. For later generations this reputation translated into wantonness: for a friend's frugal father, raising two children in the 1960s, it was synonymous with excess. If he found an overhead light *and* two lamps burning in the sitting room, he would storm in and extinguish two of them while ranting, 'It's like Piccadilly Circus in here!'

Those bright lights, electric and neon, which replaced the flickering Victorian gas lamps, were part of the technological advances that helped bring about astonishing social changes for groups who had previously led their lives in the shadows. The engineering feat of London's underground and the early financiers who had the vision to fund it made London smaller and put the capital within reach of the provinces and beyond, where travellers were also experiencing the liberation of rail travel. As the railway network accelerated through the country so did the department store's distribution network; and, later, the aeroplane would make the world smaller still and reinforce a craze for all things air-minded – from the aeroplane you could, in theory, buy at Simpsons of Piccadilly, to the less expensive aviator's helmet or flying suit available from Lillywhites. When, during both world wars, the aeroplane became part of the mechanisation of killing this, too, led to social change as more women found a role doing jobs such as bus driving, usually reserved for men.

Engineers and bankers were the true reason it became possible to meet old friends and new lovers in the underground's ticketing office, with its travertine-lined walls and classical, amber-and-black-striped columns. The Tube station is an outstanding engineering feat – a building that shouldn't really work (and very nearly didn't) – but one that combines Piccadilly Circus's architectural innovation with its hard-nosed commercialism. The Piccadilly line has always been at the heart of the London transport system that we now take for granted and which conveys millions of tourists and visitors – some straight from Heathrow Airport – to the very centre of London. In a quiet moment in a play at the subterranean Criterion Theatre it is possible to hear and feel the rumble of the Tube. It is a reminder that Piccadilly Circus's many facets work with a synchronicity that no other place in London can achieve. Likewise, the advent of electricity, coupled with planning laws that were easily circumvented, made Piccadilly Circus an advertiser's dream. The Guinness Clock, which first appeared on the northern side of the Circus in 1930, offered another example of how what was essentially a marketing tool could become a landmark freighted with romance.

The underground brought both the shop girl and her customer to central London: one to earn money, the other to spend it on clothes she could not find in the provinces. Though they came from different worlds, both might watch the same musical revue, seek the same tonic from Boots the Chemists or end their day resting their feet in the same Lyons Teashop or Corner House. When the new station opened in 1928, it delivered shoppers straight into the arms of Swan & Edgar and its own concourse of shops whetted passengers' appetites for spending. The stylish posters of outdoor life that lined its walls also persuaded travellers that a visit to sports outfitters Lillywhites or to new men's outfitters Simpsons would improve their life immeasurably. Boots the Chemists chose Piccadilly Circus for its first twenty-four-hour, seven-days-a-week shop because, according to its founder's son, John Boot, it was 'an address known to all, and convenient for bus and Tube'.[3] Even the humble shop window played its part in enhancing Piccadilly's reputation for shopping and the pavement outside Swan & Edgar department store became another of Piccadilly Circus's meeting places partly because the new plate glass windows offered a safe medium through which to eye up a possible partner. But, unlike Knightsbridge or Oxford Street, the area is not exclusively about shopping.

Piccadilly Circus has always managed to bridge the gap between sleazy Soho and unattainable Mayfair in a way rarely found in London. The area attracts so many different kinds of people that no one group can claim it exclusively, and this gives it the sense of being a people's place. In 1900 a couple in evening dress could enjoy the thrill of celebrating the lifting of a siege in far-off South Africa cheek by jowl with a seamstress or shop girl. Forty-five years later, the end of the Second World War attracted a similar fusion of nationalities, class and income to the most obvious place in London to express joy and relief.

It used to be said that if you waited long enough at Piccadilly Circus, you would eventually bump into everyone in the world you had ever known. Walter MacQueen-Pope, who worked in West End theatres from the 1920s, went even further and described Piccadilly Circus as the 'third magnetic pole'.[4] Those who have known it well, like Robert Fabian – 'Fabian of the Yard', the police officer who walked its streets before the Second World War – called it the 'pulsing heart of London'.[5] For some, a visit to Piccadilly Circus left them feeling more alive than they had ever felt, prompting them to make life-altering decisions. It's a place that for most of its history has teetered between respectability and sleaze, haunted by what one travel writer in the 1920s described as 'its epileptic lights, its feverish, lost air of searching for something it will never find . . .'[6]

Piccadilly Circus's position at the heart of London, and at the nexus of different worlds, makes it dangerous and exciting: a place where almost anything is possible and it is possible to be anyone – at least for one night. It is still *the* place to meet and to watch the world go by and to observe social change in the making. Since the beginning of the twentieth century, it has been a place for celebration and protest, although the causes being celebrated and championed have changed from imperialist battles, boat races and votes for women to concerns about the environment and consumerism. Its shifting character has always walked side by side with technological advancement – whether that is something as muscular as an underground railway network or the more prosaic, like the development of plate glass, which offered the opportunity for shopping and preening. The use of new materials, from the aluminium that forged Eros's lithe limbs to the electricity and neon that illuminated him, gave Piccadilly Circus its unique charm and attracted a cast of endlessly diverse characters. Film-makers and film stars, Bright Young Things and shop girls, music hall performers, flower-sellers and artists, con men (and women), sex workers, Tommies and GIs all arrived at Piccadilly Circus to try on different roles for size. Together, their stories form a people's history of an area that reflects many of the key moments in the first half of the twentieth century.

This book is a biography of a place and, like all biographies, it follows the preoccupations of its biographer. It is the biographer who decides where her subject's life should start, and which branches of the family tree should be pursued. My Piccadilly Circus may not be exactly your Piccadilly Circus but, like the constantly changing digital board that now illuminates the area, there will be many images that resonate.

Part One

Lights Up

I

Eros: Piccadilly Circus Takes Shape

The glow of dawn was starting to seep through the fog when a hansom cab appeared from the direction of Covent Garden. The vehicle rocked violently from side to side and seemed to be struggling to keep to the road. The passengers were in high spirits, as this was the end of a long night of drinking in the exclusive clubs of the West End. One of the passengers, a small, broad-chested man in his early sixties, was causing the cab to swerve by striking the driver, in a mock-violent fashion, with an ivory-handled walking stick, pleading with him to stop as they'd emerged into an open circus where several roads met. The driver, more perplexed than angry, kept up a half-hearted refrain: 'Mr Toole, I think you're a very objectionable old gentleman!'[1]

John Toole was a well-known actor,[2] but his audience that night consisted only of the three male friends who shared the cab with him. The tallest, who was over six feet and wore a pince-nez, not just as an actorly affectation but because he was extremely short-sighted, was the celebrated Shakespearean actor Henry Irving.[3] His hair, which was a little too long and a little too wavy for a 55-year-old to be fashionable, smelt of the bay rum he used to scent it. Toole's performance with the stick had Irving doubled up with laughter. The third friend was Seymour Hicks, an actor in his early twenties who was just starting to make a name for himself.[4] He had fine, girlish features, and probably felt as bemused as the cabbie. The whole escapade was designed as a distraction for the last member of the party: a 39-year-old, shortish man, who was, in all likelihood, wearing his customary black cape and broad-brimmed felt hat, which usually looked slightly rumpled and which he wore pushed back from his high forehead to expose his large, cherubic face. This was the sculptor Alfred Gilbert, who was agitated and anxious, despite the long night of eating and drinking at the Garrick Club.[5]

The cab slammed to a halt beside a curiously bulky shape that dominated the middle of the road. It was shrouded in tarpaulin and surrounded by a protective wooden fence that workmen were – even at this early hour – beginning to dismantle. The sudden arrival of the cab, and its cargo of strangely dressed and obviously drunken theatrical men, must have put the nightwatchman on his guard at the start of what was to be an important day. He did not recognise any of them, but their appearance surely added to his unease in an area that had gained a reputation for male assignations. It was not the first time Gilbert had brought a friend to the spot to view the statue that lay beneath the tarpaulin; earlier that year he had arrived with Bram Stoker, the red-bearded Irishman whose novel *Dracula* would appear four years later.[6]

It was only a matter of hours before Gilbert's commission was due to be revealed to the public and the artist desperately needed reassurance of its worth after facing a barrage of questions from the Garrick supper club.[7] When it was time to leave Irving had tactfully suggested they stopped off at Piccadilly Circus, or Regent's Circus as it was called then, on their way home, to view the monument.

As Gilbert lifted the protective canvas to reveal his sculpture, Irving, Toole and Hicks were clearly shocked by the figure beneath.

*

Gilbert[8] was born in 1854 in Berners Street, Soho, half a mile from Piccadilly Circus and the site of his most famous work, which would both make his name and blight the rest of his life. He grew up in a musical family: his father was an organist and editor of eighteenth-century musical texts and his mother a singing teacher and performer. Gilbert found his calling when he started to study sculpture, although the neoclassical preferences of English artists of the time bored him and he turned instead to continental sculptors such as the famous Hungarian, Sir Joseph Edgar Boehm. Under Boehm's tutelage Gilbert learnt how to breathe life into marble and bronze so that, whatever the medium, clothing appeared to ripple, skin to pulse and fur to shiver. Boehm encouraged him to study in Paris at the École des Beaux-Arts; the advice coincided with news that Gilbert's sweetheart and cousin, Alice, was pregnant, and the couple eloped to France.

Boehm was a mentor to Gilbert in many ways and his sudden death on 12 December 1890 proved a severe blow. His demise must have been even more traumatic if, as seems likely, he died at his studio in the arms of Queen Victoria's daughter, Princess Louise, who implored Gilbert, who was nearby in his workplace, to help her cover up the embarrassing truth. He wrote in his diary simply, 'Today Boehm died at a quarter before 6 !!!!!! alas'.[9] Boehm's passing added to Gilbert's workload as he took on the sculptor's unfinished commissions.

On 19 March he wrote: '1st day since poor Boehm's death that I have been uninterrupted.'[10]

Gilbert was one of the most talked-about sculptors of his time and his unconventional designs made him a bold choice to create the Piccadilly Circus statue, a memorial to the social reformer and philanthropist Lord Shaftesbury. Boehm had completed the first statue to him — an unsurprising marble likeness in Westminster Abbey – and had been too busy to tackle the second, which was expected to be a bronze likeness on a pedestal. Instead, he recommended his protégé, Gilbert, should take on the commission.

The Metropolitan Board of Works originally offered Cambridge Circus (at the Soho end of Shaftesbury Avenue) as the site for the statue, which would have offered the advantage of a circular plot, but the Memorial Committee, charged with organising a monument to the great man, preferred Piccadilly Circus. Gilbert, who favoured Cambridge Circus, complained that Piccadilly Circus was 'a distorted isochromal [sic] triangle, square to nothing of its surroundings – an impossible site, in short, upon which to place any outcome of the human brain, except possibly an underground lavatory!'[11] The committee members did bow to Gilbert's idea of a fountain to symbolise Shaftesbury's endless Christian love, but the other point of contention was that the sculptor had ambitious plans for a great, watery feature with jets that would spray the memorial, and – unintentionally – passers-by, from all sides, whereas the committee had a more modest ornamental fountain in mind. Just as Gilbert was finishing the work they made it clear that they wanted a trough of drinking water at its base for 'thirsty man and beast' as a nod to Lord Shaftesbury's philanthropic work. Their insistence forced him to add an octagonal bronze basin.

Nevertheless, the Shaftesbury memorial promised to secure both Gilbert's reputation and his finances. However, one detail about the commission robbed him of both and triggered a cascade of reckless decisions that dogged the rest of his life. Although he received £3,000 (worth about £400,000 today) – which seemed a huge amount at the time – the memorial is believed to have cost him £7,000 (about £900,000). Gilbert was under the impression that the government would provide him with old guns to melt down for the base of the memorial, but he was in fact forced to buy the copper himself at an inflated price and at a time when he was already struggling to control his finances.[12] He was overly generous to friends, giving them money and often his bronze casts, and was such a perfectionist that he thought nothing of keeping his customers waiting years – sometimes he even asked for a piece back to make final adjustments.

By the time Gilbert started work on the memorial fountain, in 1886, Alice was living in unhappy isolation at their rented farmhouse at Gomshall near Guildford in Surrey. The setting seemed idyllic – a centuries-old hideaway set in woodland and protected by the North Downs. Photos show a Hardy-esque landscape of overgrown gardens and their five children playing with a pet goat and dog. But as Gilbert started to spend more time in London, and to adopt a night-time schedule that fitted in with the actor and artist friends he met in the West End, his wife felt more and more isolated. Two days after the monument's unveiling Alice's feelings of loneliness became overwhelming, and she suffered a mental breakdown that led to her hospitalisation in a private nursing home.

*

From the moment he was given the commission, Gilbert had made it clear he was not in the business of producing a realist, 'coat and trousers'-style statue and favoured a symbolic fountain, although he changed his plans several times over the following years.[13] The statue he revealed to Irving, Hicks and Toole was certainly without coat or trousers, and it failed to resemble Shaftesbury in any way. Instead, Gilbert's friends saw a gleaming, aluminium youth with vast wings, well-defined chest muscles and taut calves, naked but for a piece of fabric draped over his groin. He stood, poised on his left foot, his right stretched out behind him, his arms holding a bow that had clearly just discharged an arrow. The creature – Cupid, Eros, Hermes, Mercury . . . no one was quite sure – looked as though he had, moments before, flown from the rooftops of the tall, narrow buildings nearby where 'sky signs' urged passers-by to indulge at Frazier's Oyster Rooms, the Hotel Piccadilly or Café Monico; although, as one modern critic has commented, the wings on his helmet point the wrong way and would resist the wind, rather than help him take flight.[14]

The statue's homoerotic undertones appeared even more marked by the time of its unveiling because in the seven years since Gilbert had received the commission the area's reputation as a venue for 'gay' (to use a modern term) assignations had grown, helped by the opening in August 1889 of underground toilets (hence Gilbert's acerbic comment about the site in Piccadilly Circus).[15] The foyers of nearby theatres and music halls, and Coventry Street, were also well-known homosexual haunts and Piccadilly, generally, was popular among men (including Oscar Wilde, who was a friend of Gilbert's) looking for romance with other men. Although not himself homosexual, the sculptor was strongly influenced by the

Aesthetic movement and its celebration of the male form.

Gilbert did not attend the opening ceremony for his fountain later that day – perhaps still desperately unsure of its worth, he sent his son Francis instead. It is not known whether the original Eros, Gilbert's model, valet and 'studio boy' Angelo Colarossi, who was just fifteen when he first posed for the artist, attended the unveiling, but it seems unlikely.

*

Hours after the cab carrying Gilbert and his friends had made a detour to Piccadilly Circus, the god was finally revealed to crowds of expectant members of the public as well as dignitaries, including the Duke of Westminster and artists such as George Frederic Watts, who, in a slightly funereal touch, brought yellow lilies. On the west side a tablet explained, in words written by prime minister William Gladstone, about the good works performed by Shaftesbury and, following a plea from the committee, a life-sized bust reminded the public what he had looked like. Gilbert attached eight ornate drinking cups by delicately wrought chains to the drinking fountain and created a shell basin for what the committee described as 'the refreshment of the canine race',[16] although there was no proof that dogs enjoyed congregating there.

Criticism of the monument began almost immediately and was most blatant in the fate of the drinking cups; by the following morning only two remained and fragments of the third were discovered at the bottom of one of the basins. Gilbert was more upset by the vandalism than the theft because, he said, it must have taken considerable time to achieve.

The new monument also produced a squall of criticism

(and a few nods of appreciation) from a range of publications. Contributors to the letters page of *The Times* were particularly exercised about it and argued over the suitability of a naked statue to honour a moral campaigner. The *Sunday Times*, ten days after the unveiling, was probably the first to suggest that the statue depicted Eros, but it took several years for the name to catch on and, as any pub quiz aficionada will know, the statue actually represents his brother, Anteros, who embodies selfless love, a fact that Gilbert explained in an interview in 1902. Anteros, he said, symbolised 'Love sending forth indiscriminately, yet with purpose, his missile of kindness, always with the swiftness the bird has from its wings, never ceasing to breathe or reflect critically, but ever soaring onwards, regardless of its own peril and dangers.'[17]

Headline writers referred to the 'Shaftesbury Fountain' or the 'Shaftesbury Memorial' and it wasn't until the 1920s that it had become known as the 'Piccadilly Fountain'; by the early 1930s *The Times* had started to call it simply 'Eros'.

Many letter-writers were troubled by the statue's missing arrow and *Punch* depicted Eros as an underhand god willing to shoot his victim in the back. Others saw it as a pun on the name Shaftes-bury – that is, to bury a shaft – and this interpretation has led to a more modern, and lewd, understanding of the wordplay that chimes with its gay associations. Other letter-writers objected to the size of the fountain and to the weakness of its jets, while a few commentators complained about the monument's ability to soak passers-by: 'It should be remembered that a fountain is a thing for squirting water, and is incomplete without water. In draughty London no fountain can be approached . . . To make a big fountain also a drinking fountain and therefore approachable is not possible,' one reader pointed out.[18] In September, the writer Edmund Gosse complained that there was not enough water in the fountain and that it looked dirty: 'The green oxide of Mr Gilbert's beautiful, curled gurnards is dulled into neutral tint. The monument already looks dingy and decayed.'[19]

The County Council was also concerned about the 'gurnards' (a fish with a large, spiny head) and installed a park-keeper to guard the fountain. The site quickly attracted the sort of boys who, without Shaftesbury's legislation, would have been shinning up chimneys. A gang of thirty or forty of them caused 'pandemonium' in and around the fountain by splashing one another and squirting water from their mouths, while others daubed the steps with mud. It was the first instance of the monument's irresistible allure for any group of revellers who found themselves in Piccadilly Circus fuelled with high spirits and/or alcohol.

A reader called F. H. Hubbard wrote to *The Times* in July 1893 to complain that the fountain 'with every breath of wind drenched the drinkers and sprinkled the passers-by on the leeside'.[20] His choice of a nautical term made the memorial sound as if it were adrift on high seas and he continued to report how the flower-sellers were forced to protect themselves from the spray with umbrellas. 'I dejectedly wondered,' he wrote, 'why he who had given us some of the best memorial work should have taken so much thought to give these people rheumatism.'

But Hubbard failed to acknowledge that Gilbert had also given Piccadilly Circus a key ingredient in its development as an inimitable location in London. His creation of Eros established a magnetic force that, for the next hundred or so years, would draw multitudes of people to linger on its steps or to scale its body. Gilbert and his friends were the first to feel the statue's pull. The sculptor needed it for reassurance and future generations of men and women would also seek it out to help them establish their place in the world. Eros has a talismanic power that attracts people of all ages, nationalities and backgrounds to celebrate, to protest, to forge friendships and romances, to shop and to be entertained. Perhaps it is its very ambiguity as a symbol that allows us all to project our own emotions upon it. But its allure would soon have faded if Piccadilly Circus had not been able to offer a battery of other attractions to draw multifarious visitors into its orbit; and, just as importantly, a speedy way of reaching those temptations.

2

A People's Place

Some of the first to come to Piccadilly Circus, to make it a people's place where different classes could interact, and a place where women, in particular, felt comfortable, were the flower girls.

Despite the danger of being drenched by the fountain, Eros provided an island in a turbulent sea of pedestrians, cabs and omnibuses from which they could sell their wares. Each staked a claim to their 'patch' on the memorial's steps, wearing brightly coloured shawls, a white or striped apron and a straw boater. They hauled their great wicker baskets around like market porters and reached out to the upper deck of omnibuses where men chose seats that allowed them to smoke. The flower girls were able to contact their loftier customers by fixing bunches of flowers to long poles, and these specially constructed flower-headed pikes stuck out of their baskets like pins in a pincushion. At ground level, the flower girls persuaded passing gentlemen to buy a buttonhole to give their jacket a jaunty air.

At Eros's unveiling ceremony, the secretary of the Memorial Committee said he hoped the County Council would allow the flower girls, to whom Lord Shaftesbury was always a friend, to stay at the Circus – so long as they behaved themselves.[1] The caveat reflected an official unease about the women, who, like the Circus itself, had an ambiguous reputation. On one hand, they were as steadfast as Eros. Come rain or shine (or, later in the twentieth century, the threat of aerial attack), they could always be found in Piccadilly Circus, or at their other main haunt, Trafalgar Square. The fact that they sold flowers imbued them with an innocent, rural gloss amid the dangerous urban streets of London.

But in other ways the flower girls presented a troubling ambiguity, particularly when it came to the role of women and to the diverse groups of people who were starting to work in the area and to use Piccadilly Circus as a meeting place. Journalist Henry Mayhew was one of the first to acknowledge the flower girl's equivocal role and his survey *London Labour and the London Poor* of 1851 noted that the typical flower girl might more accurately be described as a woman and that she might often turn to what he described as 'prostitution' by night. Even many years after Mayhew's findings, there was still something slightly transgressive about the flower girl – after all, she literally walked the streets, had intimate contact with men from all walks of life, and sold flowers – a commodity that, while associated with the countryside, was also freighted with sexual symbolism. On top of all this, she worked *outside* – a precinct otherwise controlled by men.

But as the Victorian period drew to a close her image began to shift, like that of the Circus itself, and the respectable shoppers who were beginning to be drawn to the West End grew to like the flower girl and her connection with a simpler, more rural and romantic life. Her changing image is evident in the way she was depicted. Some artists continued to paint her in a brazen fashion: legs slightly apart, planted firmly on the ground as she sat assembling her bunches or buttonholes, perhaps a bit of flesh showing through her blouse and a gaze that looked unflinchingly at the viewer. But others, like Bernard Ward in his 1895 *London Flower Girls,* placed them at the centre of a domestic scene in which they were surrounded by younger female helpers, probably family members, who sat at their feet happily arranging flowers as if they were playing in a nursery. Charles Ginner, in his 1912 painting, *Piccadilly Circus*, depicted them as homely matrons bringing a splash of nature to the busy junction.

Like the breed of 'shop girls' who would start to appear as stores such as Swan & Edgar on the west corner of Piccadilly Circus, next to Regent Street, expanded into what would become department stores in the twentieth century, the flower girls were on the front line of a commercialisation that was changing London's West End. The shops relied on the nationwide rail network to supply both goods and customers, and the flower girls, too, could only sell their wares because of the arrival of trains that brought violets, stocks, roses and lilies of the valley from the countryside – and sometimes even from abroad. And, like the department stores, they had more customers because of the arrival of motorised buses and the nascent underground railway network. The flower girls were part of a group of women who were gaining footholds in the city, a group which included women who visited the area to shop, who came to take tea – or to serve it – at J. Lyons' first Teashop, which opened at 213 Piccadilly in September 1894, as well as protesters like the suffragettes, or social investigators – as in the case of Evangeline Booth, an early member of the Salvation Army, or journalist Elizabeth Banks, who both dressed up as flower girls to see how the poor lived.

The flower girl's job had much in common with another emerging role, that of the music hall performer, and both sets of women represented a coming together at Piccadilly Circus of the notorious East End of London with the more refined West End. The image of the music hall star was starting to shift as middle-class audiences felt able to risk visiting the palaces of variety for a night out, particularly after pantomime had exposed them to its working-class stars and they had liked what they'd seen. The grand, stucco-faced London Pavilion, with its neoclassical triangle supported by columns, replaced a music hall, which in its turn had seen off a song-and-supper-room annexe to the Black Horse Inn. Occupying an entire block, the 'Pav' became famous as the place where, reportedly, the word 'jingoism' was first heard, in the song 'We Don't Want to Fight, But, by Jingo, If We Do', in 1878 and in reference to the Russo-Turkish War of the same year. A theatre of varieties, which had the innovation of tip-up seats, the Pav attracted a more respectable audience, including the Prince of Wales, Victoria's errant son and the future Edward VII, who was known to pay clandestine visits.

While the flower girls were commanding their 'patch' at the base of Eros, a few metres away music hall stars such as the diminutive, buck-toothed Marie Lloyd were strutting around the stage of the Pav. Lloyd, who was born in Hoxton in the East End of London in 1870, epitomised the seismic collision of two worlds. She had learnt her trade in raucous, smoke-filled halls and could tame audiences without the aid of a microphone and despite her size. She grew up the eldest of eleven children and the daughter of a father who spent his days making artificial flowers for hats and his nights serving as a waiter in a music hall (a mismatch of trades that crops up frequently in the Victorian census). During her early career she sometimes played as many as seven halls a night, darting around London at the same time Jack the Ripper was plying his gruesome trade. As a young girl, Marie's songs were sentimental tales such as 'The Boy I Love Is up in the Gallery' (a success that was short-lived; another artist claimed the song was her property), but as she grew older her repertoire became more risqué and accompanied by knowing winks. Now she swaggered round the huge Pavilion stage, hand on hip, daring her respectable audience to misinterpret her double entendre lyrics and flashing them a wink to ensure they *did* get the wrong message from a song like 'What Did She Know about Railways?' about a young girl who'd 'never had her ticket punched before', or in another coded song, which asked 'What's that for?' (In a curious coincidence, Marie was born Matilda Alice Victoria Wood, and her mastery of innuendo can be seen as a precursor of her twenty-first-century namesake.)

As people flocked to enjoy themselves inside the Pav and nearby theatres, it was an obvious step for Piccadilly Circus, with Eros at its centre, to become a hub for national celebration, as it did for the first time on Friday 18 May 1900. That evening, news of what was portrayed as a great victory, albeit in a far-off land, reached London at just after 9 p.m. when many people were already out enjoying themselves. The lord mayor revealed the startling development by posting a placard outside the Mansion House in the City and drivers of trolleycars, vans and cabs conveyed the reports to the West End where cabbies waiting at the ranks let out 'loud hurrahs' and pedestrians, pausing to ask what all the fuss was about, shook hands heartily with complete strangers.

The 'fuss' centred around the fact that the British Army had finally managed to relieve the garrison commanded by

Colonel Robert Baden-Powell, which had been besieged by Boer forces for seven months in the far-off South African town of Mafeking (now known as Mafikeng or Mahikeng). The lifting of the siege proved to be a decisive moment in a war between Britain and the two Boer (Afrikaner) territories of the South African Republic (Transvaal) and the Orange Free State. Historians disagree about the causes of the bitter conflict, which lasted from 11 October 1899 to 31 May 1902, but most put the struggle for control of the South African Republic, and the area's rich gold and diamond mines, at the heart of the aggression.

After listening to the lord mayor's speech, a crowd of about 200 people marched from the City and west along the Strand to Piccadilly Circus. Passengers cheered and waved flags from omnibuses and cabs, many of which had flags fluttering from their whips; groups of men commandeered vehicles and clambered to the top with reckless abandon to fly the Union flag; cyclists fitted flags to the ends of poles and careered around like knights at a jousting tournament. A few newspaper boys hurled free copies of the late edition into the open windows of hansom cabs. The sight of anyone in uniform, even a postman, was enough to spark a rendition of the national anthem.

At the theatres off Piccadilly Circus leading actors and managers announced the news to their audiences. The classical actress Mrs Patrick Campbell, whose husband had been killed in the war a few weeks previously, and who was starring in a production of *Magda*, informed the audience of the joyous news from the Royalty Theatre, Soho, and they joined in as the orchestra struck up 'God Save the Queen' and 'Rule Britannia'. In the more raucous music halls performers struggled through their 'patter' and any actor who happened to be in uniform produced cheers or renditions of 'Soldiers of the Queen'.

A reporter from *The Times*, who was passing through Piccadilly at about 9 p.m., fancied that Baden-Powell, or B-P, as he was more commonly known, would be able to hear the noise in Mafeking itself: 'At 9 o'clock all was quiet and ordinary; at 11 a.m. the West-End had gone wild.'[2] The journalist wasn't fortunate enough to obtain one of the papers a few reckless newspaper boys were giving away but had to pay twopence for the 'War Edition' of a publication that usually sold for a halfpenny. He paused to read it under a gas lamp while a young man ran up and asked him, 'Is it true that Mafeking is relieved, Sir?'

The reporter couldn't understand where all the flags had come from and as he neared Piccadilly Circus the throng grew thicker and the roar louder. A balcony above one large shop was crammed with people waving not just flags but blankets, tablecloths, towels and 'various feminine garments which are usually displayed only on a clothes line'. Matters culminated at Piccadilly Circus, where the pavements were impassable and the cabs and omnibuses bringing people from the theatre had ground to a standstill. Their passengers waved flags (which the reporter surmised many must have brought in anticipation of good news), hats, umbrellas or anything else they had to hand. A man with a cornet started to play 'God Save the Queen'; 'in a twinkling every hat was off' and thousands sang in unison. 'It was a wonderful sight under the glare of the Criterion lights.'

In the Trocadero's restaurant its owner, Joseph Lyons, announced the good news from the balcony. Everyone smiled and no one minded being stopped or crushed. 'Ladies in evening dress were squeezed in the crowd, but only smiled happily. And over all and through it all the cheers thundered on in a continuous roar, like the sound of a heavy surf on a rocky shore.'[3]

The moment is captured in a drawing from the *Graphic*. A man playing a musical instrument takes centre stage while a woman in a boater, who is caught in the blast, covers one ear and bends away from the noise like a modern-day sports fan trying to escape the screech of a vuvuzela. There are several men in top hats and tails and at least one woman in an evening gown. The horses pulling the omnibus look petrified and the vehicle itself appears to rock with the motion of the revellers on the top deck.

A reporter for the *New York Times* was shocked by the outburst. 'Sober, phlegmatic London is beside itself with emotion,' he noted, adding what a curious spectacle it was to see 'solemn, gray-haired men toss their opera hats into the air and join in the hurricane of cheers when a wreath-crowned banner with the portrait of Col. Baden Powell on it, was borne along Piccadilly'.[4] A year later the same newspaper reported that scenes of wild celebration had given birth to a new word, 'mafficking', meaning an uncharacteristic attitude of such unBritish abandonment that 'Peers walked down Piccadilly arm in arm with 'Arrys from Whitechapel'. ('Arry was a stereotypical cockney introduced by *Punch* cartoons in the second half of the nineteenth century.)

Looking back at this scene of jubilation from a twenty-first-century, post-colonial viewpoint, it might seem difficult to comprehend why so many Britons were so ecstatic at the relief, after seven months, of a strategically insignificant town nearly eight thousand miles away where the future leader of the Boy Scout movement was in charge of a garrison of 2,000 men. Interest was partly stoked by the fact that journalists from *The Times*, *Morning Post*, *Daily Chronicle* and *Pall Mall Gazette* were being held in the town too and their reports were slipped out and sent to a telegraph office fifty miles away, eventually to end up among the newspaper-sellers of Piccadilly Circus, who were either giving away their papers or selling them at an inflated price. Many newspapers devoted their entire front page to the good news and such was the public's engagement with the story that the headlines were as simple as: 'Reported Relief of Mafeking' (*London Evening Standard*) or, on the newspaper-seller's bill, 'Daily Telegraph, Mafeking Relieved . . . London's Joy'. The siege's end provoked such uncontrolled delight because B-P was a charismatic leader and Britain was desperate for good news after previous setbacks in a war that had proved to be the most costly since the Napoleonic conflict and which had involved 500,000 men on the British side, fighting against 88,000 Boer soldiers. A total of 100,000 had been killed.

This was the first time that Piccadilly Circus had become the hub of such wild national celebrations, but it would not be the last. In decades to come the Circus would hold the best al fresco New Year's Eve parties and become the most obvious place for revellers to congregate at times of national importance – its geographic position at a crossroads where so many important roads met made it an obvious place for momentous happenings to be celebrated. There would be two further occasions in the twentieth century when revellers would seek it out as a venue for jubilation. In the cases still to come, the atmosphere would be tinged with a greater feeling of personal loss and the jingoism would be less blatant.

*

Only part of Eros is visible in the *Graphic*'s illustration of the evening of wild abandon in May 1900, but his presence at the heart of the celebrations is evidence that Londoners had warmed to him. The statue is thought to be the first in the world to have been cast in aluminium, but the god's skin quickly darkened with the London smog as if he were acclimatising to his surroundings. Angelo Colarossi, the model for Eros, was also permanently tied to the place that leaves its impression on most people who visit it. While he may have longed to move on from his starring role in Piccadilly Circus, the fact that he failed to grow beyond the five feet that made him such an ideal model tied him immutably to the statue that defines the place. His size cut short his career as a model and his life was to be as humdrum and monochrome as Gilbert's would be passionate and colourful. It is now impossible to imagine Piccadilly Circus without Eros and this most ethereal of gods seems destined to rest here for all eternity.

Eros may have made Gilbert's name as an artist, but he cited it as a factor in his bankruptcy, which was declared in 1901. That August his belongings were packed into a Pickford's van and he set off for a new life in Bruges, Belgium. In the days before his departure he locked himself in his studio and meticulously smashed all of his plaster casts to avoid cheap imitations being made without his permission. The house's next owner would come across remnants of a small model of Eros.

Angry customers, growing tired of waiting for their commissions, put pressure on the Royal Academy, which had made Gilbert a fellow the year before Eros was completed, to expel him; rather than face this ignominy, he resigned in 1908. One of his supporters appealed to George Bernard

Shaw, but the writer had no sympathy for an artist who failed to complete a commission, and wrote in a letter that Gilbert should be 'drowned in the fountain with which he disfigured Piccadilly Circus'.[5] He had already been expelled from the Garrick Club for non-payment of debts.

But Eros was more resilient than his maker and, besides, Piccadilly Circus was now a popular meeting place for people from all walks of life. When Edward VII died on 6 May 1910 Piccadilly Circus's future hung in the balance. Ironically, given the monarch's love of everything the area's nightlife could offer, there were plans to replace Eros with a sombre equestrian statue and to rename the area King Edward VII Square in a bid to make it a centre for serious theatre and opera.[6] Fortunately, these suggestions came to nothing and, as would happen again later in the century, Piccadilly Circus made its feelings about the king's passing felt. As *The Times* reported:

> No one who is at all familiar with the nightly scene, especially on Saturdays . . . could have failed to have been impressed by the change wrought later by the King's death. Streets which are usually full of animation and brilliantly lighted were dark and lifeless. The majority of the restaurants remained open but had no guests. The roar of the traffic had ceased, and everywhere a strange silence brooded over the scene and depressed the few who witnessed it. The people had gone to mourn in their homes the loss of their King, and in many instances to set new names in their prayers – King George and Queen Mary.

Gilbert remained bitter about the financial and emotional cost of his work and in 1923 suggested to *The Times* that it would be a good idea to melt the whole thing down and use the money raised to build a shelter for homeless men who slept on the Embankment.[7] By then, however, Eros was thirty years old and as intrinsic to Piccadilly Circus as the lions were to Trafalgar Square.

3

Shopkeepers Take on the World

> Who and what is 'Phroso'? A phenomenally rigid human being, an ingenious electrical toy, or a legless person, supported by mechanical limbs – which is he, she or it?
>
> *Illustrated London News*, 11 October 1902

> 'Phroso', the mysterious mechanical doll – he, she, or it?
>
> *Manchester Evening News*, 30 August 1904

The crowds started to gather outside Swan & Edgar, on the corner of Regent Street and Piccadilly Circus, just before 3 p.m. on Wednesday 24 August 1904. The store had yet to acquire the icing-sugar white, majestic frontage that still adorns the south-west corner of the Circus. Its shop windows looked crowded and cluttered, like an Edwardian lady who can't decide what to wear and chooses to pile on every piece of clothing she owns. And yet those very shop windows were a revolution – a gleaming beacon for a new breed of shoppers drawn to a temple of consumerism. The plate glass, which was becoming common in many big shops as the cost of production fell, opened up a multitude of marketing ploys because its strength made it possible to instal windows that were much larger and which offered a clear and uninterrupted view of what was inside. The innovation signalled the birth of window-shopping. But on that particular summer's afternoon the windows held a promise of something more than net curtains or tablecloths, something much more unsettling and sinister.

The newspaper notice had said 'it' would appear at around 3 p.m. and stand in the window of Swan & Edgar for around forty-five minutes; there was already little room on the pavement. A 'swaying, straining mass of "human beans"', as one flower girl described the crowd, using a term Roald Dahl would have approved of, had taken over. There was a tetchiness in the air, perhaps because of the roadworks that meant most of Piccadilly, the Strand and Regent Street were 'up', or because of the chill in the summer breeze. The crowd, which included a few music hall performers and men and women of all ages, strained to catch a glimpse. The grandiose feathered hats of the time must have made that a challenge. A red blind, like a theatrical curtain waiting for the performance to begin, hid the contents of the shop window.

Inside, two burly male shop assistants grappled with what looked like a tailor's dummy, on whose face rested a 'particularly vacuous expression'.[1] Perhaps shoppers glanced up from the silks and damasks they were scrutinising to wonder why the strange object was proving so difficult to manoeuvre, or perhaps they had heard the news that Phroso would appear in the window, challenging onlookers to make him laugh. The two men positioned the doll on the shop side of the blind, where he sat on a chair, carefully framed by the existing display of pyjamas, shirts and ties. At eight minutes before three o'clock the blind was raised. 'It' stared with a 'cold, unseeing gaze into the sea of faces on the other side of the glass'.[2]

Some of the crowd had seen the doll before at the Hippodrome in nearby Leicester Square, where the novelty act had been one of the main attractions on a bill that was drawing an increasingly middle- and upper-class audience to watch an array of 'turns' that included comics, singers, performing animals and dancers. 'Phroso' the 'man-doll', as he became known, appeared to be operated using a series of levers next to him on the stage. The act's appeal was that his stiff limbs, automated way of walking and immovable face made him appear exactly like a doll, or mechanical toy, and the audience was left puzzling about whether he was human or not. He walked, bowed, and moved his arms and hands in a stiff, 'marionettish fashion',[3] and there was debate about whether he was controlled by electricity. The act – there was much discussion about its gender, probably because of its stature – usually wore evening dress, but for this debut in the shop window of Swan & Edgar he sported military uniform. Some observers thought he was dressed as a French captain, while others were convinced his uniform belonged to an Austrian officer. Whatever his allegiance, the doll's military attire made him seem even more mechanical, probably because he reminded the audience of a toy soldier. On the stage of a theatre of varieties he displayed 'all the rigidity of a machine-worked toy',[4] and here in Piccadilly Circus his pale, doll's face had 'the same inscrutable countenance that baffled Hippodrome audiences when he first astonished London'.[5]

After the initial shock of Phroso's appearance in a window normally cluttered with haberdashery and clothes, the crowd started to relax and to laugh and joke. As part of his stage show, members of the Hippodrome audience had been encouraged to stick pins in him or to press smouldering cigars into his 'flesh'; at Swan & Edgar the challenge was more humane. Anyone who could force a smile from the blank, immutable face, or a blink of the eyes on the other side of the glass, would be rewarded with ten pounds (about £1,000 in today's money); but on that first appearance at Swan & Edgar, Phroso seemed 'more doll-like than ever'.[6] After a few minutes he started to jerk and twist his head and hands in '"penny-in-the-slot" movements',[7] 'till one began to wonder where the works were'.[8]

This sudden movement may have goaded the crowd into action, and many started to 'antic' in front of the window.[9] One man frantically clawed the air to try to make Phroso blink; others pulled hideous grimaces, jeered and hooted. Someone crossed his eyes, stuck out his tongue and banged on the pane of glass. But Phroso remained unmoved. Another man conducted his own fancy dress parade by switching hats, putting on a frock coat and blinking through a monocle. The music hall turns in the crowd did their best to catch their rival's eye, but nothing worked. The crowd surged dangerously close to the window and extra police had to be called in from other parts of London. In the end, the blind was lowered and a ladder placed in front of the window to keep the mob at a distance.

Phroso appeared again, a few minutes later, but didn't stay long. The police grew concerned as the glass creaked and swayed while the crowd struggled to get a better view. One woman who was near the front announced, 'I knew he was only a doll,' but was struck speechless when Phroso leapt from his chair and disappeared back into the shop.

In his dressing room he wiped clean the make-up that gave him his doll-like complexion and shook out his limbs. He said later that the moments he had spent in the window of Swan & Edgar had been the worst of his life – he was convinced the window was on the point of smashing and he had heard it crack at least four times. Once he had removed his costume, Phroso shimmied through the crowd and hopped onto a 'penny bus', watching the commotion from the uncomfortably narrow, 'knife-board' seats of the top deck.

Although later, at Marlborough Street's magistrates' court, Phroso, whose true name was given as Frederick Travalien (or 'Trevallen' in some accounts), said he had neither been paid by Swan & Edgar to appear in the window nor had himself paid for the privilege, it was clearly a hugely successful publicity stunt, for both the music hall turn and the shop, at a time of the year when both were short of customers. Walter Morford, the managing director of Swan & Edgar, was charged with causing an obstruction, though he blamed the police for their inability to control the crowd. He felt this was part of their job – especially given the high rents charged in Piccadilly Circus. Morford was fined forty shillings and ordered to pay two shillings costs. Travalien, ever the showman, and much to the consternation of Morford, refused to confirm whether or not he was Phroso, and even offered £50–£100 to anyone who could prove the true nature of the mechanical doll.

*

Phroso's story offers a convenient metaphor for the transformative power of Piccadilly Circus: how a visitor could become a different person for an hour or two before jumping on a bus and riding home to a routine life. The man/doll's antics – and the crowd's reaction – also demonstrated how the area was becoming a public meeting place, somewhere spontaneous acts of celebration, protest or performance could suddenly burst into life. And the role played by the plate glass window – which withstood the excitable crowd – also showed how technological advance was changing shopping into an entertainment to be enjoyed by a wider group of people.

Five years after Phroso's antics in Piccadilly Circus, another talented showman would change the face of shopping in London's West End. When, in 1909, Henry Gordon Selfridge opened his imposing neo-baroque shop, with its colonnaded front and massive windows, in Oxford Street,[10] he brought with him all the pizzazz and guile he had learnt from his apprenticeship in the American department store and mail order firm of Chicago's Marshall Field & Co. Selfridge left school at fourteen and had hoped to join the navy, but his short stature ruled out a life on the ocean waves and he turned, instead, to the turbulent seas of America's new retailing industry. He joined Marshall Field at a time when the country was embracing a consumer revolution in its expanding cities and the new department store was using every trick up its fashionable sleeve to lure the new female shopper to its lavish emporium. Shopping was entertainment and the owners of the most famous of the new department stores – Wanamaker's in Philadelphia, Marshall Field in Chicago and Gimbels in New York – behaved like vaudeville impresarios in their strategies to entertain shoppers with every type of attraction, from tearooms and barbershops to fashion shows and theatrical presentations. John Wanamaker even exhibited Titians and Manets from his personal art collection. The new shopping magnates made use of advertising, lavish window displays and artfully arranged merchandise.

As Selfridge rose through the ranks to become a junior

partner at Marshall Field, he watched intently how the company treated its customers, and gathered further inspiration on research trips to London and Paris. When his employer turned down his suggestion of opening a branch in London, he decided to go it alone and used the fortune he had amassed through the canny purchase and sale of a Chicago company to launch his own department store at the then unfashionable west end of Oxford Street.

Shopkeepers on both sides of the Atlantic were becoming aware of the New Woman and Selfridge was keen to transplant the ploys that had enticed her into department stores in the United States to a British setting. The New Woman was independent – or aspired to be. She often rode a bike, or travelled alone on the underground, and might have a job in the city. She liked to explore London by herself, without worrying about what people would say, and was drawn to any place that offered a safe haven where she could meet friends without her parents demanding she took a guardian. As the suffragettes would demonstrate, shopping was one sphere in which she chose to declare her independence.[11]

Selfridge's training in the United States made him well placed to take advantage of this new customer. He was also practical and placed his store in close proximity to the new Central underground line. The shop spent £36,000 (about £4 million today) on promoting its opening and brought Marshall Field's chief window-dresser to London. The investment paid off and a million people rushed through its doors during its first week in March 1909. Visitors toured more than 100 departments, marvelling at the green carpeting and bright showrooms. Otis lifts transported them between five storeys, three basement levels and a rooftop terrace and instantly outdid long-established stores that did not have the technology to sweep customers to other storeys.[12] The lack of lifts or escalators meant that traditional shops concentrated their selling on the ground floor, while the lower was used for stock and upper floors as workshops. At Selfridges, shopping became so much more civilised as customers could recuperate in the tearoom, ladies' and gentlemen's cloakrooms or nursing station, or visit its barbershop, hair salon, library or post office. A concierge could book tickets to a West End show or a passage to New York. There was even the novelty of a rifle range. Selfridge toured the store daily in top hat and tails, writing his initials in any dust that he spotted.

Although Piccadilly's roots, at first glance, seemed very different from Selfridge's Chicago background, the area had been shaped by key personalities who, although traversing different centuries, had commerce in their blood. The very name 'Piccadilly' is thought to originate from 'piccadill', a word of Spanish origin for a stiff collar, or elaborate ruff, that was popular at court in the early seventeenth century.[13] Robert Baker, a tailor based in the Strand, made a tidy sum in the seventeenth century from selling the accessory and used it to invest in land north of what is now Piccadilly Circus. Here he built a grand home that was nicknamed 'Piccadilly House' in mocking reference to the source of his wealth. The department store Swan & Edgar also took its name from two entrepreneurs. William Edgar, the son of a Cumberland farmer, started his business selling cravats, socks and haberdashery from a stall in the Western Mail Coach offices off Regent Street, and legend has it that he slept under his stall at night until finally teaming up with a fellow stallholder, George Swan. The two moved to Piccadilly in 1812, and by 1848 Swan & Edgar had expanded to occupy an entire corner building on Piccadilly Circus. In 1886 it became a public company.

Like Gordon Selfridge, Walter Morford, Swan & Edgar's early-twentieth-century managing director, had an eye for marketing. Morford, who had worked as a buyer at Woolland Brothers[14] and Peter Robinson, returned to Swan & Edgar in 1895, where he stayed for twenty years. In the same year that Selfridges opened, he was back at Marlborough magistrates' court accused of creating a Christmas window display that was 'too attractive'. The wax dummies of ladies dressed in different costumes revolved in the shop window against a variety of settings and proved so enthralling that crowds blocked the pavement and spilled onto the road.[15] Morford agreed to put the brakes on the mannequins and to have just one scene a day. He accepted his fine – and the free publicity.

Selfridge and Morford were part of a coterie of shopkeepers who parcelled up London's growing hordes of shoppers – most of them women. In Knightsbridge, Harvey Nichols, Woollands and Harrods served the wealthiest customers, many of whom had accounts or purchased by post or on approval (meaning they could return items if they decided they didn't like them). William Whiteley, an entrepreneur from Yorkshire, had established his haberdashery store in the less fashionable area of Westbourne Grove, Notting Hill in the 1850s before developing it into a women's clothing store. These men were less rivals and more comrades-in-arms in the common battle for shoppers. As Selfridge commented: 'I wish Harrods were on one side, Whiteley's on the other and Swan & Edgar facing us, then we should all do better.'[16] But, despite this comment of solidarity, the brash new Chicago businessman certainly encouraged West End shops and restaurants to 'up' their game and when Swan & Edgar was rebuilt in 1910 it incorporated some of the grandeur presented by its Oxford Street rival.

Swan & Edgar's palatial building was part of the promise that shopping could offer a transformation, something to whisk consumers away from poorer and less glamorous homes and neighbourhoods; or, in the case of newly rich women from manufacturing towns, it provided an entrée into a more sophisticated world. For music hall star Marie Lloyd, gowns based on the latest 'continental' designs would confirm her exoticism on- and offstage and help to bridge the gap between her humble roots in the East End and her new, affluent or aspirational, fans. Shops like Swan & Edgar studied the fashion publications from Paris and adapted them to their customers' needs, even sending buyers to visit France in person. And after Marie Lloyd had strutted and preened her way through her stage act in her Swan & Edgar attire, she dazzled her admirers in fancy restaurants such as the Criterion and Romano's in the Strand.

Selfridges' many amenities – some might say gimmicks – must also have been uppermost in the minds of Lyons as it developed its Corner Houses, and, later in the century, when the Simpson company created its modernist department store. On 3 January 1909 Lyons, whose Trocadero restaurant already catered to the wealthy and whose 130 Teashops ministered to the less well off, opened the four-storey Corner House just a few metres from Piccadilly Circus, where Coventry Street intersected with Rupert Street. The building could seat over 2,000 people and provided a sort of department store for the palate. The curious public who queued round the block on its first morning, eager to pass through its bronze-framed doors and along a large marble colonnade, were able to sample an array of tearooms, bars and restaurants that sold everything from chocolates and cooked meats to cheese and fine wines. Customers could also have their shoes shined and their hair dressed; they could phone a friend at the telephone bureau or book theatre tickets for a local show. Adverts for the Corner House ended with the promise of 'Light meals. Light charges. Bright music'[17] – a combination that proved so popular that Lyons bought the next-door building to double the number of seats to 4,000.

Both Swan & Edgar and Lyons Corner House became well known as meeting places for courting couples, but Piccadilly Circus also started to gain a reputation for what was referred to at the time as 'prostitution'. After the nineteenth century sex work ebbed and flowed, but, in the public eye at least, its association with the area lingered. Even as streets became brighter and less threatening, the notion persisted that night was a dangerous time to be out and that any woman who walked the streets alone must be looking for customers.

Writers such as George Gissing and H. G. Wells raised concerns about men who came looking for sex and who sometimes stalked young women who simply happened to be in the area and who were not engaged in prostitution. In 1906 Swan & Edgar complained to the Royal Commission upon the Duties of the Metropolitan Police about the 'pests' who lingered by shop windows ready to pounce on women shoppers, 'some of whom have been absolutely terrified by the persistence of these blackguards'.[18] For the shop, the main concern was not necessarily the safety of young women but the fact that the threat kept customers at a distance and weakened the effect of their window displays.

The *Oxford English Dictionary* dates the first use of the verb 'to window-shop' to 1890 and, like so many milestones in shopping, it originated in America.[19] The move from candles and oil lamps to gaslight and then electricity played its part in transforming the shop window into a piece of theatre, a peephole into a world of glittering objects and fine clothes. Ever since glass had started to replace muslin and oilpaper in the sixteenth century, the scene behind the peephole had become sharper and more lavish. From the 1820s cheaper plate glass and the use of iron columns and bressummers (a horizontal beam over a large opening, such as a window, that supported the wall above) allowed a glittering pathway of shop windows to emerge across the West End.

But the shop window was as much a mirror on the world as it was a gateway to consumerism. As long as homosexuality remained illegal, the discreet, reflective medium of plate glass allowed two men to eye one another up without fear of suspicion. If what they saw proved intriguing, they could play a courting 'tag' until one of them felt safe enough to address the other: usually by commenting on something in the shop, by asking for a light for his cigarette or inquiring about the time. Such clichéd comments and questions made the initial approach, which was fraught with danger, a little easier and could even lead to a comic response – as when one man asked the object of his affection if he had a light and the other man replied, 'Yes. It's twenty to nine.'[20] Romance was more straightforward inside one of the area's restaurants or cafés, like Lyons' Teashops or Corner Houses, where the light flooded in past the pastries and savouries and bounced off the mirrors, crockery and bottles to envelop the customer in the warmth of female camaraderie or the haze of a male tryst.

Le Corbusier, the Swiss-French architect and designer, would rank plate glass alongside the typewriter, telephone, safety razor and aeroplane as inventions that symbolised modern life and, at the start of the twentieth century, Piccadilly's shop windows were as much about social interaction and entertainment as they were about consumerism. Indeed, plate glass, and the size of the windows it made possible, was at the heart of a protracted squabble over the fate of the Regent Street Quadrant, an area that would define Piccadilly Circus.

As Pevsner's architectural guide for Westminster puts it, 'Piccadilly Circus is the ill-shaped rock on which the hopes of many C20 [twentieth-century] IMPROVERS have foundered'.[21] Since the early nineteenth century, John Nash's sweeping white stuccoed buildings had defined the road between Oxford Circus and Piccadilly, and his architectural legacy included, at the Piccadilly Circus end, Glasshouse and Sherwood streets and the grand County Fire Office building (whose arches would, between the 1930s and 1950s, provide shelter from both the elements and prying eyes for queer men meeting there).[22] But by the turn of the twentieth century the Crown had seen the need to revamp Regent Street with a grand, uniform arcade of shops. However, they found themselves squaring up to the shopkeepers, who were dismayed by architect Norman Shaw's designs for more modest windows, which they feared would destroy the light and airy feel shoppers now expected and which they believed their existing stores offered. The lengthy spat between shopkeepers and the builder came to symbolise a crisis about London's role in the world: was it the centre of empire or the centre of shopping?

Swan & Edgar's Morford led the shopkeepers' side and in a letter to the *Daily Telegraph* on 6 April 1907 complained that even 'a professional window-dresser cannot make these cave-like windows attractive'. The *Builder* countered with: 'The idea that a great architectural scheme by one of the first [sic] architects of the day is to be stopped because a knot of tradesmen fancy there is not plate-glass enough for them, is something too ridiculous . . .'[23] The dispute continued for years; the shopkeepers had time on their side as the leases on most buildings were not due until 1919. In 1912, when Shaw was in his eighty-first year and driven to despair, he wrote to the Commissioners of Woods and Forests, which looked after Crown property, saying: 'I am sure that your department has done everything that can be done, but circumstances (and the shopkeepers!) are too strong for us, at present'.[24]

That year, Roger Fry, the Bloomsbury artist, who had strong feelings both on what London should look like and on the need for aesthetics to work closely with the practicalities of everyday life, wrote a letter to *The Times* urging compromise:

> Let us now repent and go humbly to the shopkeepers. Let Messers Swan & Edgar and the rest be as vigorous in their demands for plateglass as ever they like, and then let a really good engineer solve them their problem. If the engineer has studied proportion he will suffice; if not, let an artist (perhaps even an architect) without altering the essential features give just proportions to the building. Thus we may get something really satisfactory instead of another piece of polite archaeological humbug.[25]

Shaw resigned and the issue was taken up in the House of Commons, which appointed yet another committee. When a representative of Swan & Edgar appeared before it, he demanded windows of between twenty and sixty feet in width

– a feature that the architects who spoke to the committee claimed was unworkable. The dispute would rumble on for years until, in 1923, rebuilding finally began to a design by Sir Reginald Blomfield. It wouldn't be completed until 1928.

While shopkeepers in Regent Street were agitating about the size of their shop windows, establishments on the north side of Piccadilly Circus were raising their eyes to the skies and calculating how much money they could make from their upper floors and roofs. Although today we take the bright lights of the West End for granted, it was not until the 1890s that London's businessmen realised that they could advertise their products – or someone else's – by fixing illuminated letters to the front of their buildings. Most of these 'sky signs' appeared on the north side where the new Shaftesbury Avenue had opened an enticing frontage to passers-by. Advertising was possible here because of the lax attitude of landlords, whereas the Crown, which owned land on the other sides, resolutely refused anything so vulgar. The Commissioners of Woods and Forests have maintained this stance to the present day. Their intransigent stand can be seen in the example of the Criterion, on the south side, which opened in 1874 and in 1919 hoped to follow its neighbours' glaring lead by erecting illuminated advertising. The Commissioners dismissed its application out of hand and told the restaurant to remove immediately the large board it had already erected. The Crown stood its ground through the 1920s and 1930s and only allowed small signs announcing the name of the restaurant and theatre.

Probably the first sign to be lit up above a shop fascia in Piccadilly Circus was 'Mellin's Food', which appeared in three-foot-high, no-nonsense capitals in front of the second-floor window of Mellin's Pharmacy at 48 Regent Street as early as 1904. Its next-door neighbour, cigar merchant S. Van Raalte at 2 Glasshouse Street, advertised its own wares on a similar scale, but one floor higher, and chose to use fancier script and to make the 'V' and 'R' bigger than the other letters. Neither sign appears to have received official authorisation and a third sign, urging passers-by to 'Drink Perrier Water', appeared on the parapet of the entrance to Café Monico at 46 Regent Street in 1908, despite objections from both Westminster City and London County Councils.

As the new century progressed, advertisers grew bolder and started to erect signs that didn't simply promote the business of the building whose walls they were attached to. In 1908 London County Council (LCC) twice refused permission for the erection of eight-foot-high illuminated letters that spelt out the brand names 'Bovril' and 'Schweppes' on the top storey of Piccadilly Mansions, a site on the northern corner of Piccadilly Circus and Shaftesbury Avenue. The signs remained despite the council's rebuke.

As smaller buildings slowly began to change the look of the area, at least on the north side, Mr Huttee, the lessee of the London Pavilion, realised that he didn't need to rely solely on the venue's stage and restaurant for income. The Pav's vast portico frontage was a ready-made advertising hoarding waiting to be lit up with anything from dancing girls to an unseen hand pouring a constantly replenished cocktail. In 1913, the Board of Trade would give its unintentional blessing to the advertising onslaught by seeking permission from the LCC for the erection of two illuminated, 21-foot-high signs to promote the International Exhibition in Ghent. The introduction of rationing and restrictions on lighting in the Great War temporarily snuffed out the debate about advertising, but the battle for the bright lights would be reignited in May

1920 when the Pavilion sought permission to add another sign that flashed on and off intermittently. As one of the modern editors of Pevsner's architectural guide would note, the advertisements 'got out of hand only in the early 1920s'.

Local government, architects and other groups anxious to keep the Circus in the shadows had only outdated laws and regulations with which to combat the advertisers. Most of these had been written at a time when advertising lit up by electricity simply didn't exist and the main danger was overhanging lamps or shop signs that might endanger passing pedestrians. As the battle raged over the decades, the language used in the struggle adopted the terms of a duel. The Shaftesbury Avenue leases, for example, included two clauses in which the tenant agreed not to 'cut or maim' the walls or change the elevation of the building. However, the Piccadilly Mansions tenants had been careful to avoid this sort of injury to the building with its Bovril and Schweppes signs, and in 1914 the High Court would agree that they were not guilty of infringing this rule. The Pavilion also managed to dodge the many regulations that might have stood in its way by the very nature of its architecture. The fact that its upper storeys are set back slightly and only a tiny part of its sky sign could be said to overhang the public way gave it a useful get-out clause. The London Building Act of 1894 had stated that the local authority had to give its permission for any addition that projected beyond the line of the building, but this was not clear-cut in the Pavilion's case. Nor would the theatre 'cut or maim' the fabric of the building when it erected its signs in 1920.

Throughout the twenties Mr Huttee would battle with the council over what he was allowed to erect on the roof or facia of the Pavilion. In the autumn of 1923, a large advert for Gordon's Gin appeared in front of the second-floor window of the Piccadilly Restaurant that leased space in the Pavilion. This was just one advert among many that spread across the Shaftesbury Avenue and Circus frontages. Rather than pinpricks in the sky, the new adverts created a wall of flashing lights; there was no need for passers-by to visit the newly popular cinemas, they could stand in Piccadilly Circus and gawp at the spectacle.

But the council would have at least one supporter. When the Irish writer George Moore, who had campaigned a few years earlier to stop men and boys in London whistling, was interviewed in the *New York Times* in February 1924, he turned his attention to what he called 'the savagery of electric signs'. Just as whistling 'torments' the ears, so sky signs do the same for the eyes, he argued. He went on: 'Piccadilly Circus, because of its monstrosities in flamboyant lights, Piccadilly Circus [sic] is more ridiculous than anything savages ever invented. It would be a disgrace to any planet. A cannibal feast is not more absurd. There is one horror that flaunts somebody's gin, another that pours out port and a third that insists on putting before us inescapably the name of a popular newspaper which is always advocating the beauty of London.'[26] He ended the interview by acknowledging that the sky signs were just as flamboyant in New York, but questioned why London should imitate that city. However, that battle had been lost some time ago and Piccadilly Circus's bright lights had become as dazzling as those in New York, Berlin and Paris.

*

The white noticeboard that popped its head above the doorway in 1899 next to the splendour of the Criterion restaurant, on the south side of the Circus, was much more discreet than any of the adverts that would seek attention on the skyline of Piccadilly Circus. The sign pointed out, quietly, that this would be the site of a new underground station, although it would be seven years before passengers could use it.

From the start, the station had to entice customers to venture into its depths, unlike today when most tourists and commuters have no choice but to use the Tube. The very word 'commute' was an American invention that didn't become popular in Britain until the 1940s. One of the Victorian pioneers of the London Underground, Charles Pearson, referred to the practice of travelling into the centre of London as 'oscillating'[27] and at the time he had much shorter journeys in mind. But the railways that made commuting possible and the underground lines that started to spread like veins across the capital transformed London and – in particular – the West End. Work, home and pleasure became distinct spheres and the theatres, restaurants and shops of central London were suddenly within reach for those in the suburbs and even further afield.

The Baker Street and Waterloo Railway (now the Bakerloo line) opened Piccadilly Circus underground station in March 1906, having started to clear the site in April 1902. The platforms of the Great Northern, Piccadilly and Brompton Railway (now the Piccadilly line) followed on 15 December that year. The station was designed by Leslie Green, who was twenty-nine when he became Architect to the Underground Electric Railways Company of London (UERL), an organisation set up to build the new network. His firm designed more than fifty new stations and the ones that survive – including Belsize Park, Caledonian Road, Chalk Farm and

Covent Garden – feel like portals to Edwardian London.[28] Their exteriors' shiny, terracotta tiles, known as faïence, of a deep or *sang de boeuf* (oxblood) red, channel collective memories of old-fashioned butcher's shops and municipal baths. The glaze gleamed in the London rain and helped passengers find the entrance in a foggy, still partly gaslit night.

Green's brief was to design stations that presented one unified brand. They had to be eye-catching, practical and not too expensive to build. Drawing on his time at South Kensington School of Art and another year's study in Paris where he imbibed the principles of art nouveau, he managed to come up with a design that worked within these constraints. His steel-framed Tube stations were laid out over two storeys to accommodate lifts (before escalators became the norm for all new deep-level stations after 1912). Green indulged his artistic leanings with decorative fancies such as the oculus windows at Russell Square, and led the new underground traveller through spacious ticket halls of glazed white and dark-green tiling. His stairwells and foot tunnels were lined with moulded, dark-green flowers and pomegranate leaves that felt more like Arcadian paths than today's passageways of swarming travellers.[29]

Green's designs set a standard for clarity that still prevails in today's rumbustious capital city. The station's name welcomed passengers using a bold, all-capitals typeface that guided them down tiled tunnels – which must have seemed dazzlingly bright – by way of neat arrows and an exquisite use of colons and semicolons. It was later claimed that using tiles to pick out station names helped London's illiterate travellers, though this seems unlikely, given advances in education; but it remains true that being able quickly to identify a station has helped many a newcomer to London or, in the twenty-first century, a strap-hanging commuter who has lost track of their place on the underground network. Green's glazed tiles and station clocks were also supremely practical and lasted long beyond his early death from pulmonary tuberculosis at the age of thirty-three, two years after Piccadilly Circus station first opened.

The network that would become London Underground was in its infancy and emerging at a time when other capital cities were also starting to develop their own transport systems and to take pride in them. Budapest's first line opened in 1896, followed by Paris in 1900, Berlin in 1902 and the New York subway in 1904.[30] New York, Boston and Chicago each boasted sophisticated rapid transport lines and the quick-footed financing necessary to sustain such ambitious projects. The UERL and Green's stations were only possible because of one of the fleetest of those American financiers – and perhaps the most flamboyant character ever associated with the London Underground – a Chicago tycoon with a name that sounds like a Dr Seuss character, Charles Tyson Yerkes.

Yerkes (pronounced 'Yerkees') was born in Philadelphia, where he was brought up a Quaker. He quickly discovered a talent for speculation and had made his first fortune by the age of thirty (although he overextended himself and spent nine months in Eastern State Penitentiary), and later invested in a streetcar (tram) business in Chicago. Fascinated by speed, Yerkes was used to operating in a business environment in which underhand tricks were de rigueur; he once built a tram line in the middle of the night in four hours to outmanoeuvre fractious Chicago property-owners.[31]

On a visit to London in the late 1890s he found out about plans to electrify the existing steam-operated underground and decided to move there with his 24-year-old mistress. Joining forces with a London banker, Edgar Speyer, and Robert William Perks, a solicitor who knew his way round the legal niceties required to invest in what was going on beneath street level, over the next five years Yerkes poured money into many of London's emerging underground companies and took control of three existing Tube companies, which equate closely to sections of what became the Piccadilly, Bakerloo and Northern lines. His careful mergers and acquisitions led to the creation of UERL.[32]

Yerkes brought Americanisation to the underground via terms such as 'conductor' and 'escalator'. He extended the running hours of his underground trains in a way that destroyed the 'church interval' during which, traditionally, trains took a break between 11.30 a.m. and 1 p.m.[33] But he left London before he could see the success of his plans, and died at the Waldorf Astoria Hotel in New York on 29 December 1905.

By the end of the century's first decade Piccadilly Circus had become a shopper's delight. Encouraged by the example of Selfridges in Oxford Street, the area was hell-bent on entertaining its consumers, whether they were window-shopping through oversized panes of glass or sampling the cornucopia of a department store, or the culinary equivalent in a Corner House. Shopping and eating were entertainment and their purveyors used every technological advance or marketing tool to entice their customers. Shopkeepers became better at advertising their wares, whether in their shop window or via Piccadilly Circus's sky signs. They courted the New Woman but knew that she was a complicated consumer who could be fickle. Shopkeepers had worked out what they needed to keep their customers returning and were prepared to take on lawyers and the police to ensure their windows were big enough and that they could fill them with the most distracting displays. Everything was in place for Piccadilly Circus to attract people to shop, to celebrate, to be entertained and, unwittingly, to play their part in social change. The gleaming new underground put it on the map and the area's tantalising new shop windows and persuasive sky signs gave the people who flocked to the popular meeting place something to stare into or up at.

4

Suffragettes and Shop Girls

Given the tense atmosphere around Piccadilly Circus, the events of Friday 1 March 1912 should not have come as a surprise.[1] Rumours had been circulating for weeks that something was being planned. From five o'clock that afternoon, several hundred women began to descend on the West End. They paced up and down outside shop windows as if they were weighing up whether to buy the clothes and knick-knacks on the other side of the glass until, at a synchronised moment, they took hammers – some wrapped provocatively in black stockings – and other weapons from their hiding places – most often in demure Dorothy bags or in the muffs where they were ostensibly warming their hands – and attacked the plate glass.

From the Strand, Haymarket, Coventry Street and Piccadilly Circus the air rang with shouts of 'Votes for Women!' and the sound of tinkling glass hitting the pavement from a range of shops, from tobacconists to shoemakers, the Aerated Bread Company to Lyons' Teashops.[2] Streets were plunged into darkness as lights were smashed. In some cases, sales assistants rushed out to try to bundle the women inside. One of the attackers was Dorothy Bowker, a 26-year-old woman from Cornwall who carried on smashing the window even once the police had arrived and as she was being arrested.[3] Bowker had originally been opposed to the use of violence in the campaign for suffrage, but had changed her mind after hearing Christabel Pankhurst speak. At the same time, in Downing Street three women, including Pankhurst, drove up in a car and rang the doorbell of Number Ten, before handing over a letter, which presumably outlined their demands, and hurling stones that broke four panes of glass.

In most shops, the women's hammers had inflicted a hole that then sent a spider's web of cracks across the window, showering the display dummies with shards of glass. Nearly every shop on Regent Street had its windows smashed. Swan & Edgar, which was attacked by three women, was generally agreed to have suffered most. Selfridges and Peter Robinson were both spared, though, almost certainly because of their support for the suffragettes.[4] Shoppers said the streets looked as though a riot had taken place and it was impossible to walk on the pavement without crunching glass. As quickly as they could, the shopkeepers boarded up the gaping holes, sometimes using sun canopies or brown paper to protect the exposed goods.

*

The following day, a Saturday, crowds flocked to see the damage. Three women – including Dorothy Bowker – were charged with smashing four windows at Swan & Edgar at a cost of £210 (about £20,000 in today's money) and were sentenced to three months in Aylesbury Jail, where Bowker joined the hunger strike.[5]

On Monday 11 March 1912 the WSPU (Women's Social and Political Union) held a meeting at the Pavilion at which they defended their use of violence. The speaker – replacing Pankhurst, who was in prison – was heckled by men shouting from the theatre's gallery. A few weeks later the Pavilion hosted a talk about force-feeding in Aylesbury Jail. It was big enough to hold a big audience, and also easy to reach by public transport.

It was a period when some men were looking on in disapproval and disbelief as their wives and daughters joined the fight. They included Charlotte Emily Caprina ('Cappie') Fahey, Alfred Gilbert's youngest child, who had married a painter from his studio but left him after the birth of their son and, unusually for the time, divorced him. Although Gilbert had created the memorial in Westminster Abbey to Henry Fawcett, a blind postmaster general and husband of the National Union of Women's Suffrage Societies (NUWSS) founder, Dame Millicent Garrett Fawcett, he disapproved of the movement and wrote from Bruges to his son, Alfredo, 'Cappie [is] a thumper of drums or a "tootler" on Flutes and a banner waver in a rotten Cause!!!!'[6] But in 1910 the 'tootling' suddenly became more serious when Cappie decided to go on hunger strike and was force-fed in prison.

After the window-smashing of 1912, representatives from West End shops, including Swan & Edgar, Harvey Nichols, D. H. Evans, Harrods, Marshall & Snelgrove, and Liberty, met to discuss what to do about the damage. Businesses like Swan & Edgar feared that women would give their windows a wide berth lest they were perceived to be about to assault them.[7] The *Daily Mirror* reported that the 'hammer women have done more than break windows – they have killed a fashion', because shoppers were afraid to carry portmanteaux in case they were suspected of carrying weapons.[8]

This was not the first time that the suffragettes had targeted

Piccadilly Circus. On the night of 21 November 1911, Swan & Edgar's windows had been smashed by a stone hurled by two women who had pulled up in a motor taxi; the assault caused £20 (about £2,300) worth of damage. Evelyn Huddlestone and Margaret Robinson – who were later sentenced to two months in prison – were among 233 women arrested that night after the London and North Western Railway company in Parliament Street, the Canadian Northern Railway Company in Charing Cross, and Messers Dunn, the hatters in the Strand, all had their windows smashed.[9] The WSPU chose the windows as the focus of their protest to make the point that the government cared more about property than women's lives. It was also a very public way of punishing the shops, which many of those protesters frequented, for not lobbying the government for change.

This strange set of affairs reflected the complex and symbiotic relationship between protest and consumerism. While the WSPU's newspapers, *Votes for Women* and the *Suffragette*, were urging their readers on to violent action, the very shops who were the target of those attacks were buying advertising space in the two publications. The shop owners obviously didn't relish having their windows smashed, but, at a time of greater awareness of the power of targeted advertising, the retailers recognised that many of their customers supported the suffragette cause and stores such as Swan & Edgar couldn't afford to turn their backs on such enthusiastic shoppers. Likewise, the hammer-wielding women were fully aware of how valuable shops were to their campaign. The stores provided significant income via the classified advertising sections of their publications and added legitimacy to the cause by selling stylish items of clothing that promoted the campaign (as well as more discreet items such as underwear in the suffragette colours of white, green and purple). In June 1913, for example, a Swan & Edgar advertisement in *The Common Cause*, the organ of the NUWSS, sang the praises of a set of sensible clothes to be worn on the Great Pilgrimage, a march that lasted several months and aimed to promote the peaceful side of the campaign. A series of drawings of elegant young women showed one wearing a Manilla straw hat trimmed in the NUWSS colours; another, tall figure sporting a tailored 'Dumfries' coat and skirt in wool-shrunk flannel, 'for countryside and seaside'; another wearing a voile blouse mounted on a Guipure lace yoke; and a final sketch of the lower half of a woman with an impossibly tiny waist in a 'Boyden' tailored walking skirt. A year later the store was selling the dark-green coat and skirt of the Active Service League of the NUWSS. The League pledged to use open-air meetings to welcome on board new sections of society such as shop assistants – presumably shop girls could sell the uniform for £2 2s to the very women who were trying to convert them.

*

While women were discussing how to look their best while campaigning, Kitty Marion was trying her hardest to promote the cause outside Swan & Edgar, and doing so by using the skills she had learnt as a stage performer. Despite being German by birth, she had lived in London for some time and worked in pantomime and then music hall and, while she never achieved star billing, she managed to make a living – although her striking eyes and auburn hair meant that she had continually to fight off unwanted attention from booking agents and managers. In the first decade of the twentieth century, when she was in her thirties, Marion started to write to the industry paper, the *Era*, to complain about how women were treated in the halls. After she joined the Actors' Association and the Variety Artists Federation (VAF), she disrupted one meeting by responding to a speech about general corruption among agents by blurting out 'they won't give me work because I won't kiss them!'[10] It was a natural next step to join the WSPU, which she did in 1908, as well as the Actresses Franchise League (AFL), which she became a member of the following year.

Marion's experience of projecting her voice in theatres, which didn't have the advantage of modern sound systems, and of dealing with rowdy theatre crowds, made Piccadilly Circus the obvious place for her to fulfil the movement's maxim of 'deeds not words'. It was here that she sold the WSPU's publication, *Votes for Women*. Marion described the experience in her autobiography:

> The first time, I took my place on the 'island' in Piccadilly Circus, near the flower sellers. I felt as if every eye that looked at me was a dagger piercing me through, and I wished the ground would open and swallow me. However, that feeling wore off and I developed into quite a champion paperseller.[11]

Her work in the halls may have made the public attacks less of an ordeal for her. Another seller of pamphlets, who worked the same patch at Piccadilly Circus, described how she became a target from opponents to the cause or those who viewed her as competition:

> Two old men, one a professional paper-seller and one a military looking gent, had spat at me, and one lady with a dog had poked me with her umbrella, remarking that I ought to be boiled. For the rest, the public had been more than friendly.[12]

The newspaper-seller's reaction is perhaps understandable because of the competition she posed; the vendors, along with the flower girls, certainly viewed Piccadilly Circus as their domain.

Piccadilly Circus wasn't just an ideal place in which to protest; it also offered two convenient, and familiar, venues for large gatherings and rallies behind closed doors. By 1909, the year Marion joined, the AFL had started to meet in the hushed, genteel tearooms of the Criterion.[13] The organisation chose the venue because it was conveniently close to the West End theatres, in the heart of London, and renowned for the quality of its ladies' cloakrooms. It was easy to fill the Grand and Victoria Halls as members listened to speeches from MPs and from Christabel Pankhurst. Men also attended and seemed to enjoy being surrounded by actresses.[14] The AFL aimed to attract both supporters and detractors to these 'safe', middle-class 'at homes', where they might be persuaded to lend their influence or cash to the cause.[15] It was also a good place to celebrate and in April 1909 400 WSPU followers joined a breakfast to celebrate the release of their treasurer, Mrs Pethick Lawrence, from a two-month stretch in Holloway Prison. The tables were decorated in the movement's colours of white, green and purple picked out in ribbons and flowers – irises, stocks, tulips and smilax. Emmeline Pankhurst and Mrs Lawrence both gave speeches and the evening ended with singing.[16]

Lyons' Teashops – not just the original at Piccadilly, but others, such as the one at Parliament Square – were less intimidating to women unused to the glitz of the Criterion, and also offered a base from which protesters could muster their courage over a cup of tea and a fish paste sandwich. However, as opposition to the suffragettes' demands grew among some members of the public, these cafés lost their reputation as safe havens. On the evening of Saturday 23 May 1914, for example, customers started to pelt two women who were handing out leaflets at Lyons Corner House in Coventry Street with cutlery, sugar, bread and cake. The assault was the culmination of a day of high tension; members of the WSPU had smashed West End windows and two women had attacked the glass case of a mummy in the British Museum. As a result, women were banned unless they had a letter of recommendation from someone willing to take responsibility for their behaviour. The Tate Gallery closed its doors until further notice. The women who were attacked at Lyons Corner House were put in the lift for their own safety, but when it stalled between the ground and first floors hundreds of diners, joined by passers-by, gathered in the hallway to hurl missiles through the cage for about fifteen minutes.[17]

Piccadilly Circus's place at the centre of the struggle was highlighted when the funeral procession for Emily Wilding Davison, who died when she threw herself under the feet of the King's horse at the Epsom Derby, passed through on 14 June 1913. The pavement outside Swan & Edgar teemed with people, and crowds, many in boaters, gathered on the steps of Eros to catch a glimpse of what is sometimes seen as the last great suffrage march. The women in the cortège wore white, purple, scarlet or black. That same month

Swan & Edgar was one of four companies to accuse Christabel Pankhurst and other members of the WSPU in the High Court of maliciously conspiring to procure members of the WSPU to commit trespass and damage.[18] After a three-day trial the jury took forty-five minutes to find in favour of Swan & Edgar and the other plaintiffs.

For the first time in its history, Piccadilly Circus was at the very heart of a nationwide protest movement that proved to be bitter and prolonged. Its position and reputation made it a focus for a campaign that was as nuanced as its followers. The area's reputation as a people's place attracted women who wanted to smash windows or were prepared to be heckled as they sold copies of their movement's newspapers. But it also drew individuals whose protest might be as genteel as attending a meeting at the Criterion, where the colours of the flowers were as important as the harrowing talk of hunger strikes, or who wore the suffragette colours on items of clothing normally hidden from view. This early protest movement showed that individuals could take Piccadilly Circus's familiar landmarks and repurpose them for their own cause: Swan & Edgar could be both a target for violent protest and a resource from which to raise awareness and funds; Eros's steps were a battlefield where suffragettes vied with newspaper vendors and flower girls to peddle their wares, but also a respectful vantage point from which to acknowledge the funeral cortège of a martyr to the cause; Lyons Corner House was a refuge for women devoted to their ideology but enough of a democratic meeting place for them to have to dodge bread rolls hurled by those who didn't share their views. The outbreak of the First World War would put paid to this range of dissent, but the demonstrations left an indelible mark on Piccadilly Circus's collective memory and added protest and procession to the site's inimitable personality traits.

*

Piccadilly in the first decade of the twentieth century was also starting to welcome women from a wider range of jobs who would work, and spend their free time, in the West End. The 1911 census revealed an estimated 50,000 additional women, who lived in inner London, had joined the working population (compared to the additional 4,000 extra men) and were earning a living from an increasing range of urban occupations.[19] Significantly, many of these new jobs were not based at home. Technological advances meant that women might now spend their days at a typewriter or telephone as the nature of clerical jobs changed. Other women worked in the expanding industries of food manufacturing, paper and printing, while teaching and nursing remained reliable sources of income.

But of all these new jobs, the role of the shop assistant was the one that intrigued the public, as well as writers and dramatists, more than any other. The growth of department stores such as Swan & Edgar offered new prospects for young women and the shop girl quickly caught the public's imagination and became a 'type' who appeared in songs and plays. She was among at least 2 million shop assistants who appeared in the 1911 census and half of them were female.[20] Domestic service, by comparison, fell to nearly a tenth of the 1901 figure.

At the end of the nineteenth century the shop girl's life was sometimes portrayed as a respectable option for a genteel woman who had fallen on hard times or for someone from a lower class trying to claw their way up the social ladder. In upmarket shops, at least, the job was a promising alternative to domestic service; you often didn't have to wear a uniform (although your clothes had to look similar to your co-workers') and you were always addressed properly and not simply by your first name. An article in the *Sketch* on 28 November 1894 described a shop girl in a Bond Street shop as, 'a very superior young woman. At first glance she appears all eyes, black hair, and black satin gown . . . an exceedingly long, slim waist, a throat to match, and a bearing which at once renders other people conscious of their inferiority.' The woman being interviewed earned twenty-five shillings a week and considered herself better off than many governesses, and added that she worked alongside the daughter of an army officer. In her spare time, she read, went to the music hall or theatre or attended a dance, although she admitted that she had to change out of her black satin dress before going home.

However, the Bond Street shop girl was in the minority and the reporter's next stop was 'an insignificant shop window, which displays a motley collection of pink flannel nightdresses, cheap stays, and stockings, at a bargain, with a background of knitted petticoats of an ugliness appalling'. Inside he found a 'tired-looking girl' in a brown skirt under a badly fitting 'jersey'. She is suffering from a cold and stiff neck. 'She is meant to be a pretty girl; she has tired shadows under her eyes, the colour in her eyes is fading, and her lips are pale and cracked.' She can barely live on the ten shillings she earns a week, although she has got used to an aching back and feet. On Saturday evening she often goes to the Pav with her fiancé.

Some shop girls were expected to work ninety-hour weeks,

others, typically, started at 8.45 a.m. and finished as late as 8 p.m., five days a week, with another long, busy day on Saturday. At the start of the twentieth century shops vied with one another to stay open later and the wider use of high-quality plate glass and better lighting offered by gas and then electricity made this possible. Shop girls were at the mercy of their manager, who could fine them for a petty offence such as being slightly late or being untidy in appearance. They were also beholden to customers, who could demand they fetch endless stock but might leave without buying a single item. Within department stores like Swan & Edgar there was a strict hierarchy. The store and department managers were at the top, followed by the floorwalker; there were various levels of 'sales women' and the most senior had the choice of customers and therefore a better chance of making a commission. Showroom assistants carried books to record the customers' purchases and were helped by apprentices.

Philip Carey, the main character in Somerset Maugham's *Of Human Bondage* (1915), joined that hierarchy when he became a floorwalker at a department store called Lynn and Sedley that is widely believed to be based on Swan & Edgar. At his wits' end after an unwise investment that forces him to give up his medical studies, Carey spots an advert for a job in a department store and takes what he believes to be a desperate decision, which leads to 'a curious little sinking of the heart, for with his middle-class prejudices it seemed dreadful to go into a shop'.[21] Maugham had paid Gilbert Clarke, who worked at the store at the start of the twentieth century, thirty guineas to write 6,000 words about his time at Swan & Edgar, and Clarke later claimed that Maugham used his account 'practically word for word'.[22] Clarke was a 'shop-walker' whose job it was to loiter in a particular department making sure that the assistants were being attentive and to swoop down on customers who looked as though they needed help finding an item. Swan & Edgar inspired Clarke to an even starrier career and he progressed to Paris, New York and Chicago, finally ending up in Hollywood as chief costume designer for MGM.

Of Human Bondage stresses the long, monotonous hours worked by Philip and how, after a few days, and just like the thousands of shop girls who were keeping the West End's shops going, his feet hurt so much that he could hardly stand. The store's thick, soft carpets made his legs burn and it was painful to remove his socks at night. The other 'floormen' in his lodgings in Harrington Street, just off Shaftesbury Avenue, slept with their feet dangling out of their beds to relieve the discomfort, and Philip was forced to sit with his in a pail of water. Often the discomfort was so extreme that he couldn't walk and was obliged to stay in the hostel's sitting room, where the agony was exacerbated by a co-worker from the haberdashery department who spent his evenings consumed by his stamp collection. To add to Philip's torture the man whistled as he pored over his hobby.

Many contemporary writers worried about the physical effect on the shop girls and warned about the danger of varicose veins from the widely enforced rule that shop girls were not allowed to sit down while at work. The *Pall Mall Gazette* on 30 December 1887 reported how shop girls in 'one of our biggest West-end shops' all wore elasticated socks to ease the stress. In some shops girls had to dress in a uniform with a waist of 18–20 inches, no matter their own measurements. The workwear was also awkward for anyone who was taller or shorter than the average woman of the time.

By the start of the twentieth century legislation had gone

some way towards lightening the shopworker's load: the Shop Hours Regulation Act of 1886 had limited the working day for staff aged under eighteen and reforms between 1904 and 1914 brought in further legislation to cut hours, provide a weekly half-day holiday and to regulate mealtimes. But the job was still demanding and the shop girl still had an ambiguous image.

Like the flower girl before, the public was in two minds about her. Theatregoers viewed her fondly because of her depiction in plays and musical comedies such as *The Shop Girl* (1894–6), the first act of which is set in a department store and centres around a shop girl who inherits a fortune, and *Our Miss Gibbs* (1909), about a young woman from Yorkshire who finds work in a London store. But the shop girl was also the butt of ribald jokes whose punchlines often ended with clothes being removed in the changing room or innuendo about her sexual availability. The sensual fabrics and partially clad mannequins of a department store – where the emphasis was on dressing and undressing bodies to produce the most alluring result – carried a sexual charge that was hard to ignore. While she served women, the shop girl was often harassed by male shoppers and colleagues.[23] She was also encouraged to develop unseemly skills of persuasion that made her potentially dangerous. In his memoir, Fabian of the Yard gives an account of Denise, a former shop girl, who defrauded a young man by persuading him she was well off.[24] She established the persona of a wealthy 'girl about town' by carrying boxes wrapped in paper from upmarket shops in Old Bond Street and Burlington Arcade. The packages were, in fact, empty but the props persuaded the young man that she would have no problem repaying the cash she borrowed before popping into Fortnum & Mason while he stayed in their cab. He waited in vain and she appeared to have slipped away using a door he couldn't see from the taxi. Clearly, shop girls were not to be trusted.

*

Swan & Edgar was among the large department stores that offered accommodation for many of their staff. Other shop girls had to endure grim dormitories above their workplace that made them feel like they were engaged in domestic service,[25] but Swan & Edgar insisted that its hostel offered a homely atmosphere in which shop girls shared a living room with a piano and other amenities not on offer in the average lodging house. Many families of shop girls, too, could see the advantage. And so when, in 1908, Swan & Edgar announced that it would end the living-in system so that it could convert the girls' recreational and dining areas into extra showrooms, the parents of seventy-six young women protested.[26] Eighty of the women refused to leave their accommodation and Morford had to find a compromise whereby they were offered bed and breakfast at another site, and an additional payment to cover their tea and dinner. He told a reporter:

> A number of our girls, who had been looked after by a motherly woman, to whom they are devoted, are terribly upset at the change. They have been like a large happy family. They have made their rooms pretty and surrounded themselves with their favourite knick-knacks and treasures. They feel as if they were leaving home.[27]

One of the shop 'girls', who must have been, at least in her late twenties, responded:

> I am quite miserable at the new regulation. I have been here for 11 years and cannot bear the idea of such a change. My own home is some considerable distance from town, and I do not want to go into rooms. Happily, the news of the premises to which we are going has cheered us up a bit.[28]

The protest was a sign of things to come in an industry that had been slow to unionise.

Although the hostels had the feeling of a girls' dorm – the young women abided by a curfew and a set time for lights out – the rooms offered a sense of safety in the middle of the West End's temptations. Swan & Edgar's employees also had an impressive sporting reputation and competed as the Quadrant Athletic Association. The shop's general manager, W. G. Emery, played water polo for England and the company did particularly well at swimming and rowing. The *Sporting Life* noted in February 1907 that nearly half the company's employees were members of the association, a percentage that the paper thought unrivalled by any other store.[29] Staff trained at a ten-acre farm at Shepherd's Bush and male swimmers had their club night on Fridays at Holborn Baths, while female swimmers 'disported themselves' every Tuesday evening at Marlborough Baths.

*

Department stores such as Swan & Edgar also employed a team of seamstresses who toiled away, out of sight, from 9 a.m. to 7.30 p.m., hand-sewing made-to-measure dresses in workshops that had their own specialisms such as bodices, sleeves (which in the Edwardian period were elaborate), skirts and tailoring. The work was highly skilled but the pay modest – about 12s 6d a week – and workers had to wear white overalls to protect the fine fabric from dirt brought in on the seamstresses' clothes. The seamstresses were expected to tame any material they were given and to get the better of whalebones and other fiddly parts of a gown's hidden scaffolding. The only clothes that were ready-made were those that ended up in the shop window. Occasionally, the seamstresses were challenged to see which of two teams could produce the best gown. In one instance the winning dress was a confection of green chiffon with panels of blue panne velvet. Members of the triumphant group were each given a credit note with which to buy a new pair of gloves from the glove department. Marie Lloyd bought the dress for sixty guineas. It almost certainly needed adapting to fit her curvaceous form.[30]

Shop girls, seamstresses, typists and other working women needed somewhere to go after work and on their days off. Although equal pay was still a distant dream for most women, there was a growing awareness of the concept of leisure in a sphere set apart from work that was becoming accessible to more people at the lower end of the social ladder. Suffragettes had shown how useful Piccadilly Circus could be as a centre of protest and other women from a range of backgrounds, including shop girls and shoppers, were exploring their new-found independence in its cafés, restaurants and hotels. However, it was the mechanisation of war that was to bring about arguably the biggest change in female lives in the first quarter of the twentieth century and, again, Piccadilly Circus's central position and its range of music halls, theatres, restaurants and cafés meant it was well placed to give women the chance to savour those opportunities.

Part Two

The Dim-Out

5

'Now You've Got Yer Khaki On'

Tea at the Criterion that afternoon in December 1914 was a tense affair for Vera Brittain, a twenty-year-old who had just struggled through her first term at Oxford University, where women students were a rarity. Vera, who had ambitions to become a writer, had fallen in love with a close friend of her brother Edward, and was about to meet her sweetheart's mother for the first time.

Roland Leighton was a few months younger than Vera, but had the assurance of someone much older. She described how his 'powerful frame and big head with its stiff, thick hair gave him the appearance of a very large person'.[1] They had got to know one another during walks and heated discussions about God and literature at her home in Derbyshire. Long letters had helped to stoke that ardour. Edward and Roland were both at university, and had applied for commissions when war was declared on Tuesday 4 August 1914. Roland was the first to receive his and joined the 7th Worcestershire Regiment.

Vera and Roland had met a few days after Christmas and before the nerve-racking introduction to his parents during his few days' leave. He was in uniform and sported a new, rather sparse moustache; she wore a new, rose-trimmed hat and squirrel coat her father had bought her. She would later describe her appearance as 'childish chocolate-box prettiness'.[2] At 5 foot 3 inches tall Vera felt tiny next to Roland, as she tried to steal glances at him from beneath her hat. Vera was staying for the Christmas break in her grandmother's house in Purley, south London, from where she took daily trips to the West End to meet Roland. Chaperoned by Edward or her aunt, they went to the theatre, restaurants or on shopping expeditions.

London was changing and for young couples like Vera and Roland it was an even more thrilling place for trysts. Searchlights swept the skies hunting for Zeppelins, and the West End turned its lights down to make it harder for the enemy to find a way through. Although those who experienced both world wars would say the first 'blackout' was more like 'a dim-out', the area had, nevertheless, shed some of its lustre. Shops obscured their outside lights, tramcars turned theirs off and pedestrians had to negotiate pavements with less help from streetlamps. Thrillingly, the encroaching darkness meant that Roland was obliged, as the gentleman he was, to take Vera's arm as he guided her across the gloomy streets.

Tea in the upholstered calm of the Criterion, while Piccadilly Circus continued its bustle outside the five-storeyed building, represented the culmination of an intense day during which Vera and Roland had barely spent a minute apart. He had insisted on accompanying her to the dressmakers, the milliners and even the underclothing department of D. H. Evans as she gathered items for her next term at Oxford. The shopping made them late to meet Roland's mother, Marie Connor Leighton, and sister, Clare, and so they took a taxi to Piccadilly Circus, where the two women were waiting for them in the Criterion's lounge.

Clare, who would later become a famous artist, had two, long, thick plaits and seemed to Vera very young for someone who was sixteen. Marie wore furs and velvets and appeared to Vera the 'embodiment' of the world of letters. Roland had proclaimed himself a feminist through the fact that his mother, a journalist and novelist, had contributed to the household expenses and to his school fees at Uppingham. In fact, Marie probably earned more than her husband, Robert, who was also a journalist and novelist. Marie idolised her eldest son and was wary about his association with a woman who was studying at Somerville College because she thought Vera would be 'very academic',[3] telling him that Oxford was no use to a writer 'except of treatises'.[4] Marie disapproved of the 'modern' type of woman but was reassured that the object of her son's affection was 'too much the pretty-pretty type ever to seem aggressively up to date'.[5] Vera remembered very little of the tea, but she appeared to pass the test.

The following day, after Roland saw Vera and her aunt on to the train for Purley, which left from Charing Cross, he returned to Piccadilly Circus, where he welcomed in 1915 standing next to Eros (which wasn't taken away for safety until the final year of the war). Later he wrote to Vera:

> It was a glorious night, with a full moon so brightly white as to seem blue slung like an arc-lamp directly overhead. I had that feeling of extreme loneliness one is so often conscious of in a large crowd. There was very little demonstration; two French men standing up in a cab singing the 'Marseillaise'; a few women and some soldiers behind me holding hands and softly humming 'Auld Lang Syne'. When twelve o'clock struck there was only a little shudder among the crowd and a distant muffled cheer and

> then everyone seemed to melt away again, leaving me standing there with tears in my eyes and feeling absolutely wretched.[6]

Vera and Roland were experiencing a new, muted Piccadilly Circus. The first, hesitant glow of neon light, which had arrived in 1913 and had once again changed the way brands advertised on the Circus's streets, had been smothered due to the outbreak of war. In Britain, the word 'neon' has since become a catch-all term used to refer to any brightly coloured light, even one filled with other gases. However, the original, magical substance of neon was first discovered in a lab in University College, London in 1898 by a chemistry professor and his assistant. Neon (which means 'new' in Greek), like argon, helium, krypton and xenon, is a noble gas – the term for a gas that doesn't react to anything. When a current is passed through a tube containing neon gas the tube emits light, which makes it perfect to use in advertising and signage. The first neon sign to be used in advertising is thought to have appeared on the Boulevard Montmartre in Paris in 1912 to highlight a barber's shop with the words, 'PALAIS COIFFEUR'.[7]

The West End Cinema Theatre in Coventry Street was one of the first buildings in central London to make use of the gas. Cinemagoers flocked there to enjoy the new entertainment of film either from one of the theatre's 500 seats flanked by baroque plasterwork or by taking the marble stairs to the stalls; they could sip a cup of tea in the café or dine in the subterranean Elysee Restaurant, which, in the 1920s, would be transformed into the Café de Paris nightclub.[8] Soon after the theatre opened, in March 1913, its name appeared outside in red neon lights and its monumental, arched window was framed with white tubes. But it lasted just a few months before London had to turn off its bright lights to protect it from aerial attack. Neon lights would return to London in the Jazz Age of the 1920s and 1930s to illuminate rainy London streets with their muted glow and to blur the distinction between night and day. Later still, neon would come to provide a too-easy shorthand for sleaze and solitude.

*

War also quickly changed the cast of players drawn to Piccadilly Circus. German, Swiss and Austrian waiters and music hall turns, or anyone with a Teutonic-sounding name, suddenly became the enemy. For many this meant concealing their ancestry or readjusting a persona originally adopted to seem glamorous. The magician Carl Hertz, for example, announced publicly that he was American, and the comedian George Mozart admitted that his real name was David John Grilling and that he came from Great Yarmouth.[9]

Suffragettes, who had mounted a campaign of attacks in art galleries during the early summer of 1914, agreed a ceasefire so that they could support the national emergency. But while their official campaign was put on hold, they made inroads into male-dominated worlds by replacing men who joined up or, after 1916, were conscripted. During the war women could be seen delivering the post, lighting streetlamps and cleaning windows, and they drove all sorts of vehicles – from cars to ambulances – and worked as dispatch riders, donning breeches to leap onto motorbikes. In their spare time they even dared to relax over a cigarette.[10]

London's traffic changed too. Some buses operated by the London General Omnibus Company (LGOC) were commandeered and many employees were called up or volunteered.[11] If you could find a taxi – and many had been converted to ambulances, while hundreds of hansom cabs lost horses to the war effort – placards reminded customers that 'Your King and country need you' in an echo of the posters pasted on walls around the capital. By August 1916 it was forbidden to hail a taxi at night with the traditional method of a shrill whistle in case it disturbed injured soldiers trying to rest in London's hospitals.[12]

As men stepped down from their familiar jobs, the thousands who found themselves in uniform were funnelled through London; for many, Piccadilly Circus was a natural port of call and it became associated with a unique mixture of urgent hedonism and nostalgia in the area's latest version of a people's meeting place. As the war progressed, those soldiers started to come from further afield: from New Zealand, Australia, Canada and the United States. Once casualties increased, the injured returned and it became common to see not just a wide array of uniforms but also those uniforms adjusted to take account of missing limbs: sleeves folded back over absent arms and men hobbling along on sticks. There was less colour on the streets as more women dressed in mourning black, like crows shuffling along the pavements. Vera Brittain joined that growing crowd of bereaved women on 26 December 1915 – a year after her unforgettable tea at the Criterion – when she heard of Roland's death at the hands of a sniper. She was, by then, serving as a nurse in Camberwell, south London. He was the first of many losses she would endure.

*

Until a few years ago, it was widely believed that the song 'It's a Long Way to Tipperary' sprang to life in 1912 in response to a five-shilling bet that Worcestershire-born Jack Judge, a music hall performer and former fishmonger, could not compose and perform a brand-new song within twenty-four hours. However, a more recent interpretation suggests that Judge adapted an existing song that he had co-written in 1909 with Henry 'Harry' James Williams, whose family ran a pub in Warwickshire and who became a wheelchair user after a childhood accident.[13] The original version was called 'It's a Long Way to Connemara' and told the story of a homesick Irish boy writing to his sweetheart from London. Judge changed the place name to Tipperary because that was where his grandparents were from. When, in August 1914, a *Daily Mail* reporter heard a battalion of the Connaught Rangers (an Irish regiment based in Galway) singing the song to boost morale as they arrived in France, the paper printed the lyrics in full and it became one of the biggest hits of the war. Soldiers from around the world marched to its beat or sang, as they rested between assaults, about an Irishman who visits London Town eager to see the attractions of Piccadilly, the Strand and Leicester Square but waves them goodbye in favour of the sweetest girl he knows, who is back in Ireland. The sentiments sum up the curious place the Circus held in the psyche of people who may only have visited it a handful of times – or even just once. Despite its whirlpool of visitors, Piccadilly Circus represented something that was comforting in its immutability. Today, the song is one of the oldest still bringing in royalties, which a few years ago amounted to around £30,000 a year for Williams's descendants. Judge, whose own son was killed in the war, sold his rights to his co-author for £5 when he fell on hard times. Despite its surprising origins, it remains steeped in nostalgia and a longing for London – particularly Piccadilly Circus – even by people who may only ever have had a fleeting acquaintance with the area.

Soldiers who passed through London needed entertaining, but the nature of that entertainment changed during the war years. A disproportionately high number of men employed by London's theatres, restaurants and hotels joined up and those who remained had to drum up trade without the help of advertising signs, and find a way to welcome customers into foyers where the lights had been dimmed. Alcohol was hard to come by and food shortages became more acute as the war progressed: bread rolls contracted in size and taste, and food prices rose. War led to a moral panic about increased drinking among women and soldiers on leave. As a result, pub opening hours were squeezed and it became illegal to buy someone else a drink – even if you were married to them. Moral crusaders grew increasingly worried about the enjoyment to be had in music halls and cinemas and both faced a continued battle against the type of entertainment they could portray.[14] Organisations like the National Council of Public Morals and the Crusade of the Workers for Self-Denial worried about audiences gathering in the dark to watch debauched scenes of violence or of a sexual nature, and about the opportunity for both heterosexual and homosexual fumbles in the dark.[15] The phenomenon of 'War Babies', conceived in the heat of new freedoms, or as a result of the encroaching khaki, exercised campaigners. As news from the front became grimmer nearly every non-essential activity, from window-dressing to using scented soap, could be seen as excessive consumption.[16]

*

In 1914, Marie Lloyd was forty-four and continued to be one of the most popular music hall performers in Britain. On the day war was declared, she was appearing at the London Pavilion. Her complicated private life increased the audience's enjoyment of songs such as 'A Little of What You Fancy Does You Good' (1915), and of the innuendo in 'Now You've Got Yer Khaki On', which is about a soldier and his girlfriend worrying about his furlough being cut short. The lyrics to most of Marie's songs are best listened to with an ear cocked for saucy subtext. 'The Piccadilly Trot' (1912), written and composed by George Arthurs and Worton David to a tune that capitalised on the popular ragtime beat, is no exception. The second verse, in particular, describes an encounter that could easily be with a prostitute in a busy, night-time Piccadilly Circus. By the time we reach the final line it seems an obvious conclusion that the 'fatted calves' are plump limbs, rather than anything biblical.

*

The war put Lloyd in an awkward position. She wasn't the sort of person to follow rules – in either her private or public life. She had joined the picket lines during the music hall performers' strike of 1906–7 – which objected to the long hours and low pay forced on stagehands, musicians and minor acts – when her protest became an extension of her stage act and she strutted along the pavement in her sumptuous gowns, jewellery and furs, silencing hecklers with her well-practised one-liners. When a second-rate singer called Belle Elmore, who fancied she bore a resemblance to Lloyd, took advantage of the shortage of good acts to brave the strikers, Lloyd is reported to have shouted, 'Don't be daft.

Let her in. She'll empty the theatre.'[17] (Belle Elmore, whose real name was Cora Crippen, met an unhappy end three years later when her husband, the homeopathic practitioner Dr Crippen, killed her and hid her body under the brick floor of the basement in their home in Hilldrop Crescent in north London.)

The dispute was part of a shift away from the raucous music halls of the Victorian period. In the years leading up to the war, 'variety', as it was increasingly known, was becoming more respectable and the theatres in which the stars performed grander and more comfortable. Lloyd's involvement in the music hall performers' strike may have cost her a place on the bill of the first Royal Command Performance, held in July 1912 at the Palace Theatre on Cambridge Circus, at the other end of Shaftesbury Avenue from Piccadilly Circus. But it wasn't just her picket line history. At that time, Lloyd had moved in with Bernard (Ben) Dillon, a champion jockey who was closer to her daughter's age, and this fact, together with her existing reputation, made her less respectable than many of her rivals; she was also well known for ad-libbing, often with a saucy aside, and this and her tendency to run over time made her a liability. The royal performance proved to be a stilted version of music hall, but Lloyd's omission was, nevertheless, a painful snub. On the night itself she was on stage at the London Pavilion and it was rumoured that she had arranged for placards to be put up saying, 'Every performance by Marie Lloyd is a command performance – by command of the British Public'.

On the day war was declared Lloyd wore a pink gown twinkling with diamonds and carried a matching parasol to strut along the stage at the Pavilion singing 'The Dress of the Day', a song about techniques for attracting men, before changing into a white gown with a green sash (perhaps a nod to the suffragettes) for subsequent numbers. In case there was any doubt about her intentions she sang 'The Next Best Thing – Being Careful If You Can't Be Good'. Lloyd's fans had joined the audience in a bid to forget about the harsh world outside – the rumours of collapsing banks and shops running out of food. The crowd, fired up with patriotic pride, was said to have sung the French, Russian and British national anthems – although it seems more likely that they hummed along to all but 'God Save the King'. Whichever it was, their enthusiasm showed how keen the audience was to join in the entertainment.

The war posed many challenges for performers. Some changed their acts to accommodate the prevalence of soldiers and their sweethearts, wives and mothers in the audience, but Vesta Tilley, a male impersonator from Worcester, went further than most by setting herself up as a one-woman recruiting machine.[18]

Tilley, whose real name was Matilda ('Tilley' for short) Powles, was born in 1864, the second of thirteen children. She began her professional singing and dancing career when she was five and, finding that she enjoyed dressing as a boy, three years later adapted her act to one in which she assumed a male persona. Her success was such that her father abandoned his job as a music hall 'chairman', or master of ceremonies, to manage his daughter, who became the sole earner for their ever-increasing family. She made her debut in London in 1874, aged ten, and it was during her season in the capital that Edward Villiers, manager of the Canterbury Music Hall, suggested she change her name to reassure audiences who seemed confused by the child's gender. He suggested 'Vesta' after the popular brand of matches and to acknowledge the precocious nature of her talent as a 'bright spark'.

The new train and underground railway network made it possible for music hall performers to attract a more middle-class and suburban audience and, while Marie Lloyd always stayed close to her East End roots and could be relied on for her trademark innuendo, Vesta Tilley's act was famously clean. However, while Tilley's material was predictably wholesome, her admirers were attracted to her act for a range of reasons. Most of her fans were women, and contemporaries spoke of enjoying the wit with which she, as a female, mocked her male characters. Other women found a maternal appeal in her depiction of young boys. And, of course, there was always the novelty of seeing a woman dressed as a man and this brought with it a certain amount of titillation. At the Royal Command Performance, the queen was reported to have urged her ladies-in-waiting to cover their eyes with their programmes rather than see female legs in trousers.

Always introduced as 'Miss Vesta Tilley', she never tried to deepen her voice – even when singing songs such as 'Burlington Bertie' or 'Algy, the Piccadilly Johnny with the Little Glass Eye' – or disguise her body; photos of the time clearly show an obvious bust and her face makes no pretence at having stubble. Tilley was meticulous in her costume – her authenticity extended to wearing men's underwear and she insisted on carrying a genuine soldier's knapsack because the lighter, straw-filled kind didn't swing properly as she marched.[19]

By the 1890s Tilley had become one of the highest-earning women in Britain. Like Lloyd she had toured America several times but, unlike her rival, she was hugely successful in an overseas market that was usually difficult for British performers to prise open. Her marriage to a music hall manager, Abraham Walter de Frece, also gave her the respectability and stability that Lloyd lacked. But it was the First World War that provided her and her husband with the chance to move from the stalls to the royal box of Britain's elite.

At a time when many music hall songs were about sailors, Tilley turned her attention to songs about soldiers and her repertoire at theatres such as the London Pavilion included numbers such as 'Jolly Good Luck to the Girl Who Loves a Soldier', 'Jack Tar Home from Sea', 'The Army of Today's All Right', 'A Bit of a Blighty One' and 'Six Days' Leave'. She even, unusually, took the lead part in the three-reel film *The Girl Who Loves a Soldier* (1916), playing a young nurse who poses as a man to deliver an important message to her wounded fiancé. The film had its premiere at the Pavilion. Audiences wallowed in the patriotism and many men were persuaded to join up there and then.[20] In one week alone Tilley enlisted a whole battalion, which became known as 'The Vesta Tilley Platoon'. She also sold war bonds, and donated all the proceedings from the sale of her picture postcards to charity.[21]

Lloyd also did her part raising money for wartime charities, but not on the same scale as Tilley or Scottish singer and comedian Harry Lauder, whose son was killed on the Western Front and whose fundraising efforts were honoured at a lunch at the Criterion. Lloyd's only relative in uniform was her third husband, Ben, but he had unsuccessfully applied for exemption from duty after conscription was introduced for men between the ages of eighteen and forty-one in 1916 because he had two parents and four brothers to support. In 1917 he was arrested for being absent without leave and accused of beating his wife. This pattern of violence was to be repeated over several years and became an aspect of Lloyd's life that the public was well aware of and which added a poignancy to one of her final songs, 'One of the Ruins That Cromwell Knocked about a Bit'. For many, the lyrics were a subtle reference to her own experience of domestic abuse. On 8 April 1921, the year before Lloyd died, Virginia Woolf, who enjoyed music hall, described her in her diary as 'a mass of corruption – long front teeth – a crapulous way of saying "desire", & yet a born artist – scarcely able to walk, waddling, aged, unblushing. A roar of laughter went up when she talked of her marriage. She is beaten nightly by her husband.' Lloyd's act kept domestic violence at arm's-length and acknowledged that a woman could have two distinct personas: a very public, glamorous life and a darker, private struggle. She was unusual in depicting a highly successful woman on stage and one who brought together the East and West Ends in the most public of arenas. Throughout her life she made few compromises to what the Establishment wanted of her and when she died in 1922, aged fifty-two, West End pubs draped their beer taps with black and an estimated 100,000 people attended her funeral in north London.

The Great War dimmed the lights at Piccadilly Circus and changed its atmosphere. It became an even more important site at which to meet, but war added a new dimension to many of those meetings; they were urgent and wistful and carried the threat that this might be the *last* meeting for some couples. While Piccadilly Circus would always be a place at which to try on different personas, the war forced people to take sides – not just in the obvious sense but by choosing what was important to them. For music hall stars like Marie Lloyd, it proved impossible not to show war through a saucy, flirtatious lens; others, such as Vesta Tilley and Harry Lauder, felt compelled to bring a more active element to their stage performances and beyond. The war changed the sort of entertainment visitors to Piccadilly Circus experienced; it changed where they stayed and what they ate. The conflict was all-consuming and made the need to let off steam more urgent. While the lights were dimmed, they still offered a release from the shadow of the trenches.

6

'The Wickedest Pavement in England'

Squashed under a bed among the lint and hairballs, desperately trying to scribble down shorthand in a notebook, was not the ideal way to experience the pleasures of Europe's largest hotel.[1] But there was no other option for Detective Sergeant Brewer, who had been forced into hiding in the Regent Palace in order to track down a criminal in an area of London famous for the range and frequency of offences committed there, an area that Fabian of the Yard described as 'the wickedest pavement in England'.[2]

The Regent Palace, which opened in 1915 and had 1,028 bedrooms, was yet another outpost of the Lyons empire.[3] Oliver Bernard, who also worked on Corner Houses and hotels, designed the interior. He had no formal architectural training but had fallen in love with art deco while working in theatres in London, Manchester, New York and Boston, and his ornate bars and restaurants feel, at times, like stage sets. As one twentieth-century commentator put it, he was creating settings for hotel customers who were 'slightly better off and more sophisticated without being in the least open to the charge of being fast . . . he was out to design interiors which communicated a sense of fun, a feeling that you were very definitely not at home but need not be nervous all the same.'[4] A 1935 description of the hotel's cocktail bars confirms this delicate balancing act; they were 'just a trifle dissipated and naughty, but not sufficiently so to be vulgar'.[5] It was, perhaps, this broad-minded attitude that allowed Quentin Crisp, author of *The Naked Civil Servant,* to choose the hotel as the venue for his only public outing in drag, probably in the early 1930s. He was living at Baron's Court at the time and took the Tube to Piccadilly Circus dressed in a black silk dress and velvet cape. His escort to the hotel wore a dinner jacket. 'The evening was a triumph, in that it was boring; nothing happened,' he wrote later.[6]

From the outside, the Regent Palace looks as if it is holding its breath to allow it to squeeze into its one-acre, triangular plot on the north side of Piccadilly Circus, where it is bordered by Glasshouse, Sherwood, Brewer and Air streets. But its height more than makes up for the tight fit. Nine floors climb to its green-tiled roof, while a lower ground floor, basement and sub-basement burrow in the opposite direction. An ornate 'Bridge of Sighs', with terracotta and green roof tiles, links the main building to its massive laundry and 160 staff bedrooms. Its slim height is reminiscent of New York's Flatiron Building and the *Burlington Magazine for Connoisseurs* described it in 1917 as 'resplendent in its white terra-cotta dress and making a showy contrast to the distinguished Ritz in Piccadilly'.[7]

Lyons liked to stress the building's connection with film stars and actors but also, very subtly, and in a tactic used in their Teashops, emphasised its affordability. The company confronted the social anxiety about whether or not to tip through its telegraphic address, 'UNTIPPABLE PICCY', and the full-page advert on the front of the *Daily Mail* on 26 May which reassured, 'A Palace hotel – LITERALLY' above

'NO TIPS' in bold.[8] Prices ranged from 6/6 a day (single) to 13/- a day (double).[9] This is similar to the daily rate charged by the Imperial Hotel in Russell Square and slightly more expensive than the Gower Hotel in Euston Square, where rooms started at four shillings. However, the Regent Palace was much more glamorous and centrally placed. Soon after it opened much of its accommodation was requisitioned for the war effort – Wilfred Owen stayed there in October 1915, three weeks before he joined up[10] – and it later became a favourite destination for honeymooning couples who might only be able to afford one night in the centre of London. The hotel was also popular for trysts and saw more than its fair share of shootings, scams and suicides. There was always the slight whiff of sleaze about the Regent Palace Hotel. Hence the policeman lying in wait under one of its beds in 1917.

The two men Detective Sergeant Brewer was waiting for entered the hotel via the main entrance facing Piccadilly Circus. They went through a hall into a circular lounge lined with marble and then took either the marble staircase, a lift or the more modest staircase beyond the large swing door. They continued into the Rotunda Court where stairs off the ladies' and general writing rooms led to bedroom floors. One of the men Brewer was awaiting was Warrant Officer Howard Hawkins, who was staying at the hotel under the pseudonym Burgess. He had already had dinner – perhaps in the Louis XVI Restaurant or, more likely, the huge Grill Room on the lower ground floor. The other man was Mordecai Markham, a 34-year-old ladies' tailor who worked in Great Portland Street.

Hawkins had been introduced to Markham through the strange case of an Australian soldier, Albert Orr. In January 1917 Orr, a 21-year-old from Adelaide who had joined up three years earlier, had arrived back in London, having served in both the Sinai Peninsula and France. He was desperate not to return to the front and conveyed these fears to a prostitute, who put him in touch with Markham. The tailor in turn introduced him to John Henderson Bell, a forty-year-old doctor from Chelsea who worked at Brompton Hospital and Edinburgh Royal Infirmary. For £25 Bell injected Orr in the knee with a substance that caused the joint to balloon to the extent that he had to be hospitalised. The soldier told the authorities the injury happened when he fell off a bus, but later confessed. The army decided to set up a 'sting' to provide enough evidence to trap Bell and Markham.

Hawkins – posing as Burgess – contacted Markham claiming to be a soldier seeking the same injection as Orr to avoid active service, and Markham arranged for them to meet in a Regent Palace room. From beneath the bed Detective Sergeant Brewer jotted down their conversation. Markham arranged for Hawkins to have the injection and said it would put him in hospital for four months. Hawkins handed over another £10 (he'd already placed a down payment of £10 towards the total fee of £50 – about £3,000 today) but Markham decided that the procedure would take place at the prostitute's home because Dr Bell didn't fancy performing it in a hotel bedroom.

And so, a few days later Brewer was hiding under another bed – this time belonging to the prostitute. There he recorded a discussion between his undercover officer and Dr Bell about whether Hawkins's injection should be in the knee or the nose – the latter was likely to prove tender as Hawkins was suffering from a cold. As Dr Bell produced a bottle of iodine and prepared the syringe, he promised the operation would put the soldier in hospital for at least two months, adding reassuringly, 'When I have finished with you, you will not be able to do any more military service.' At this point Brewer scrabbled out from under the bed and arrested both Bell and Markham. Their reactions are not recorded, but they must have been dumbfounded.

Although this was clearly a case of what would today be seen as entrapment, the White City recruiting case (in which men liable for conscription paid doctors to give them a low medical classification or medical exception) was cited as an example of a police technique that had reached the High Court without any quibbles from the judges. By this point in the war – after three years of fighting, a growing casualty list and the introduction of conscription – the authorities were becoming increasingly alarmed at the techniques men were using to avoid being called up or returning to the front. In June 1918 Dr Bell was convicted of 'attempting to produce a disease' in a man belonging to HM Forces and of 'doing an act preparatory to producing a disease or infirmity' in another member of the Forces. He was sentenced to six months' imprisonment with hard labour – later modified to six months' imprisonment in the second division (that is, without hard labour). Surprisingly, the General Medical Council, after hearing evidence from Dr Bell, decided not to remove his name from the medical register. Indeed, it went as far as to say that the procedure seemed 'perfectly usual and [a] proper medical routine'.

Despite its claims to propriety, the Regent Palace was the venue for several attempts at deception, perhaps due to Piccadilly Circus's reputation as a place where the whole world gathered and where dressing up was encouraged. In 1915 Ernest Andrews, a 23-year-old, was arrested for wearing an officer's uniform there, an offence that had first become law in 1894 under the Uniforms Act and which excluded actors dressing up for a play. Andrews 'came of good stock' and had been educated at Oxford. He had left New York to join up but had 'got into bad company', been found absent without leave and faced a court martial. In sentencing Andrews, the magistrate said the unauthorised wearing of an officer's uniform was 'obviously an open door to fraud and misdeeds'. He might have added that the Regent Palace Hotel's affordable glamour made it the ideal setting in which to perpetrate such deeds. The magistrate took into account the defendant's age and gave him the option of paying a £20 fine.[11]

There were many reasons why a man might wear a uniform, or parts of a uniform, to which he was not entitled. It was a good way of avoiding the recruiting sergeant or a white feather from a censorious woman. Some men felt they were entitled to a uniform – either because of past service or because they were contributing to the war effort in other ways. Some simply liked the glamour it bestowed, the chance to be someone else. Twenty-year-old Louis Fodell, for example, appears simply to have relished the 'look'. In April 1915 the police told him to stop wearing puttees and breeches (he was also wearing a khaki collar, tie and shirt), but he ignored this warning and was later arrested in Piccadilly Circus.[12] Probably the most outrageous case of impersonation was Humphrey Pomfret in 1922; he claimed to have lost his sight in active service and was selling bootlaces and match-boxes near the hotel. His military-hospital-blue uniform boasted the Croix de Guerre, Mons Star, General Service Medal and Military Cross and he usually attracted a crowd, dominated by women – many of whom were moved to tears. He was arrested when it was discovered he had no right to wear the uniform or the medals and that he had been blinded while trying to brew up nitroglycerin for safe-breaking in his basement kitchen in Clerkenwell.[13]

*

As well as deceit, newspaper reports confirmed Piccadilly Circus's association with other vices. The *Weekly Dispatch* posed the rhetorical question of why a young officer walking from a hotel in Regent Street to Piccadilly Circus had been accosted sixteen times.[14] Prostitutes were a common sight at the Circus during wartime. Arnold Bennett wrote in his diaries of the 'grues' (sex workers, or 'prostitutes' as they would have been described at the time) he saw going backwards and forwards on the north side of Coventry Street and how the gloom seemed to put each woman, whether young or old, pretty or otherwise, on an equal footing, until they lurched into the unforgiving arc of a lamplight.[15] Some observers believed the war was attracting more, younger women, a few only fifteen years old, to sex work, and that many had been forced into it by economic hardship, unlike the older 'professionals' who frequented the area in peacetime. In reality, the number of arrests and convictions for soliciting and related offences fell during the war, although it may still have been the case that more young women were attracted to earning a living this way.[16]

The Women Police Service (WPS), which emerged during this period, was particularly keen to rescue young women.[17] The organisation was founded in 1914 by Nina Boyle from the Women's Freedom League and musician and philanthropist Margaret Damer Dawson. Volunteer constables and officers were patrolling towns and cities across the UK by the following year, although the chief commissioner took against them and refused to make them a permanent part of the police. The WPS was particularly interested in young women, whose age seemed to make them more vulnerable to the temptations of immorality, and drove away the men who were waiting to take advantage of them. WPS officers patrolled in pairs, their moral probity reinforced by their serge blue jacket, skirt and hat, adorned with 'WPS' in silver letters. Piccadilly Circus and Coventry Street were favourite spots on their patrols, which lasted from 8 p.m. to 12.30 a.m. Their strategy was to follow any young woman who looked as if she was about to commit an immoral act and simply to stare her down as a way of deflating the ardour of both parties.

Age was also cited as a contributing factor in another case, but in this instance it was the male who was portrayed as the victim, as the *People* announced in its headline on 18 February 1917, 'How Boy-Officer Was Inveigled into Marriage by a Lady He Met in Piccadilly'. William Amsden was nineteen when he met his future wife, 23-year-old Norinne Fournier Schofield – although the report does not name her – who was listed in the 1911 census as a 'professional dancer'; her father was a 'professional vocalist' and her mother had been born in France. Amsden had been a boarder at Charterhouse public school and was working at his father's firm in the City when he joined the army in 1915. He met Norinne one evening on a trip up to London from Woodbridge, in Suffolk, where the 12th (County of London) Battalion (known as The Rangers) was stationed. Norinne told him she was an actress and they spent the night at a room in Soho, where Amsden said she appeared to be known. He returned to Woodbridge, but after Norinne wrote to say she was worried about her career and unhappy living at home with her parents Amsden sent for her to join him in Suffolk. After three days together in Woodbridge, Norinne insisted that they should marry, claiming he had made a promise and that she had been 'compromised'. Norinne arranged the wedding in a Catholic church in Ipswich, although Amsden was a Protestant, and told him he must say he was twenty-one so that he could marry without his parents' consent. On a visit to Amsden's parents after the wedding they 'tried to make the best of things, but it was a failure' and a separation was arranged whereby Norinne received an allowance. In the subsequent divorce case – which Amsden did not attend as he was on active service at the time – two waiters, who had lived at Piccadilly Circus Mansions where Norinne had had a flat, gave evidence that she had been visited by a man, thought to be an officer. In a signed affidavit Amsden accused Norinne of drug and alcohol addiction and said she had attacked him physically in public. A decree nisi was granted.[18]

Norinne and Amsden's story was the sort of misadventure that moral crusaders felt was becoming common in a period when it was too easy for wayward women to prey on young soldiers. Indeed, some might have felt that Amsden got off lightly. The Reverend Frederick Brotherton Meyer, for example, a minister in south London,[19] was convinced that women were luring soldiers to their bedrooms where they drugged them and robbed them of their possessions. The *People* gave the story several column inches on page four and stoked prurient interest with details that emerged in court. The union was a perfect storm of all the ingredients that might make up an encounter in Piccadilly Circus: the difference in age (Amsden was described as 'the boy husband'), class, nationality (as Norinne's mother was French), religion, income and experience. And then there was much that wasn't made explicit in the account but which most readers would have inferred: the word 'actress' was heavy with suggestion, the picture of the meeting with the in-laws allowed the reader to add their own details (it was easy to imagine the look on Amsden's parents' faces as they recognised what their son was unaware of or did not want to acknowledge) and the final detail of the officer visitor (who was surely a client).

The court case was a reminder of the sort of encounters to be had at Piccadilly Circus and how the war had made them easier. In the past someone like Amsden might not have ventured there alone, but now he was a soldier eager to experience something different on his furlough. Norinne may not have been the temptress the press depicted her as, but the meeting, nevertheless, put her in touch with a world that, in normal times, would have been well beyond her reach.

*

The threat of moral danger was taken seriously by sections of the public, church leaders and the new Women Police Service and made titillating reading for newspaper consumers. Enemy action, in the first few years of the war at least, seemed trivial by comparison. In fact, the government took an unusual approach to air raid warnings – there weren't any.[20] It was decided that raising the alarm might worry the public and, since there were very few anti-aircraft guns, the sound of their rat-a-tat-tat failed to alert Londoners to an approaching air strike in the way that became usual in the Blitz of 1940–41.

The first Zeppelin airship drifted over London's sky one night at the end of May 1915 and caused awe rather than terror. People hung out of their bedroom windows to gaze at the spectacle or rushed into the street to peer up at the ethereal, silvery-blue cigar. On the night of the fifth and final attack of that year, Wednesday 13 October, however, it became clear just how deadly these vessels could be. Three Zeppelins bore down on the capital. One bombed East Croydon and a second caused mayhem at the riverside near Woolwich. The third airship, which was a new vehicle, approached from the north-west. Its captain, Joachim Breithaupt, was aiming for Whitehall but miscalculated and instead dropped his bombs north of the Strand. Figures differ about exactly how many people died that night, but the toll would have been much higher if a theatre had been hit. As it was, seventeen people were killed as they queued to buy refreshments from a street vendor during the interval.[21] The extent of the attacks was passed on solely by word of mouth as newspapers were forbidden from reporting the details. The carnage, however, did stop people grumbling quite so much about the restrictions on lighting. Their tetchiness was replaced with a jumpiness around even the smallest light, such as a smouldering cigarette butt. And as spy mania took hold, any unusual behaviour could lead to arrest. Philip de László, a distinguished Hungarian artist, for example, became a British citizen as soon as war was declared, but this was viewed by some as suspicious in itself, and a rumour later spread that he had been using his cigarette lighter to signal to Zeppelins from Piccadilly Circus.[22]

By 1917 the capital was exhausted. It had become a quieter and smellier place as church bells were rarely allowed to ring out and rubbish was often late to be collected. Paper and paste shortages made it difficult for music halls to advertise and there was an air of desperation to the editorial in the industry's newspaper, the *Era*, which argued that everyone who lived in a town or city should be forced to go to a music hall rather than sit at home wasting coal and, in some cases, electricity. Shortages increased and in April a Public Meals Order banned light pastries, muffins, crumpets and teacakes from restaurants, hotels and clubs. This followed the introduction of voluntary rationing of bread, meat and sugar among ordinary people in February. Lyons' Teashops and other tearooms could only serve cakes and buns to the value of 1s 9d per person after 6 p.m. to try to limit consumption.[23] Performers bravely carried on during raids by Zeppelins and, later in the war, bombings by the twin-engined biplane, the Gotha. Before an attack the lights would unaccountably dim; then the audience might hear the whistle of shells, followed by the all-clear bugle blown by a Boy Scout. In July 1917 the government re-evaluated its view on warnings, but still maintained this was only necessary during daylight hours. Certain police and fire stations would release two maroons and policemen would leap on their bikes, blowing their whistles and brandishing the 'Take Cover!' notice. If it hadn't been so tragic, it might have made a music hall skit.

The new system did not engender confidence and many Londoners, including Virginia Woolf, preferred to study the phases of the moon or to linger on the underground train until a raid was over. A full moon was believed by many to make it easier for Zeppelins to find their way to their target; as Woolf commented, 'Still no raids, presumably the haze at evening keeps them off, though it is still, & the moon perfectly clear.'[24] Others were convinced that the moon would keep the enemy away because it made them more visible to defenders on the ground. Dark, foggy nights were thought to offer particular protection, and this was why the attack by L45 on the night of 19 October 1917 was such a shock. It was a shock for the airship's crew, too, as they had been heading for the industrial target of Sheffield.

Strong winds had swept Zeppelin L45 to Hendon, where they bombed the aerodrome, and through north London, where they attacked Cricklewood railway station. At 11.30 p.m. the pilots spotted a concentration of lights and one of the men shouted 'London!' The Zeppelin then hurtled past Regent's Park and down Regent Street. The ghostly presence flew high above the clouds (as much as four miles above street level), and the sound of its engines went undetected and the crew untroubled by any defence gunfire in an attack that became known as the 'Silent Raid'.[25] L45 dropped its bombs randomly but their effect was deadly. A 300 kg high-explosive bomb gouged out a twelve-foot-diameter crater next to Swan & Edgar, which lost the whole of its frontage. The explosion smashed two gas mains and damaged telephone lines. Buildings in Regent Street, Shaftesbury Avenue and Jermyn Street were also hit. Seven people, including three soldiers on leave, were killed, and some twenty-five pedestrians injured by flying glass, shrapnel and masonry. One woman was so disfigured that she could only be identified by her jewellery and clothes. L45 careered on to cause more damage in south London – in Lewisham ten children died, seven from one family – until, with only two engines functioning, the crew surrendered in France.

The attack, which had appeared to come from nowhere, was a terrible shock to Londoners. The gash in Piccadilly quickly became a gruesome tourist attraction. Virginia Woolf heard two 'soft distant but unmistakable shocks'[26] at about 9.30; a third shook the windows in her house and then there was silence. Her friend Alix Strachey had been in the West End at the time and Woolf wrote in her diary:

> Happily, or she might say unhappily for Alix she [sic] didn't presumably wander in Piccadilly all night, or the great bomb which ploughed up the pavement opposite Swan & Edgar's might have dug her grave.[27]

Woolf was disturbed when she saw the crater for herself on Monday 22 October, and wrote in her diary:

> The moon grows full, & the evening trains are packed with people leaving London. We saw the hole in Piccadilly this afternoon. Traffic has been stopped, & the public slowly tramps past the place, which workmen are mending, though they look small in comparison with it. Swan & Edgar has every window covered with sacking or planks; you see shop women looking out from behind; not a glimpse of stuffs, but 'business goes on as usual' so they say.[28]

The bomb may have contributed to the decision to move Eros in what turned out to be the final year of the war – though clearly the public still wasn't sure which god he represented; on 19 May 1918 the *Daily Mirror* complained of a 'Cupidless London' and the *Western Gazette* explained why 'Cupid' had flown: 'One of the flower girls, who were his guardians, says he has gone "for the Duration", being afraid of getting a bomb or a bit of shrapnel on his little head.'[29]

When the ceasefire did come, many people heard it from paperboys shouting the good news. On Armistice Day, 11 November 1918, Piccadilly Circus became a place of celebration: bells rang out again, flags appeared from nowhere and crowds poured onto the streets, just as they had after the Relief of Mafeking in 1900. Although it started to rain, the mood could not be dampened. Searchlights swept playfully across the skies, dazzling passers-by as their beams caught up with the glare from newly illuminated theatres and restaurants whose early closing restrictions had been lifted. The Trocadero, not to be outdone, put up a necklace of additional lights. Bonfires blazed in both Piccadilly Circus and Trafalgar Square and Eros's base became 'festooned' with theatre musicians.[30] A well-known music hall performer took the place vacated by Eros, playing his bass clarinet while, once again, a diverse crowd came together to celebrate: officers, ordinary soldiers and nurses, chorus girls and well-bred women in evening gowns linked hands to dance a ring-a-roses below him to the popular hit, 'Over There'. Meanwhile, ambulances continued to carry the injured from France to their hospital beds.

The king and queen went on an informal tour of the West End. The American poet Ezra Pound found himself just two feet away from the couple when their open-topped carriage arrived at Piccadilly Circus, where crowds cheered despite the drizzle. Their only protection was 'a couple of cops' and Pound noted how happy the king looked.[31]

Alfred Gilbert, who had fled Britain and angry customers in 1901, continued his exile in Bruges, fully aware that he was putting himself at risk. The city was placed under martial law and bombed. Gilbert was arrested twice but managed to use his knowledge of German to avoid punishment. His friends in Britain, who had heard little from him, feared the worst but he survived, only to discover after the ceasefire that his son Alfredo had died in a naval battle.

A year later the UK marked the first two-minute silence to

remember those who had lost their lives in the Great War. The next day Sir Arthur Steel-Maitland, a Conservative MP, described being in Piccadilly Circus during the moment of stillness. The quiet was so profound that he was sure he could, very faintly, hear the eerie tones of the 'Last Post' sounding, he supposed from the Cenotaph in Whitehall, to mark the end of the silence.[32] The anecdote is remarkable – not because it shows how far the sound of a bugle might reach but because it demonstrates the damage to the national psyche inflicted by the Great War. Only something so terrible could produce a sustained silence in a place more normally associated with celebration and revelry.

The war had made Piccadilly Circus a meeting place for people from around the world, not just Britain. Thousands of khaki-clad soldiers came from countries on the other side of the globe and their visits, no matter how brief, left them with a sense of longing. Piccadilly Circus now symbolised not just bright lights but the lights of home, even if your home was miles away. And the place now had its very own anthem, 'Goodbye Tipperary', which summed up a sense of loss and nostalgia. The people who visited Piccadilly Circus during the war years were desperate: desperate to escape the war, themselves or their uniform. Hotels like the Regent Palace allowed them to do that – if only for a night – while others wanted new experiences, recognising that this might be their final opportunity. For young Tommies, that might be the embrace of a woman they would never see again or a hastily arranged wedding that soon fizzled out. The war gave women opportunities, too, and changed the face of Piccadilly Circus, proving that females could drive taxis, deliver letters and even act as police constables (although not officially). No one was quite as they seemed and that engendered suspicion as well as excitement. When the enemy finally managed to leave a vast crater in Piccadilly Circus it became a tourist attraction because it seemed remarkable that such a familiar landmark should be so altered. Although the area was quick to reassert its normal identity, it had been a glimpse of what was possible in the worst of all possible worlds: that a glittering playground could so quickly have its appearance refashioned.

Part Three

Bright Young Things

7

Under Ground in the Jazz Age

Louise Brooks, with her shockingly blunt bob and precise fringe, was the epitome of the Modern Woman. In December 1924, she had just turned eighteen as she became one of the first people to perform the Charleston in London. It was a curious, jerky dance that involved side-kicks from the knees and airy circling of the hands; dancers no longer glided across the dance floor as they did in other ballroom styles, but looked like they were stubbing out a persistent cigarette. No doubt part of the Charleston's appeal was that the dance was delivered with abandon and with a glimpse of those busy knees.

The Charleston symbolised a changing attitude to entertainment: it was as much about being seen, about showing off, as it was about simply having a good time. Piccadilly Circus after the First World War had an urgency, a sense of making up for lost time and of pushing boundaries. There was a compulsion to try new things: new food and drinks, a new style of dancing, new clothes, even dressing up to look much older or younger than you really were or to flirt with gender. Before the war the main entertainers, and certainly the ones most likely to be seen as subversive, were music hall performers like Marie Lloyd or Vesta Tilley who weren't afraid to startle their audiences. As music halls gave way to theatres of variety it was the nightclubs where the newest, most daring acts could be found, and it was the richer, more privileged members of society who were entertaining themselves by dreaming up stunts to cause havoc among polite society. They were also confirming that Piccadilly Circus wasn't just a meeting place but a meeting place where being seen was as important as the encounter itself. For decades it had been a place to blend in with the crowds, but for the Bright Young Things, in particular, this part of London now became the ideal place to stand out from the crowd.

Brooks, who was originally from Kansas, became a professional dancer at the age of fifteen when she joined the Denishawn dance company in Los Angeles. After appearing with them in Paris she made a detour to London and the oval-shaped dance floor of the subterranean Café de Paris, just off Piccadilly Circus, that December. Her act started at midnight and afterwards she returned to her apartment in Pall Mall, where her only friend was her maid. She was so lonely that she cut short her engagement and returned to America on 14 February 1925. Piccadilly Circus's bright lights weren't for everyone and were generally best enjoyed among friends.

She may not have stayed long at the Café de Paris, but Brooks played her part in making the two-tiered nightclub in Coventry Street the place to be seen and to catch the latest musical acts in the 1920s and 1930s. The club shared some of the values that made Piccadilly Circus so popular: anyone was welcome, the more exotic the better, and, just like its street-level counterpart, Café de Paris had an air of unpredictability and danger; it was a place to let off steam and where your excesses would be noticed. The only difference was that, unless you were a performer or waiter or served the guests in any other way, you needed a certain level of income to enjoy all that the club had to offer.

Booking Brooks was a typically astute marketing ploy by the club's manager, Martin Poulsen. Poulsen was a dapper little man with a pencil moustache and a stomach that bulged under his waistcoat and tailcoat. His height meant that he had to look up to many of his guests, but his stature belied his background: he was born in Denmark and first came to London as a gymnast to take part in the 1908 Olympics. In later years, when he had lost much of his litheness, he would still, when overtaken by high spirits, spring onto his hands and walk quickly across a room. To customers, at least, he was always smiling and spoke with a fast, parrot-like delivery, but among his waiters, hostesses, performers, cooks and coat girls he was viewed with something close to fear.

In the period immediately after the First World War, Poulsen had his work cut out to make the Café de Paris popular and profitable. His desperation is evident in one of the early performers he booked: Willy Woltard specialised in juggling apples while taking bites in mid-air until the fruit was reduced to pips and a stalk. The nightclub wasn't helped by its location in Coventry Street – a short, but wide, thoroughfare between Piccadilly Circus and Leicester Square – which had gained a reputation as the place to pick up prostitutes and for gay assignations: it was a place *not* to be seen. The Foster Theatrical Agency had bought the lease of what was the Elysee Restaurant as a vehicle for trying out new cabaret acts and dance bands – many from the USA – and changed the name to the Café de Paris. Initially, the name confused potential customers because the lettering on their sign was in the same style as the Rialto Cinema and so passers-by assumed that 'Café de Paris' was the title of a film that was showing. The venue's modest front door gave the impression that it led to a fleapit rather than a glamorous nightclub.

But daring new acts from abroad, and a glittering array of guests that kept the Café de Paris in the gossip columns, secured the venue's lasting popularity as diners enjoyed a range of acts from conjurors to dancers to comedians. Nancy Mitford, who would become famous for novels such as *The Pursuit of Love* (1945) and who, despite her aristocratic family, was often short of money, recalled her friend's sister being nearly killed when a roller-skater swung her around his head. The Café de Paris also become well known for signing Black artists – most famously Josephine Baker, the American-born French singer and dancer who caused a sensation at the Folies-Bergère in Paris by performing a provocative number wearing a skirt made of bananas, and as the place where guests were likely to hear future hits. It also featured slightly risqué turns such as Douglas Byng, a deliciously camp performer popular with the future queen mother, who sprinkled his comic songs with double entendres, and Florence Desmond, who specialised in wicked impersonations of famous women. Music hall performers Gwen Farrar and Norah Blaney sang comic songs and made no secret of the fact that they were a couple.[1] Farrar's plainness became her trademark. Her dull brown hair was 'straight as string',[2] she had a long, sad face and on stage dressed solely in black and white; her only make-up was a shock of scarlet lipstick. She had her suits fitted in Savile Row, drove fast cars[3] and was known as the one woman in show business to play the cello. Her father had been a mining magnate and politician but she refused to be presented at court, telling her mother that if she was forced to appear she

Not everyone approved of the statue of Eros and some observers were troubled by his missing arrow. A few months after its unveiling, *Punch* depicted the god as an untrustworthy character willing to shoot a passing cab driver in the back.

Piccadilly Circus' has long been used as a shorthand for London and as a reminder of home. Here it forms a backdrop for a stage production by Second World War prisoners at Stalag Luft III, Sagan.

Vol 9 The War Illustrated Nº 207

SIXPENCE — Edited by Sir John Hammerton — MAY 25 1945

IN HAMBURG, FOUR DAYS BEFORE GERMANY'S UNCONDITIONAL SURRENDER, a corporal of the British 2nd Army, watched closely by a German policeman, erected new street-signs; the Grosse Allee became "Piccadilly Circus." Germany's second largest city, with a peacetime population of over 1,700,000, surrendered to General Dempsey's troops on May 3, 1945; the vast dock-yards were less badly crippled than had been anticipated, and many U-boats were found on the stocks. *Photo, British Official*

NO. 208 WILL BE PUBLISHED FRIDAY, JUNE 8

Renaming a busy thoroughfare 'Piccadilly Circus' has often been used as a way to stamp a British identity on foreign soil. Four days before Germany's unconditional surrender in May 1945 a local policeman watches as a British corporal transforms the 'Große Allee' in Hamburg.

This wooden sign was part of a trench in Gaza, Palestine, during the First World War. 'Piccadilly Circus' was often used by homesick troops to denote a bustling location and may have indicated a London association with the unit.

Sir Alfred Gilbert in his studio, The Avenue, Fulham Road, where he started work on the Shaftesbury Memorial. The photo is taken some time between 1887 and 1890. He is wearing his familiar, wide-brimmed hat and smoking a pipe.

Flower girls became familiar characters and guarded their patch jealously. This seller, on Eros's steps, extends bunches on long poles to men who were required to sit on the upper decks of buses to smoke. She probably caught their coins in her boater.

The *Graphic* shows wild celebrations on the evening of 18 May 1900 to mark the relief of the British Army garrison at Mafeking in South Africa. It was the first time revellers from different backgrounds met at Piccadilly Circus to join in a national celebration.

Swan & Edgar used its plate-glass windows to entice a new breed of shoppers who arrived in London by train and Tube. Suffragettes smashed the windows as part of their campaign for the vote, and would-be lovers eyed one another up in the window's reflection.

Phroso drew crowds of curious shoppers when he sat in Swan & Edgar's window as part of an early marketing stunt in 1904. Onlookers could not decide whether the music hall turn was a real man, a doll or an automaton.

" There they all were, a very representative sprinkling of the Café de Paris' usual clientèle which includes princes, poets and politicians, and a goodly leavening of American and other visitors "

In the 1920s the subterranean Café de Paris nightclub, with its elegant double staircase, became the place to be seen and to watch the latest acts from America and Europe.

OF THE SALE
OF THESE CARDS
WILL BE HANDED
BY MISS TILLEY

OF WALES' FUND

Vesta Tilley, the music hall performer and male impersonator, sang songs dressed as a 'Tommy' at venues such as the Pavilion. During the First World War she encouraged young men to enlist and won admirers among both sexes.

Colonel Victor Barker worked as a reception clerk at the Regent Palace Hotel in 1929. Barker is an example of someone who felt able to try on a new identity within the confines of Piccadilly Circus.

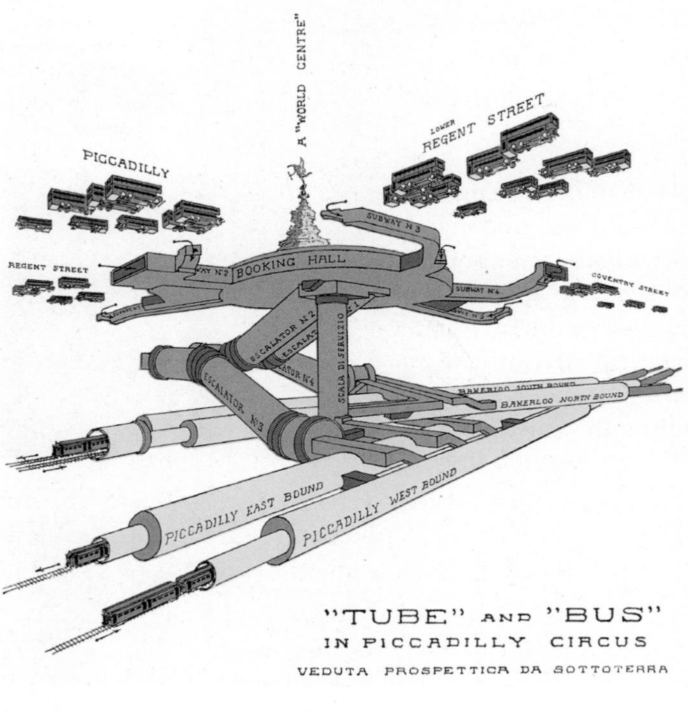

Architects from around the world admired Charles Holden's design for the new Piccadilly Circus Tube station, which opened in 1928. Renzo Picasso, an urban planner from Genoa, recorded his impression when he visited London and produced an illustration that made the site look startlingly futuristic.

Douglas MacPherson's poster, which became known as 'the stomach', revealed 'a new Piccadilly Circus below the Old' and showed the hive of activity going on underground.

Anna May Wong, the American actress who starred in the silent film, *Piccadilly*, captivated British audiences with her beauty and her acting ability. Women cut their hair to adopt her trademark fringe and the outfits she wore to the theatre were reported in fashionable magazines.

would approach the dais with a Charlie Chaplin-style gait. Blaney, a more conventionally attractive brunette, came from a less wealthy background but had already established herself as a reciter of monologues, singer and composer when she met Farrar during the First World War. They formed a double act to entertain troops in France and, shortly before her husband died from wounds, set up home together in Chelsea. A few years later they toured America and continued their on–off partnership for the rest of their lives.

Poulsen set about making the club the most talked-about in London by calling in favours and raiding the little black book of contacts of his previous employer, the Embassy Club in the more refined Old Bond Street, where he had previously been head waiter. He sent out 400 telegrams to regulars offering a free night at his new workplace and was bold enough to telephone the Prince of Wales (the future Edward VIII, who would later abandon the throne for Mrs Simpson) to ask him to visit the struggling venue. The prince started to come regularly and brought with him his then mistresses, Mrs Dudley Ward and Lady Furness – although not at the same time. He was so keen on the Charleston that he would visit in the afternoons to practise his moves with Mrs Ward on the deserted dance floor. On other occasions he brought close friends such as Brigadier-General Gerard Trotter, who had lost an arm during the Second Boer War, and Edward Dudley 'Fruity' Metcalfe, as well as American stars Fred and Adele Astaire. A secret passageway led from the balcony of the Café de Paris to Rupert Street, which allowed royals and VIPs to make a discreet entrance. It was also a useful exit for drunks, who were thrown out by what was known as a 'flying wedge' – ejection by a team of six waiters.

The Café de Paris only sprang to life after nightfall and yet it epitomised the word 'bright' – an adjective that summed up the intent of the group of rich and privileged young people who hoped to shake off the drabness of the post-war period by staging elaborate dressing-up parties such as 'come-as-you-were-twenty-years-earlier' (which for many meant dressing up as a baby) or the night-time party held at St George's Swimming Baths, near Victoria, in which guests swam and played with giant inflatable horses while overheated waiters served a Bathwater cocktail invented for the occasion.[4] The Bright Young Things, as they became known, represented a clique of eccentric socialites who frequented places such as the Café de Paris and who specialised in exuberant and often outrageous behaviour. The capital was their playground and they used it for scavenger hunts and bizarre social gatherings. One such event occurred in Piccadilly towards the end of their reign and when the press and public were growing tired of their antics, when they held a Mozart-themed party that was captured in a photo of April 1930. It shows the future society photographer, Cecil Beaton, appearing to use an industrial drill to attack the road surface; he is dressed in the clothes of the eighteenth-century Viennese court – stockings, breeches, a wig and long sleeves – and stands next to other guests wearing similar attire and one flat-capped road worker who stands, looking slightly embarrassed, with his hands on his hips.

Although usually included as one of the Bright Young Things, Nancy Mitford much preferred to watch their antics – which she would then write about – and the Café de Paris provided an ideal venue from which to gather material for her novels. When she visited in the early 1930s with Hamish St Clair-Erskine, with whom she was in love – despite his obvious homosexuality – they were left, after paying the bill, with only seven and a half pennies between them and had to be bailed out by her brother, Tom, who helped them to get home.

Even when the allure of the Bright Young Things had dimmed, Mitford would continue to return to one of their favourite haunts, because the Café de Paris was always the stage on which something dramatic might happen – and with great style. A few years later she was there with Sir Hugh Smiley, a rich and handsome Grenadier Guards officer. This time the tables had been turned and it was Smiley courting his less than enthusiastic companion and who made the last of a series of unsuccessful proposals. The Café de Paris became renowned for the sort of dramatic scene Mitford noted in a letter:

> I had another proposal from Sir Hugh, in great style orchids etc at the C de Paris with Hamish giggling at the next table & I gave him the final raspberry. He was very cross & said I should be left on the shelf (impertinence) so I went off with Hamish to the Slipspin (new & horrible night club) which made him still crosser. Lousy young man, I don't answer any of his letters now even.[5]

Other couples were more eager to accept proposals and there was a growing feeling among some members of the press and public that these hasty unions showed that the topsy-turvy world of Piccadilly Circus had gone too far. These fears appeared to have been borne out by two events that occurred in 1929 and which both involved weddings.

Socialite Elizabeth Ponsonby was at the heart of this group of enthusiastic partygoers who cavorted their way through the 1920s. Many of the events happened in Piccadilly and revellers often ended up at the Café de Paris, especially after the 1921 Licensing Act allowed customers of licensed premises to continue drinking late into the night, so long as they had something to eat. The press was fascinated by their antics and liked to report on them in shocked terms.

On 24 January 1929 Elizabeth Ponsonby, daughter of the Labour MP for the Brightside Division of Sheffield, who was said by one newspaper to earn a living working as a model in a high-class clothes shop, married John Rayner. Ponsonby has been seen as the model for the doomed Agatha Runcible in *Vile Bodies*, the satirical novel by another Bright Young Thing, Evelyn Waugh.[6] The bride wore a beige dress with a corsage attached to her fur-trimmed coat and a cloche hat; the groom was dressed in a 'violently'[7] striped shirt, huge white bow tie, oversized morning suit, brown boots and what looked like a trilby. The best man, novelist Robert Byron, sported a 'ragged' waxed moustache, a 'flaring red buttonhole',[8] a tatty bowler hat and frock coat. As if to stress how the wedding transgressed the normal social order, journalists said his moustache made him look like the music hall turn Billy Bennett, who was best known for his comic performance of the dramatic monologue 'The Green Eye of the Yellow God'. The guests, many of whom were members of the aristocracy, chose a mismatched jumble of outfits and each wore an array of curious outfits, which included a double-breasted silver waistcoat, a raincoat with the collar turned nonchalantly up, and a white felt hat with an enormous bunch of multicoloured cherries. Everyone looked as though they had raided their parents' wardrobes – which might well have been the case because this was a 'mock' wedding. The nuptials were a sham and the meal afterwards at the Trocadero was eaten in the middle of the dining room so that bemused diners could not fail to notice the outlandishly attired party of diners. The bride and groom left in a taxi amid a hail of confetti and rose petals.

The mock wedding was one of the Bright Young Things' last huzzahs and newspapers were generally not impressed. The event probably caused such affront because the Bright Young Things were poking fun at one of the cornerstones of respectable life: marriage. The *Sheffield Daily Telegraph* commented: 'After a period of quiet, Society's "bright young people" have burst out again with one of their eccentric stunts which they fondly believe are the outward and visible sign of their superior intelligence'.[9] The *Graphic* described the event as Ponsonby's 'latest idea for a surprise-cum-creating-attention party'[10] and the *Daily Mirror* wondered whether such a prank should be enacted at a time of severe national unrest (the General Strike of 1926 was still fresh in many people's minds).[11] At least two publications noted that the hoaxers may themselves have been hoaxed because the vicar, who happened to be in the Trocadero while they were tucking into their wedding breakfast, and who signed their menu and offered advice on the holy state of matrimony, may himself have been a fraud. It seems no vicar of that name existed in the parish of South Mimms and, as one newspaper suggested, he may have been lying in wait for the wedding party.[12]

At the Regent Palace Hotel, a few hundred metres away from the Trocadero, there were certainly couples who were ignoring the sanctity of marriage, but they were doing so behind closed doors. The hotel had a veneer of respectability, and one that was reinforced by the stolid, six-feet-tall presence of its reception clerk, Colonel Victor Barker, who worked there from 15 September 1928, when he earned £5 a week.

Barker, who was married and in his early thirties, and who had earned medals during the Great War, fitted in well at a large hotel like the Regent Palace where there was a fine line between accepting guests at face value and not being duped by visitors who pretended to be richer than they were. Barker's military record gave him the sort of authority that the hotel, which often employed ex-Scotland Yard police officers, needed to keep an eye on clients. The most unscrupulous visitors were adept at using fake crested writing paper[13] and income tax returns to create a wealthy persona that encouraged staff to lower their guard while the guests made off with everything from towels, ashtrays, mirrors and glasses to paintings, bedside lamps, silk bedding, and even corridor carpets. Hotels couldn't be seen to be encouraging prostitution, and so employed their own 'hotel detective' whose skills included being able to distinguish between couples who were genuinely in love or, at least passionate about one another, and cases where the room wasn't the only element for hire.

London's big hotels developed a cunning code to alert one another to guests who had demonstrated a track record of misdemeanours that ranged from the minor crime of poor tipping (although tipping was, as has been mentioned, in theory, discouraged at the Regent Palace) to more elaborate cons. Although the details of this system have not survived, it appears to have been based around the positioning of the labels porters and concierges stuck to the luggage of troublesome customers as they waved them on their way to their next hotel booking. In the most elaborate scams, unscrupulous guests had been known to smuggle in a cockroach in a matchbox or a baby rat in a shoe and then use the creature to demand blackmail money.[14]

Barker made a stolid addition to this frontline against

disreputable visitors. There was nothing unusual about a veteran taking a modest position and, in the 1920s, Britain was full of ex-soldiers looking for work. However, there were many aspects of Barker's life that *were* unusual, but, for most of the 1920s there was no one to connect up the dots in his unusual career. Barker had been married twice and had two children from a third relationship. His jobs over the years had ranged from acting (he'd performed with Mrs Patrick Campbell) to working in an antiques shop in Hampshire; his tally of medals had grown since the end of the war and included a Distinguished Service Order (DSO) and Croix de Guerre. In 1926 Barker had received a letter at his lodgings in Soho for a different Colonel Barker inviting him to join the National Fascisti (a forerunner of the Union of British Fascists), and he threw in his lot with the emerging organisation, offering to help by training young men from the NF to box and fence. He had also had brushes with the law and in July 1927 ended up in court when a gun found in his possession did not match a firearms certificate. He avoided a sentence on that occasion, but the law finally caught up with him after a café he opened off Leicester Square failed and Barker was ordered to appear in bankruptcy court. For the second time, Barker's life was knocked off course by a letter that went astray when he overlooked the note that was pushed through the café's letter box and a bailiff arrived at the Regent Palace Hotel on 28 February 1929 to arrest him for contempt of court.

After he was taken away the hotel manager opened Barker's locker. Inside he found male clothing, an eyebrow pencil, a well-worn powder puff, a few safety pins, two pieces of ribbon and a razor. Once Barker arrived at Brixton Prison it proved impossible to keep his secret any longer, although he begged the doctor not to reveal that he had been assigned female at birth. He was transferred to Holloway Women's Prison and when he was released had to be helped to flee via the prison's garden as reporters and a crowd of around a thousand people, most of them women, were waiting at the main entrance, though his Eton crop and bulk made him easy to spot.

Women crowded into the courtroom when Barker's case came to the Old Bailey in April 1929, when he was charged on two counts of perjury for having falsely signed the register when he married his wife Elfrida (also 'Elfreda') Haward. The defendant appeared in a collar and tie under a fawn raincoat, which sported a red rose in the lapel; he wore heavy boots and golf socks. When she was questioned, Haward said that, although they had shared a bed, she had not realised that her husband had been assigned female at birth. The defence put forward the argument that Baker had believed he could earn more money in a male guise, but for the judge, Ernest Wild, Barker's main crime was that he had 'profaned the House of God' by falsifying a marriage certificate. He was sentenced to nine months in prison. When Barker returned to Holloway a special uniform had to be made to accommodate his sixteen and a half stones, but he found it hard to eat and drink in prison and his weight dropped to thirteen stone.

The story of his complicated life, with all its twists and turns, emerged in the three versions he sold over the years to different newspapers. Avid readers discovered that he was born Lillias Irma Barker on the island of Jersey and that at the end of the First World War he married an Australian soldier. The marriage didn't last long; he returned home and started a relationship with a second Australian soldier, which led to the birth of a daughter and a son. He began to favour more masculine clothes, but was still living as a woman when he met Haward, telling her that he was behaving as a woman because his mother had wanted a daughter. He assumed the name Sir Victor Barker and lived with Haward at the Grand Hotel in Brighton. They married in 1923.

Once Barker was released from Holloway he was able to live as a man again and careered through a typically broad range of jobs: he worked in a furniture shop in Tottenham Court Road, sold cars (until a customer recognised him), worked as a film extra at Elstree Studios, sold cleaning products door to door, assisted a fortune teller at an end-of-pier show on the Isle of Wight, moved back to Sussex as a kennel man, worked as an assistant chef at two large hotels in the West Country and as personal assistant to a millionaire. He appeared in court several times accused of theft and took his most ignominious job in Blackpool, when he appeared in a freak show.

The Second World War was a particularly trying time because double-breasted jackets, which helped him to conceal his womanly chest, were hard to come by and because the national emergency required everyone to carry identity papers. Tragically, his son, who was a bomber pilot, was killed in 1944. Barker, who had lived under so many names, was buried, at his own request, in an unmarked grave, near Lowestoft, Suffolk, in 1960.

One wonders if his life might have turned out differently if Barker had not missed the important letter that plopped through the letter box of his café near Leicester Square. Would he have been able to live on as the trusted and respected reception clerk at the Regent Palace Hotel, where an important part of his job was to turn a blind eye to the unusual and the nonconformist? There were plenty of men who dressed up as painted ladies and enjoyed themselves in Piccadilly Circus. Had Barker lived a century later, would his chosen life have been less painful?

Piccadilly Circus's history is littered with examples of men and women living secret lives that allowed them to be true to themselves decades before official legislation sanctioned their choices. However, Barker's criminal conviction meant he lost his job and endured months in a setting that must have been torture for him. The Bright Young Things sailed close to what was seen as improper behaviour but rarely broke the law. As entertainment became more about audience participation and spectacle, they felt emboldened to flirt with different personas and sexualities. Piccadilly Circus, and establishments such as the Café de Paris, gave them free rein to experiment and they did so with abandon. Their way of life was only ever challenged in the press, not in court, and their antics only faded from view when it ceased to create the sort of provocation the Bright Young Things were looking for. Professional acts such as Gwen Farrar and Norah Blaney paraded their lifestyle in plain view and, in doing so, barely raised an eyebrow in a setting where the audience expected to experience something different. The twenties and thirties showed that Piccadilly Circus could offer different things to different groups of society, but that class and money were key factors in how far you could push that experience and how much you could get away with.

8

The Moving World of the Underground Railway

While the Café de Paris had established itself as a subterranean retreat for revellers, a few minutes' walk away the underground transport system was burrowing deeper beneath Piccadilly Circus to create a station that looked more like the complicated interchange familiar to Londoners and tourists today and which would cement the area's position as the heart of the capital.

Douglas MacPherson's poster of 1928 referred to the new station as 'the stomach', and there is definitely something anatomical about its intertwining network of walkways filled with corpuscular passengers and arrows indicating the direction of travel of the station's lifeblood: its trains. The second diagram in the *Illustrated London News* (12 March 1927), which filled the lower half of a full-page spread that included Tottenham Court Road and Charing Cross stations, made the engineering feat look more like a nest of worms grubbing their way into the clay.[1]

Just as Leslie Green's original station on the corner of Haymarket would not have been possible without the entrepreneur Charles Yerkes, so its replacement, in a more central position, represented a happy combination of the distinct, and yet complementary, talents of two men: the architect Charles Holden and the enlightened transport administrator and town planner Frank Pick. Both men were the sons of drapers, and both were shy and yet determined.[2]

Holden, who was born in Lancashire, studied at Manchester School of Art and developed a love of the writings of the American poet Walt Whitman. He moved to London to work for the Arts and Crafts architect C. R. Ashbee and then joined Percy Adams, where he helped build several hospitals before collaborating with him and Jacob Epstein on Oscar Wilde's tomb in Paris's Père Lachaise Cemetery. He became a partner in the practice in 1913 and also that year visited the USA. During the war he served with the London Ambulance Unit and later worked for the Imperial War Graves Commission and architects including Edwin Lutyens. He met Pick, the administrator of the Underground Electric Railways (later London Passenger Transport Board), during the same war when they discovered a shared taste for good, clean design and when Pick helped to devise a system of coal rationing.

Pick, whose very name seems to have singled him out to create a new-look Piccadilly Circus, was born in Lincolnshire and trained as a solicitor. In 1902 he joined the North Eastern Railway Company and when, four years later, his general manager Sir George Gibb took over the management of the Metropolitan District and London Underground Electric Railways, Pick went with him. In the following year Gibb retired and Pick was transferred to the staff of his successor, A. H. Stanley, later Lord Ashfield, and become deeply involved in running London's underground railways and with the associated company that joined the group in 1912, the London General Omnibus Company. After the First World War he returned to the group of underground companies, and became joint managing director in 1928. When the London Passenger Transport Board was formed in 1933 he became vice chairman and chief executive officer. Today we take his London-wide transport system for granted, but in the first half of the twentieth century it was a startlingly new concept.

Pick was a man who attracted extreme opinions. For some he was a cold martinet whom it took great courage to approach or challenge; others attributed his manner to shyness and described him as kind and modest. Whatever the truth, it is indubitable that he, more than anyone else, managed to create the various elements that make the London Underground system what it is today. He brought order – and even beauty (Man Ray was among the famous artists who designed new posters for the Tube) – to the disreputable splatter of posters that cluttered up the underground's walls; he approached Edward Johnston to design a typeface that came to be associated with the transport system, and commissioned the red, white and blue Tube roundel that is one the most instantly recognisable signs in the world.[3]

Once Holden had finished his first sketches of Piccadilly Circus underground station the engineering shop at Earl's Court built a full-scale model so that the various sections could be taken apart and rearranged.[4] His plans provided an elegant solution for a station that needed seven entrances – each for one of the roads that converged at the junction.[5] The station took four years and £500,000 (£31.6 million in today's money) to build and caused huge disruption at one of London's busiest junctions, and yet there were few complaints in the press – perhaps the novelty of such upheaval was enough to reduce any grumbles. Or pedestrians may have been too busy moaning about the introduction of a gyratory system for the Circus and coloured lights (i.e. rudimentary traffic lights) in summer 1926, followed, a year later, by the repaving of Piccadilly, which sent buses and taxis off on major detours.[6]

The new station aimed to be able to handle 50,000 passengers an hour, compared to the 24,000 who passed hourly through the original station,[7] and everything about the new design aimed to speed up the experience of using an underground train. Travellers could reach the 25,000-square-foot circular booking hall via seven subways, leading from Lower Regent Street, Regent Street, Glasshouse Street, Shaftesbury Avenue, Coventry Street and two from Piccadilly. They could buy a ticket from one of thirty automatic tickets machines that, *The Times* noted, 'stand like robots guarding the head of the stairways',[8] or use one of four 'passometer' turnstiles. The revolutionary ticket machines were coin-operated and could even give change. Tests showed that the new machines helped to shave an average of two and a half minutes off the time it took a passenger to get from street level to Tube platform compared to the old station on the corner of Haymarket.[9] Other innovations, such as the press-button, compressed-air carriage doors, also reduced journey times and took the passenger further away from the original single-leaf door, which had been modelled on a horse and carriage and had room for only one person at a time to pass through. The new carriages, designed in the early 1920s, had sliding double doors that were accessible from most seats and which left room for two streams of passengers – one alighting and the other getting on.[10]

Although the booking hall was only nine feet tall, its careful lighting made it feel cavernous. Columns of red imitation marble with bronze bases and caps helped to give a feeling of airiness, as did the brown travertine marble walls and the big white tiles on the floor. Holden's aim was to create something like a night-time arcade of shops. A passenger who was running late could make a call from a phone box in a special corridor.[11] As they descended the escalators, passengers could study a huge map of the world painted in oils in which artist Stephen Bone (the son of the etcher Muirhead Bone, whom Holden had got to know in Manchester) had picked out the British Empire in bright colours and added simplistic details about some of the countries: for example, a lion in central Africa. The mural was later removed, although the World Time Clock in its wooden housing still remains. The central strip of Roman numerals moves across the globe so that you can follow the time around the world. When it was first unveiled, tourists queued to peer at it and place their life in a wider context.

Eros had enjoyed a thorough cleaning during his wartime break and his reappearance in 1930 was viewed as a sign that normality was returning. The *Illustrated London News* pointed out that when he first made a comeback his arrow had been reversed so that he looked as though he was trying to take his own life,[12] but the joshing was all part of the general affection that the public now regarded him with. As work started on a facelift for the area above the Tube, though, his fate again hung in the balance as his detractors said it was the ideal moment for him to go, while others felt the setting wasn't good enough for a god. Sir Frank Dicksee, president of the Royal Academy, described Piccadilly Circus at night in 1925 as 'without doubt the most vulgar place in Europe' and the 'hideous illuminations'[13] as 'most degrading'. Theatrical impresario Charles B. Cochran disagreed: 'Until the advent of the sky signs Piccadilly Circus was shabby. It was a dreary place, with insufficient light. In fact, I can remember when it was so dark as to be unsafe to cross the road.'[14] A leader writer in *The Times* pointed out that the buildings on the west side of Piccadilly Circus were now much higher than they had been when the statue was first installed. In its new, more central site Eros would have as background 'the electric advertisements, which are as ramshackle-looking by day as they are fussy and gaudy by night'. The traffic was now so bad that the only chance the viewer had to obtain a good view of the memorial was to visit 'in the small hours of a summer morning'.[15]

Everyone had a stake in Eros's future. Alfred Gilbert, who was now living in Bruges and hadn't been heard of for years, suggested the statue should be moved to St George's Hospital near Hyde Park, and there was talk of it adorning the Tate Gallery. Indeed, Herbert Hampton, the new owner of Gilbert's house in Maida Vale, had lovingly pieced together the fragments of Eros's plaster cast and arranged for them to be cast in bronze and exhibited at the Tate. The Royal Academy paid for a second cast and Gilbert gave the proceeds from this to the Artists' Benevolent Fund.[16] The *Daily Graphic* created a quasi-Photoshop effect that put Eros in Hyde Park, but the architect Sir Reginald Blomfield argued that the statue, 'undoubtedly the finest work of outdoor monumental sculpture ever designed and executed by a British sculptor', should be returned to its original home.[17] The 'real' Eros was taken from Piccadilly Circus in February 1925 to one of the Embankment's small parks for safety while the new Tube station was being built. Women pushing prams and office and shopworkers lingering over lunch breaks replaced the hurly-burly he was used to. The basin was stored at Stockwell Power House, until its return on 28 December 1931.[18]

Eros's flight left the flower girls who congregated around

the fountain's base homeless, and one wrote to Gilbert to say she considered the departure tantamount to a death in the family.[19] A few moved to a plot outside the Criterion but one, who claimed she had been selling flowers in Piccadilly Circus for over forty years, was determined to cling on to her pitch and sat on the central refuge, just outside the double gates that led down to the excavations.[20] The Duke of Westminster offered to provide alternative pitches for the flower girls on his Grosvenor estate and promised to build shelters over the stalls to protect them from the rain. Letter-writers to *The Times* suggested they be moved to Trafalgar Square and that brightly coloured awnings, as seen in continental towns, should be introduced to shield them from the elements. Mrs Pennington-Bickford, wife of the rector of St Clement Danes on the Strand, acted as a go-between and helped the women to settle in new locations: six found alternative sites around the Circus, two moved to Leicester Square and the rest took the Duke up on his offer of pitches at Hereford Gardens, near Oxford Street.[21] In time, many of the flower-sellers couldn't resist returning to their old haunt – at considerable risk to their own safety.

Journalists who were invited to observe the progress of the building work marvelled, in particular, at the way the 150 men who were constantly at work picked their way through the tangle of telephone cables, sewers and pipes that supplied water, electricity and gas. All the tunnelling had to be done by hand because it was too expensive and too tight a spot to use a large rotary excavating machine. The workmen shovelled a thousand tonnes of London clay each month and unquantifiable amounts of gravel to the surface by squeezing it through the tiny exit where the fountain had been and where an 18-foot shaft had been sunk.[22] From here it was taken to be dumped at sea. As the men worked, they came across reminders of an earlier London: jars containing dregs of wine pointed to a cellar, and a fossilised nautilus suggested a lost prehistoric marine world.[23]

A few months before the Tube station was due to open, on 27 September 1928, just after 5 p.m., one of those pipes that featured in all the diagrams of the station and which the construction men had been doing their best to avoid suddenly threatened to make the grand scheme look like hubris. Eyewitnesses at first thought a bomb had exploded, until an account by one of the workmen, a Mr G. Roberts of Kilburn, explained what had happened. According to Roberts, he and about eight other men were working on a subway when one of his mates drove his electric drill through a high-pressure gas main. As the gas rushed out two men hurried off to find some clay to plug the hole while the rest of the crew stood back. The two men had just returned when there was a 'terrific explosion and the place seemed to rock about us'.[24] Roberts was thrown twelve feet in the air and something hit him on the neck; the other builders were hurled to the ground. Roberts believed the earth walls were about to burst. There was only two feet of concrete and earth between them and the road.

Above ground the flagstones on the island where Eros had once stood, and where flower-sellers and shoe-shiners still plied their trade, started to erupt as if the Circus was experiencing an earthquake. One of the shoe-shiners, James Carey, was sitting on his box when he saw an elderly woman staggering away from a shop. A manhole she'd stepped on had been thrown into the air and he heard a deafening crash and saw a cloud of yellow smoke; everyone who'd been on the central island rushed for safety. No one was hurt but he described the smoke and flames as 'blinding' and reported that the woman was taken away by ambulance. His friend narrowly missed being hit by falling wood. Police arrived on foot and horse to calm the traffic.

Roberts had no idea what caused the explosion but speculated that someone had flicked a lighted cigarette through the grating. He added, perhaps with a little too much haste, 'I was not smoking, nor were any of my mates.'[25] Eight men were taken to Charing Cross Hospital, where they were treated for burns and shock; no one was detained. The near-miss was a foreshadowing of another subterranean explosion that was twelve years in the future but which would not have such a happy ending.

The new station copied and improved elements already in place at existing underground stations. The tall pylons that threw up light from either side of the stairway echoed a design at Waterloo and the large booking hall was reminiscent of Bank station, although more artistic in its ornamentation. The double flight of escalators had been tried at Tottenham Court Road, but commentators were particularly impressed by the set at Piccadilly Circus.

The concept of being transported by a moving staircase as the world passes you by was not new, but it was still novel. The escalator in Harrods is usually cited as one of the earliest, if not the first, example in Europe; the store introduced the device in 1898, six years after its invention in New York. The experience was so unnerving that shop assistants had to be on hand to calm shoppers with smelling salts and cognac.[26] Earl's Court was the first underground station to transport travellers in this way in 1911. The *Illustrated London News* described how the new service worked in a two-page spread of rather alarming sketches and cross-sections that revealed the hidden mechanisms that connected the Piccadilly 'Tube' to the District Railway. The article explained that a passenger could run or walk on the contraption, but that they must not sit down. However, because the original escalator used a 'shunt' mechanism rather than the modern 'comb', the stairway ended sooner for the right foot, which made it essential for the passenger to be prepared to step off using their other foot – as they were 'shunted off' the device. As a result, passengers were told to stand on the right-hand side of the escalator.[27]

Earl's Court is reported by some to have hired a man named 'Bumper Harris', who had a wooden leg, to show just how straightforward the escalator was to use. Other sources doubt his existence, but he has appeared in miniature form in models used by the London Transport Museum, where his left leg appears to be wooden, and relatives have stepped forward on the internet to acknowledge their link to him, adding that he was an employee of London Underground.[28] Whether he is apocryphal or not, it seems unusual that a man with just one leg should be used to demonstrate an activity in which alighting with your left foot carried such importance.

The *Illustrated London News* noted that the escalator saved the passenger exertion and brought London in line with New York. The article added that the new device was proving thrilling for both Londoners and 'country cousins'. Passengers had been known to break their journey at Earl's Court simply to go up and down the escalators as a form of entertainment before continuing on their way. An illustration showed a startling array of passengers enjoying the invention in close proximity: a plump flower-seller, a well-to-do family with a son in a boater, a fusty colonel type carrying a set of golf clubs and several women wearing hats weighed down with a range of plumage.[29] What is unusual about this group of passengers is their alertness; they seem amazed by their surroundings and not one has the dead-eyed gaze of today's commuter, who has learnt not to make visual contact with other passengers.

Piccadilly Circus had eleven escalators – a record for an underground station. Five of these in two tunnels could transport a total of 40,000 passengers at 'rush' hour (in 1928 *The Times* still put the adjective in speech marks) from the booking hall to a common landing. Four of these ran during the busiest period of the morning. From the common landing, six escalators divided between two tunnels, to take passengers to the Bakerloo and Piccadilly lines.

Escalators made it possible to transport huge numbers of passengers into the depths of the station, but they also opened up vistas. The walls became art galleries, promoting everything from the penguins at London Zoo and the greyhounds at Wood Lane's racetrack to sporting events such as Molesey Regatta and the Olympia Motor Show. The escalators could also sweep shoppers straight into the welcoming retail arms of Swan & Edgar. The store had gone through a difficult trading period in the 1920s, partly due to a rebuilding that had tripled its size and given it two acres of floor space. Harrods bought it in 1920 and then an investment trust specialising in department stores assumed control in the same year that the station opened. The new owners, Drapery Trust, made much of the fact that the store had secured space in the display windows leading into the station and that an exit would lead directly into the store's lower ground floor.

The escalators provide a moving narrative, the chance to guess at other passengers' life stories from their clothes, facial expression and what they're carrying, and then to readjust your assumptions as they near you. The moving stairs offer the thrill of searching out a familiar face in the crowd as you wait for your friend or lover to emerge from the station depths. Sam Selvon captured this excitement in *The Lonely Londoners*, a novel about a group of new arrivals from the West Indies settling into 1950s Britain. Galahad starts to feel he has the measure of the city when he tells his new girlfriend, Daisy, to meet him at Piccadilly Circus Tube station.

> Many nights he went there before he get to know how to move around the city, and see them fellars and girls waiting, looking at they wristwatch, watching the people coming up the escalator from the tube. You could tell that they waiting for somebody, the way how they getting on. Leaning up there, reading the *Evening News*, or smoking a cigarette, or walking round the circle looking at clothes in the glass-case, and every time people come up the escalator, they watching to see, and if the person not there, they relaxing to wait till the next tube come. All these people there, standing up waiting for somebody. And then you would see a sharp piece of skin come up the escalator, in a sharp coat, and she give the ticket collector she ticket and look around, and same time the fellar who waiting throw away his cigarette and you could see a happy look in his face, and the girl come and hold his arm and laugh, and he look at his wristwatch. Then the two of them walk up the steps and gone to the Circus, gone somewhere, to the theatre, or the cinema, or just to walk around and watch the big life in the Circus.[30]

Once their relationship is more secure, Daisy becomes the one scanning the crowd spewing out from the escalator and, when they meet, Galahad shows her Trinidad on the clock that tells the time around the world but regrets the island is so small that it is no more than a dot with a name.

*

Despite the seemingly chaotic nature of the mass of shafts, most newspapers were proud of the engineering feat of Piccadilly Circus underground station. The *Illustrated London News* boasted that the new station would be 'the finest subterranean station in the world'. The fact that the builders were working in London clay and that they were, at their closest, a mere nine feet below the shoppers who went about their business oblivious to the extreme efforts going on beneath them added to the project's kudos. When it opened in December 1928 the newspaper had no hesitation in declaring it better than anything in New York; in fact, it was 'one of the sights of London'.[31] A photo showed flappers wearing cloche hats, Peter Pan collars and ties consulting a series of discs under a heading 'See how they run' that told them when the trains were due. Other women gazed at dresses in one of the shop windows in the 'circulating hall' and booking office that made it 'another Piccadilly Circus just below the street level'.[32]

Architects around the world admired Holden's design and the concourse was particularly influential in the crafting of the Moscow Metro system.[33] Renzo Picasso, an urban planner from Genoa who travelled to cities such as London, New York and Chicago to record the innovation he hoped to introduce in his home town, recorded his impression in an illustration that gives the new station a futuristic appeal, like a prototype of the starship *Enterprise*.[34] And for many visitors to Piccadilly Circus the Tube station represented a portal to new galaxies.

Eros was swung into position on 28 December 1931, but there was no ceremony to mark his return. The statue, shining in the light of new high-wattage tungsten lamps imported from America, proved too much of a temptation for New Year's Eve revellers. Just before midnight Hugh McKenzie, a 22-year-old clerk from Lewisham, climbed the statue, mounted Eros and started to rock it backwards and forwards, singing and shouting. When police told him to come down, he said he would – when the clock struck twelve. His acrobatic feats became more elaborate and at one point he was actually standing on Eros's wing, causing it to wobble in its socket.

Piccadilly Circus now had a world-class underground station and a spruced-up Eros for revellers and protesters to flock to. As the young clerk from Lewisham discovered, the setting and atmosphere made it all too easy to lose yourself in the headiness of the moment and to indulge in a caper that might have long-lasting consequences.

9

Private Passions behind Closed Doors

For many, a glamorous hotel in London's West End was the ideal backdrop for a marriage proposal, but for a tragic few the anonymity made it easier to contemplate suicide. When Herbert Turner and Mabel Hill signed the visitors' book as 'Mr and Mrs H. Turner' on 29 October 1932,[1] neither expected to see the world outside ever again.

In the 1920s and 1930s the Regent Palace Hotel proved popular among couples from outside London who wanted a night of glamour, although that glamour excluded a private bathroom, which, because of the narrowness of the building, was absent until the 1950s when a few were introduced. Room after room offered the whiff of an elegant and privileged life that was out of daily reach for most of its visitors: the marble-lined, circular lounge; the airy winter garden with its domed roof and seventy feet of stained glass, the Louis XVI touches and the neoclassical style of plasterwork. Its Lloyd Loom chairs and palm trees made its rooms feel like they were on an ocean liner.

Indeed, the hotel was run with the precision and scale of a giant vessel. Huge washing machines laundered sheets and table linen with an industrial intensity and in the kitchen rows of eggs were lined up on the table waiting to do battle with diners' requests. In one photo dozens of moustached kitchen staff in grubby chefs' overalls and floppy white hats gather around a pile of silver tureens and platters, steam rising above them. They look like stokers hard at work in the bowels of a ship. As in the Lyons Teashops and Corner Houses, there was a below-stairs camaraderie among the staff and the company boasted that at one time there were thirteen families working in the restaurant, including two sets of three sisters. The hotel was also proud of its 'mod cons', and bragged about the supervisor of the new 'super-telephone exchange', Edith Anderson, who could not only tame the myriad of wires that burst from the exchange but also had an OBE, awarded after she'd raised the alarm about the first 'Zepp' raid on London in 1915 when she was just seventeen and working for a naval telephone exchange in Immingham, north-east Lincolnshire.

*

Before leaving for London, Herbert Turner, a 21-year-old motor mechanic who lived with his parents in Shipley, Yorkshire, and Mabel Hill, who was eleven years older, separated from her husband and childless, and also from Shipley, had both told their parents they were off to Blackpool. They stayed first in a hotel in Bloomsbury, from where they went to the theatre a few times before moving to the Regent Palace. At 9.20 p.m. on Saturday evening Turner asked the chambermaid to arrange for him to have a bath. When he returned to the bedroom the couple discussed suicide; Turner had already bought the prussic acid and perhaps the fact that they were running out of money persuaded them that now was the moment to carry out their plan.

Hill poured out two glasses of poison, giving herself more than Turner. They lay down on the bed together in the tiny room and said goodbye. Hill drank the poison first and handed the glass to Turner, who put it on the table before downing his draught. Early the next morning a chambermaid knocked on their door. When there was no response, she raised the alarm and staff opened it to discover Hill dead and Turner unconscious. He was rushed to Charing Cross Hospital, where his stomach was pumped out. On 2 November he was charged with his lover's murder and, later, a further charge of 'attempted suicide'.

When Divisional Detective Nurse (his first name doesn't appear in newspaper accounts) arrived at the hotel he found a bottle labelled 'prussic acid' in a chest of drawers; it appeared to have been sold by a chemist in Yorkshire. There was a glass on a shelf and some shards of glass on the floor. In Turner's coat pocket, he discovered an unaddressed envelope containing two letters, one to each of Turner's parents. The letter to his mother read:

> Dear Mother – Can you ever forgive me for the trouble I have caused you? By the time you have received this I shall not be on this earth. Please ask father to forgive me, as I have been a rotter to him. No doubt you will know who I am with. Please do not blame her. We cannot live without each other.[2]

Another letter, in Hill's hand and written to her mother, explained, 'I cannot think of any other way out for a bad girl, I have caused enough trouble for you, my dear, in this world.'[3] The case was widely covered in publications ranging from *The Times* to regional papers. Reports focussed on the perceived difference in their characters and – importantly – ages in a way that suggested that such factors in a relationship doomed it – although it might be viable for one night in Piccadilly Circus. There was an implication that Turner, a keen cricketer who had sung in the church choir, had been led astray by 'an independent, strong-minded woman who wanted her own way'.[4]

In a statement, Turner told the detective that he had been 'sweethearting' with Hill for about seven months before they agreed to take their own lives in London. He knew the chemist because the latter was a customer at the garage where Turner worked, and Turner was able to convince him that he was buying the poison to destroy two puppies.[5] In his statement he added:

> We were so unhappy we decided to commit suicide together. Mabel Hill suggested it and I agreed . . . she said we should go to London to do it. I carried the poison about for a day or two, and then gave it to her . . .[6]

It's not known exactly why they chose the Regent Palace Hotel and Piccadilly Circus as the place to end their lives. The hotel certainly offered an anonymity that may have helped to detach them from the reality of their everyday. Perhaps the headiness of the bright lights may have allowed them to take that bold, irreversible step, and given them the fatal push they required to propel them into oblivion. Travelling to another world, so far from home, might have been enough to tip them over the edge. It seems unlikely that they would have taken the same desperate course in Blackpool.

When he appeared in Marlborough Police Court, Turner looked very ill and wore a light overcoat and no collar. He collapsed when the charge was read and had to be given first aid. When asked by the magistrate if he had anything to say he whispered, 'I didn't do it, sir.'[7]

Turner stood trial at the Old Bailey and was sentenced to death, although the jury recommended mercy when the judge pointed out the difference between deliberate murder and a suicide pact. Instead, his sentence was commuted to penal servitude for life. After a respectable period of time had passed this, too, was reduced to two years' imprisonment, following his barrister's petition to the Home Office in which he pointed out that Turner was only twenty-one at the time, and that he had been under the influence of an older woman.

Sadly, Hill and Turner were not the only people to travel to the hurly-burly anonymity of Piccadilly Circus and the discreet comfort of the hotel's myriad rooms in order to take their lives. Only two years before the suicide pact that went horribly wrong another motor mechanic, George Crisp, who was forty-five or fifty-five – accounts differ – checked in one Tuesday. Chambermaid Lilly Hilliard noticed that he was in his room all day on Friday and that she could hear him moving around inside. On Saturday morning at 10.45 a.m. housekeeper Nora Stevens called to him through his bedroom door to make sure he was all right. Crisp, a director of City Garage Limited in Birmingham, which he ran as a hobby, according to his son-in-law, replied that he was quite well and was just getting up.[8] It was Hilliard who discovered Crisp's body lying on the floor in his pyjamas with a shotgun between his feet, a piece of string attached to the trigger; his face was horribly mutilated. The inquest found that Crisp did not seem to have any money worries but had become depressed because of his wife's illness, which had been going on for two years and which had, in effect, turned him into her carer. The official ruling from the coroner found that Crisp had died from self-inflicted gunshot wounds while temporarily insane.[9]

Two such horrible instances in the space of two years must have shaken the hotel's staff and added a new dread to the moment when a chambermaid gingerly pushed open the door of a bedroom she had been sent to clean.

The sad cases of Mabel Hill, Herbert Turner and George Crisp highlight the range of people who sought out Piccadilly Circus and their motives for visiting. It shows how visitors could be sucked into London in one frame of mind, in good enough spirits to visit a show or two, but how the bright lights, and all that they promised, might contribute to a fatal shift in mood or highlight the contrast in their own bleak mood. While for most people a visit to Piccadilly Circus meant the chance to try on a different persona for size, it gave others the courage, so far from home, to end their life.

Hill and Turner's suicide pact also demonstrated how your station in life could play an important part in its final act. Their humble background attracted the couple from Shipley – a 21-year-old motor mechanic, still living with his parents, and his older, married lover – to Piccadilly Circus in the first place. But Turner's lack of a good lawyer and the fact that his crime did not involve a high-society setting both worked against him. As Justice Charles put it: 'There is in the minds of some of us a sort of sense of unreality when we are dealing with murder of this sort.'[10]

Another tragedy showed how privilege and money could produce a very different ending and how the gender and social standing of the defendant may well have influenced the outcome. While Turner whispered, 'I didn't do it, sir,' Dolores Elvira Barney, the 27-year-old daughter of a chief government broker, assumed a sharply contrasting attitude when she was accused of killing her lover in the same year as Turner faced the death penalty. Her brazen confidence served her well and Barney's trial was as brash and circus-like as Turner's was subdued and shameful.[11]

Elvira is often described as one of the Bright Young Things, but she was only on the periphery and lacked its members' *joie de vivre* and wit. She was the eldest daughter of Sir John Mullens, stockbroker to George V and Lady Evelyn, and lived the spoilt life of a debutante;[12] she loved partying and driving cars and was involved in one, high-profile crash. She was also believed to be bisexual. Elvira's husband was the American singer John Sterling Barney, who often performed at the Café de Paris in top hat and tails as part of a trio called The Three New Yorkers. But, although Elvira was a regular at the night-club this was not where she met him. Much to the disapproval of her parents, who were dismayed that their daughter should stoop low enough to become infatuated with an American entertainer, the couple had fallen in love in 1927 when John was being paid to perform at a function organised by her mother. They tied the knot a year later, though the marriage did not last long and appears to have been abusive. John returned to the United States a year after their wedding and rarely troubled his British family. Elvira stayed in London and took up with a range of lovers; rumours were rife about the sexual practices she liked to indulge in.

On 30 May 1932, Elvira arrived at the Café de Paris for dinner at just after midnight. The late hour was not unusual for the club's customers and it was not uncommon for Elvira to be as drunk as she was that night. She was accompanied by her lover, William Scott Stephen, a 24-year-old former fashion designer who had been cut off by his parents and who made ends meet by drug deals and with support from Elvira. They had come from a party at the flat they shared but which Elvira owned, at number 21 William Mews, near Sloane Street.[13] Neighbours had grown used to the arguments they heard from number 21 and the loud parties that kept them awake.

After dining at the Café de Paris they couple went on to the Blue Angel Club in Soho before heading home. At 4 a.m. neighbours heard Elvira screaming that she would shoot someone and then one or more shots rang out. The neighbours, perhaps inured to this sort of pandemonium, did not raise the alarm, and so it was Elvira who called a doctor at 4.45 a.m. The doctor arrived to find Stephen's body lying next to an American .32 revolver on the upper landing near the bathroom door. Police and the famous pathologist Sir Bernard Spilsbury were called to assess the scene of discarded glasses and gin bottles. The gun was Elvira's and on 3 June she was arrested and charged with murder.

The trial at the Old Bailey made for thrilling newspaper columns and the police struggled to control the crowds outside. One officer was pushed to the ground; another had his helmet knocked off and reinforcements had to be called. The thirty-six seats in the public gallery were packed with Elvira's glamorous and well-connected friends, many of whom knew her from the Café de Paris. The press reported that Elvira was a 'pale, beautiful woman dressed entirely in black' who was 'fighting for her life' in an 'electric' atmosphere.[14] She sat like a statue, according to the *Daily Mirror* reporter, 'the sun's rays striking her golden – almost platinum blonde – curls', though the truth was that alcohol and drug abuse had robbed Elvira of her looks and transformed her into an overweight figure who looked much older than her years. There were plenty of dramatic moments: when Elvira had to be revived, when the judge asked to be given the revolver and turned it over in his hands so that the highly polished barrel, like Elvira's curls, shone in the sunlight.

As the daughter of wealthy parents, Elvira was able to secure a leading barrister to help her avoid the noose. She was acquitted. This may also have been helped by the fact that, although women were allowed to act as jurors,[15] the property ownership rule meant that juries were dominated by men, who tended to be more sympathetic to female defendants.

After her acquittal the press continued to hound Elvira, reporting that, back at the Café de Paris, she had responded to prying eyes by shouting out from the dance floor, 'I am the one who shot her lover – so take a good look at me.'[16] Although she had escaped hanging, Elvira didn't live much longer; her life ended on Christmas morning 1936 when another unwitting chambermaid found her lifeless body, still clothed in a black-and-white check dress and fur coat, in the bedroom of a hotel in Paris. She appeared to have died of an excess of drugs and alcohol.[17] Piccadilly Circus was capable of offering anonymity but there were those, like Elvira, who could never resist the limelight.

Her case demonstrates the extent to which the nature of entertainment had changed after the dimmed, austere war years. Leisure had become more exuberant and more about standing out from the crowds. The young, rich and privileged made their mark and enjoyed preening and experimenting with drink, drugs and sexual identity in venues such as the Café de Paris. Often those experiments took place as part of an elaborate stunt such as a mock wedding or an elaborately themed party. However, by the 1930s the press and public opinion were starting to grow tired of their antics; as the world faced economic hardship and worrying new political orders, there was little room for such frivolity.

The new underground made it easier to reach Piccadilly Circus and, once there, the world travelled at a faster pace as you sped towards street level on one of the new escalators or waited, heart pumping, for a romantic rendezvous in the Circus itself. For the less privileged, Piccadilly Circus was still a place of bright lights and excitement, somewhere you could lose yourself and feel so far from home that the unthinkable might suddenly become a possibility, whether that was living in a different gender from the one you had been assigned at birth, enjoying a weekend with an older lover or taking a more tragic route through suicide. Most people returned changed in some, small way; for a handful their lives would never be the same again.

Part Four

Lights, Camera, Action!

10

A 'British Hollywood'

It's easy to look back at the early stars of the silver screen and wonder what all the fuss was about. Many performers seem baffled by the new medium and are still grappling with the acting conventions of the Edwardian, or even Victorian, theatre and a script written with the stage in mind. The challenge is even harder if the film is a silent movie in which actors are required to gurn and rely on over-exaggerated hand gestures. But this is not the case with Anna May Wong (Wong Liu-tsong),[1] the Asian-American movie star, who arrived in London in 1928 to shoot the silent film *Piccadilly* – a movie that made the most of the danger, glamour and transformative possibilities associated with the area and its growing international reputation as a meeting place.

Anna May Wong was the perfect actor to represent the possibilities of bringing different worlds together and also to readjust the public view of people of Chinese descent.[2] Almost a century later, the many photos of her that appeared in magazines and newspapers, from the high-profile *Tatler* and *Bystander* to the more parochial *Leven Advertiser* and *Staffordshire Sentinel*, show that all the fuss was entirely justifiable and explain why she was so popular in Britain. As the film's leading lady her character epitomised all that

Piccadilly Circus stood for: she was daring, glamorous, alluring and unpredictable. Her private life, which revealed her to be, at times, shy, thoughtful and determined, also mirrored a place that could change dramatically, depending on the circumstances.

*

Wong was born Wong Liu-tsong in 1905 and grew up in Los Angeles, where the family lived above a laundry owned by her Chinese-American parents. From an early age, Wong was fascinated by movies. The industry was still in its infancy and establishing a base in California, where guaranteed sunshine made filming easy. As a young girl she modelled for a furrier (a job that ignited a lifelong love of fur coats) and, despite her father's concerns about the loose morals of the business, started to win small parts in films. At the age of fourteen she was an uncredited lantern bearer in *The Red Lantern* (1919)[3] and later she secured her first lead in the feature film, *The Toll of the Sea* (1922), which was also the first film to be shot in Technicolour. The following year Wong appeared opposite Douglas Fairbanks in *The Thief of Baghdad*. The film did well in Europe, where she was beginning to establish a fan base.

But, while Hollywood was *the* place to be for an aspiring performer, it was not a comfortable setting for a beautiful young actress of Chinese heritage. Scriptwriters were steered away from stories that even hinted at interracial romance and kisses between actors from different ethnic backgrounds were banned, a prohibition that severely limited Wong's ability to take on romantic roles. Many films included racist themes and she was frequently cast as a prostitute, servant or slave. Too often her character stabbed herself to death or overdosed on drugs in her final scene. It's no wonder that the young Wong spent hours in front of a mirror practising a scream.[4]

America's laws also restricted Wong's private life. Interracial marriages were illegal, which meant she couldn't marry a white European-American. This may be why she never settled down and instead enjoyed several long-term affairs with older, white men, many of whom were actors or who were high up in the movie business and not intimidated by her intelligence and success. Her friendship with the German playwright and screenwriter Karl Vollmöller, proved particularly useful when she tried to expand the range of parts she was offered by spending time in Germany. Despite the abhorrent racism that would dominate the Nazi period, the country was surprisingly liberal in many ways in the 1920s and early 1930s when German modernism flourished.[5] Some Black journalists and other visitors from the USA were pleasantly surprised by the warm welcome they received – particularly in contrast with the discrimination they faced at home. *Piccadilly*'s German-born producer Ewald André (E. A.) Dupont, who had quit Hollywood partly due to its insistence on stereotypes, was conscious that Wong risked being typecast in the USA and, instead, offered her a complex part that allowed her to reach beyond the normal clichés reserved for an actor of her racial background.[6] He came from a German tradition that was making bold steps in the new art form through films such as Robert Wiene's *The Cabinet of Dr Caligari* in 1920 and Fritz Lang's *Metropolis* (1927), which uses uncanny sets and camera angles that are still unsettling today. These masterpieces brought the German film industry to the attention of the rest of the world and made it easier for German film directors to find work in Hollywood.

*

By the time Wong reached London in 1928 after visiting Hamburg and Paris with her sister and secretary, Lulu, her fame had spread. The *Sketch* on 25 July 1928 told its readers that Wong was a 'modern American girl'. Despite the delicacy of her Chinese name – Wong Liu-tsong – means 'frosted yellow willow', she was a keen all-round sportswoman (newspapers overlooked how impractical her long nails would have made this) and had worked as her father's accountant, although she now had her own mansion in Hollywood and a retinue of servants. Shops sold postcards and cigarette cards of her in Chinese or European dress. Her fans viewed her as a Chinese flapper: a young, independent woman who liked fast cars, smoking and wearing daring clothes and a sharp haircut. Most images highlighted her elegant hands with their very long fingernails. The *Sketch* published a whole page of four photos in which her talons are given prominence.[7] The caption explained that, traditionally, in China long fingernails were a sign of high birth because they were proof that the owner had no experience of manual labour. (This fascination with her fingernails continued in the British press; in 1933, newspapers reported how she hoped to start a trend for clip-on gold nails,[8] which she thought were more elegant than the painted version; by 1938 it was revealed that she would be trimming her nails for the first time in twenty years and that she was only doing so to meet the requirements of a part.)[9]

Wong embraced everything about London – from the fog,

which she found romantic, and the rain, which she said made everything so clean, to the friendliness of local people. She even tried playing bagpipes, though was unable to coax a note from them. Newspapers and magazines were fascinated by her and, on the whole, reported her life story with an accuracy not usually associated with coverage of film stars (though one reporter claimed she was discovered in a Chinese laundry by Douglas Fairbanks).[10] She and Lulu rented an apartment in the Park Lane Hotel overlooking Hyde Park and journalists visited her there for interviews. One American, who was ushered in by a Chinese servant, was struck by an understated room of books, cushions, Chinese vases and a lavishly embroidered Chinese shawl. Wong entered the room quietly, putting him at his ease by offering him a Players cigarette.[11]

In *Piccadilly* she plays an unsmiling siren who has the upper hand in her romantic relationships. Wong has a luminous beauty that speaks straight to the camera; her movements are elegant and minimal and her facial gestures subtle and spare. The many images and interviews that record her time in England confirm her star quality and wit, and she comes across as animated and eager to engage with the country she was visiting. She told one reporter that when she visited Limehouse it would be by bus as it didn't seem right to take a taxi.[12] She said how proud she was to be Chinese and that she always tried to introduce a Chinese motif into her dress, although she didn't point out that she hadn't yet visited China. When she had time, she added, she would make a 'little Chinese home here in London, furnished and decorated in our own manner, so that sometimes I can pretend I am in China, and then, when I want a change, I can look out of the window and see one of your very kind policemen on point duty, and remember that I am in your very charming London'.[13]

After the film had secured her fame, Wong appeared on the front page of the *Tatler* in all her vampish splendour. She has a Louise Brooks hairstyle, a perfectly shaped Cupid's bow and a look of disdain. She's sitting on a bench, holding a long-stemmed musical instrument, probably a modified shamisen, that shows her elegant hands to maximum effect and which draws attention to her exposed legs. Her other arm is resting on the bench as if she's about to leap up. A bird in a cage hangs above her head, perhaps to make the point that Anna May Wong cannot be contained.

In Austria, an artist painted her topless in front of a stylised backdrop of Piccadilly Circus for the fifteen-foot-tall poster used to promote the film; one arm is above her head, the other languidly lifting her flimsy gypsy skirt. In this version, which would not have shocked liberal Viennese audiences, Wong's body is much more voluptuous than the reality of her slight frame. At 5 foot 6 inches tall,[14] she was taller than the clichéd Asian female character, typically a prostitute or victim of violence, that Hollywood tried to force her into being.

The following summer, in June 1929, the *Sketch*'s gossip column reported that she had been spotted at Covent Garden on the arm of the composer Constant Lambert.[15] She wore a red 'mandarin's coat' over her evening gown in the same shade, and the magazine noted that her 'wonderful golden complexion is just the fashionable "sunburn" shade we are all vainly trying to achieve!'[16] Wong was becoming so popular that young women powdered their faces to try to capture her complexion and some cut their hair to adopt her trademark fringe. Others took the less drastic measure of wearing lavishly embroidered mandarin coats and jackets to the theatre. There had since before the First World War been an interest in China, but this latest focus on fashion was driven by Wong's charisma. By the time Lulu returned to the USA later in 1929, Anna May had made many friends in London – including minor members of the royal family, who appear as extras in *Piccadilly*; they are in the audience when her character, Shosho, performs her dance.[17] At the height of her fame it was hard for her to leave her apartment without being mobbed.

Wong represented to the public a very different image of people of Chinese descent from the version that had been prevalent in the British press just a few years earlier. During the Great War, when Britain felt particularly threatened by foreign powers, fears spread about Chinese men carrying off young women for the white slave trade and linked Chinese communities with gambling and opium dens. Brilliant 'Billy' Chang, whose real name was Chan Nan, was a Chinese-born restaurateur and dealer who personified the drug menace that began to be associated with the Chinese in London.[18] Chang, who dressed in a luxurious coat with fur lapels and wore grey suede shoes, was alleged to have caused the death of 21-year-old dance hostess Freda Kempton, after he sold her a bottle of cocaine at his restaurant at the Piccadilly Circus end of Regent Street in March 1922.[19] Newspapers quickly labelled him the 'Dope King' and told of his technique of luring women into his circle by sending over to their table an invitation to meet him as they dined in his restaurant.

Little was known then about the true properties of the drug and it was believed, for example, that cocaine was a relaxant rather than a stimulant, and that prostitutes used drug-laced cigarettes to sedate their clients.[20] It was easy to procure drugs at a chemist's and sheets impregnated with morphine and cocaine were seen as ideal presents for soldiers serving at the Front.[21] The drugs menace was regarded as an addiction that women and effeminate men were most likely to fall prey to – two reasons that made Piccadilly Circus the obvious place for the police to seek out traffickers since it had a reputation as a meeting place for gay men and for women who worked in the sex trade. In 1916 a young man who was caught soliciting in the area was found to be carrying a powder that was pink rather than white, and designed for his face, not his nose. A more successful arrest took place in Glasshouse Street when a man was spotted giving a woman a packet of cocaine worth £5 (£290 today), which he claimed he had bought from Brilliant Chang's restaurant.[22]

Many writers exploited this fear of Chinese immigrants and the misconception that they used their criminal activities to control certain parts of London. Authors such as Sax Rohmer in his Fu Manchu books (published between 1913 and 1917) depicted Limehouse as a place of menace, a country apart from the West End. Thomas Burke's collection of short stories, *Limehouse Nights: Tales of Chinatown* (1916) perpetuated the perceived link between the area and the white slave trade. The book was turned down by twelve publishers who all worried that his tales of interracial romance and prostitution would lead to prosecution, especially since D. H. Lawrence's novel, *The Rainbow* (1915),[23] had fallen foul of the Obscene Publications Act because it was seen as damaging the nation's moral wellbeing during wartime. Eventually the publisher, Grant Richards – whose authors included Arnold Bennett, a prolific novelist and the writer of *Piccadilly*, who had also worked at the Ministry of Propaganda – accepted the book, although it was banned by both Boots' and WHSmith's circulating libraries, which 'rented' out books and helped make reading affordable to ordinary people. Bennett warned Burke that prosecution was likely.

As the plotline of *Piccadilly* would show, Bennett had clearly studied Burke's Limehouse setting. *Piccadilly* opens with a view of the Circus in silhouette. Adverts for 'Gordon's London Gin' and the Monico twinkle out of a gloom established by Dupont's blue filter, and a sign above the London Pavilion announces 'THE CENTRE OF THE WORLD'. From here we are taken inside the fictional Piccadilly Club to meet the customers and the waiters, performers and cooks who keep it going. The venue, with its twin staircases sweeping down to the dance floor either side of the band's podium and with its row of balcony seats and glass wall, must surely be modelled on the Café de Paris in Coventry Street.

The club is struggling and its star turn, Mabel, is considered, at the age of twenty-eight, too old. In desperation, the owner, Valentine Wilmot, who is in a relationship with Mabel, remembers a beautiful scullery maid, Shosho, played by Wong, he had dismissed for performing an impromptu, and extremely sensual, dance on the club's kitchen table. Could her exotic dancing save the business? Wilmot tracks her down to Limehouse and persuades her to perform. She agrees on the condition that she wears an authentic warrior's costume and that her Chinese friend, Jim, played by King Ho Chang, accompanies her on the shuangqin, a traditional Chinese instrument.

Wilmot starts to fall in love with Shosho and Mabel is driven mad with jealousy. One evening she follows Shosho and Wilmot to Shosho's home and, once Wilmot has left, persuades Jim to let her in. She begs Shosho to give up Wilmot and, in the most melodramatic scene in the film, Shosho sees that Mabel's handbag contains a pistol and lifts a ceremonial Chinese dagger off her wall to defend herself. The screen cuts to black as the camera homes in on Mabel's outstretched hand holding the gun, and then fainting.

Jim tells the police that Wilmot was the last person to see her alive, and he is arrested. Mabel insists on telling her story to the coroner's court, but can remember nothing after she fainted. Jim is discovered in the police mortuary, dying near Shosho's body from self-inflicted gunshot wounds. With his last breath he confesses to killing her.

Piccadilly is a curious confection. Although the denouement includes the familiar trope of a Chinese woman lying dead, the film is, nevertheless, refreshingly subversive in other ways. As all the reviews acknowledged, Anna May Wong and King Ho Chang, who was a famous restaurant owner, steal the show, and her dance in the warrior costume is stunning. Most reviews also give a special mention to Charles Laughton's comic interlude as the 'greedy nightclub diner', who complains that his plate is dirty. This was Laughton's first, full-length film. In 1927 he was appearing in Arnold Bennett's play *Mr Prohack* in London, and he would go on to win fame for his onscreen portrayal of another glutinous character in *The Private Life of Henry VIII* (1933). Although his part in *Piccadilly* was small, it allowed Valentine to meet Shosho – he visits the kitchen to remonstrate about the state of the crockery and finds her dancing on the table.

A short interlude from the main story in which Shosho and Valentine visit a pub in Limehouse elevates the film beyond a traditional melodrama, in both its style and the themes it tackles. The scene is notable for a tracking shot along the bar that ends with Valentine's hand closing over Wong's famous fingers. This sequence is also memorable for the confrontation that explodes over a white woman dancing with a Black man. While some aspects of Shosho and Jim slide into familiar stereotypical portrayals of Chinese people, Wong, in particular, brings depth to her part and the episode in the pub suggests a more sophisticated appreciation of racial tension. While a scene in which Valentine and Shosho kiss was cut, it is clear that they have a passionate relationship. We see rare insights into the private lives and living spaces of members of the Chinese community, and while *Piccadilly* shares tropes with the traditional Cinderella story, Shosho is not a conventional rags-to-riches heroine. She is taller than Jim and has considerable power over him; she owns her body, too, and we're reminded of this in her choice of warrior costume for her important dance number.

As some commentators noted at the time, the film perfectly encapsulated the contrast between London's East and West Ends, and Piccadilly Circus's pivotal role in connecting both. Just like the Circus, the film brought together an eclectic mix of actors and artists and allowed them to interact in surprising and often transformative ways. Perhaps most startling of all was that such a daring and innovative screenplay should have been devised by a writer more often associated with formulaic Victorian storylines. Arnold Bennett, a journalist and novelist who at the time was world famous for his novels set in the Potteries in north Staffordshire that began with *Anna of the Five Towns* (1902), has since become associated with a staid kind of writing during a period when modernist writers like Virginia Woolf were reinventing the novel. He certainly wasn't considered to be the kind of writer to address controversial subjects such as interracial romance. *Piccadilly* was to be Bennett's only screenplay and he didn't enjoy the experience of working on the film, although it was adapted as an illustrated novel for the Readers Library publishing company. Although he didn't go into detail about why he found the experience of working on *Piccadilly* so painful, he commented in an essay on movies generally that: 'The screen has laid hands on some of the greatest stories in the world and has cheapened, soiled, ravaged and poisoned them by crudest fatuities.'[24] From the comment, he sounds as though he didn't relish the collaboration that is necessary in film-making and the unavoidable reduction of the original story.

It may have been the theatre critic James Agate's waspish attack in the *Tatler* that caused the novelist so much pain. When he first heard that Bennett was going to write the screenplay for *Piccadilly*, Agate considered all the stories he might have chosen, given the unique setting he had at his disposal:

> . . . he might take the people debouching from the Tube on to Piccadilly Circus and follow them to their homes, or a selection of them. I imagined that he might give us a little file of figures coming up from the bowels of the earth and declaring that he would work out for us the lives of an arbitrary number of them, say the seventh, eleventh and sixteenth. It would have been good to see the procession one by one and to wonder what the protagonists would be like when their turn came. Or I thought that Mr Bennett might choose Piccadilly on Mafeking Night, in the throes of war fever, on Boat-race Night, on the afternoon of a Cup-Final. Perhaps he would burn down for us the London Pavilion . . .[25]

But, while he was disappointed by the plot, Agate praised Laughton, Wong and Ho Chang: 'The truth of the matter is that Miss Anna May Wong and Mr King Ho Chang run away with all the honours that are going.'

The *Illustrated London News* was also critical of what Bennett had done to a place that Londoners were starting to feel protective of:

> Piccadilly – what a subject! What an ever-flowing, ever-varying time of humanity the mere word conjures up! Dignified somnolence of palatial clubs, buses breasting the slope with lumbering determination, silver fox furs and white camellias, and the mud spattered art-silk legs of little shop girls. Piccadilly! . . .

The journalist went on to acknowledge the growing sense, intensified by the First World War, that Piccadilly Circus had come to assert a special place in people's hearts, even if they no longer lived in London, or even Britain. It had become the heart of the British Empire.

> I doubt whether the homesick Britisher would find his Piccadilly in the legendary night club to which Mr Bennett has narrowed it down, and to which Mr EA Dupont leads so cosmopolitan a flavour. The night club has apparently ousted Eros permanently from his position in the 'hub of London,' Piccadilly Circus.[26]

Many reviews made much of the international nature of the production – which mirrored the cosmopolitan make-up of Piccadilly Circus itself. 'Herr' Dupont (as he was often referred to in the press),[27] Werner Brandes, the cinematographer, and the set designer, Alfred Junger, were all German. Mabel was played by Gilda Gray, who was born in Poland and grew up in the USA, and who claimed to have invented the Black Bottom and 'shimmy' dance (apparently produced when her nerves while singing 'The Star-Spangled Banner' caused her to shake uncontrollably). Journalists who visited the British International Pictures studios at Elstree, seventeen miles north of London, saw this international talent as helping to create a 'British Hollywood'.[28] As Hollywood had yet to become the behemoth it is today, this was a realistic aspiration. One reporter noted: 'The visitor speaks to a Briton one moment, to a Russian or a Dane or a Frenchman or a German, perhaps, the next.' Anna May Wong confirmed his impression, telling him, 'Oh, we are very cosmopolitan here!'[29]

The same reporter described the painstaking detail that the production team had taken when designing the set of *Piccadilly*. Some 120 carpenters – a figure that doubled or tripled for particularly detailed scenes – created the main dance floor, which at 200 feet in length, rivalled any ballroom in a West End hotel. The workmen also built a three-quarter-size replica of Piccadilly Circus and in the opening credits London buses, carrying the film's cast and credits on their sides in place of adverts, trundle round the tarmacked roads. The set included fully stocked shops such as a tobacconist's that had £2,000 worth of cigarettes, cigars and tobacco.[30] One interior was furnished with thousands of pounds' worth of antique ivory; another included a historic fireplace, which was lent to the film-makers, and plasterers created fake marble busts and statues for another scene. Lights hidden in the tables allowed the champagne glasses to sparkle in front of the guests, who were mainly 'well-known society people from the West End'[31] and who emerged blinking from the club to stumble into Elstree's quiet country lanes.

Piccadilly opened at the Carlton Theatre on Thursday 31 January 1929 in an event that the *Daily Mirror* believed may have marked the first time a British film had premiered in a theatre. The temporary takeover was prophetic and in 1934 the London Pavilion became a cinema. Wong's star quality was such that she was given the lead in a production of *The Circle of Chalk*, an adaptation of a thirteenth-century Chinese play, just as *Piccadilly* was opening. The play, which was produced by Basil Dean, was also notable for the West End debut of a young Laurence Olivier, but was not well received; and reviewers criticised Wong's speaking and singing voices – both of which had remained hidden in the era of silent movies – for sounding too American.

Piccadilly, the film, epitomised what the area of London stood for and how it had changed since the war. It showed how class, status, nationalities and ethnicities collided at a place that was also thought of, nostalgically by those living abroad, as the centre of the British empire. Anna May Wong's onscreen world was vivid and complex; she portrayed a determined woman who makes her way in a dark and fraught London. Offstage, the actress wooed her fans with her charisma, stylish dress sense and evident enjoyment of all London had to offer. The film represented the dichotomy of Piccadilly Circus; some reviewers saw it as too dark a representation of the centre of empire, while audiences thrilled to the sinister underbelly that threatened to close in on the area and its occupants.

*

If anyone could rise to Agate's challenge of putting Piccadilly Circus's dark side in the spotlight, it was Alfred Hitchcock, a director whose distinct and disturbing style was starting to find audiences at a time when cinemagoers were gasping at Wong's performance. Hitchcock, a Londoner through and through, relished the transformative darkness and how Piccadilly Circus's bright lights could puncture that sinister gloom with the same dramatic menace as the jarring music that would accompany the stabbing knife in the iconic shower scene in his later film of 1960, *Psycho*.

Hitchcock was twenty-seven when he started work on his 1927 silent film *The Lodger: A Story of the London Fog*. It was his third film as director, although the first to be made in England (the others were created in Germany), and one of the earliest to reveal his talent for suspense. Later, he told the French film director François Truffaut that the film was 'the first true Hitchcock movie'.[32]

The Lodger was based on a novel by Marie Belloc Lowndes, sister of Hilaire, and inspired by a dinner party at which the hostess described how her butler and cook were convinced that their lodger was Jack the Ripper. In the film version the killer is obsessed with young, blond-haired women like Daisy. This detail is often cited as the first example of Hitchcock's preference for blond leading ladies – he would later cast Tippi Hedren and Grace Kelly in his films; however, he pointed out, with justification, that fair-haired actors produced a sharper image, particularly in black and white where lighter hair offered a crisper, better-lit contrast.[33]

The film opens with a screaming woman and then we follow news of the latest assault from the printing presses of Fleet Street via a van carrying the wet-inked newspapers to the newspaper vendors of what appears to be Piccadilly

Circus, who announce the outrage like old-fashioned town criers as customers clamour for a copy. Above them crowds read the headline picked out in bright lights: 'Another Avenger Crime – Late This Evening – The Body of a Fair-Haired Girl Was Found On the Embankment'. As the news spreads Hitchcock appears, in what is usually cited as his first cameo role, as a journalist at the news briefing. Post-production editing made the film even sharper as Hitchcock agreed to cut the number of title cards from 350–500 to a bare minimum and allowed E. McKnight Kauffer, the American artist whose posters were brightening up the London Underground, to design opening credits that set the tone of mystery and menace.

The Lodger presents a chilling, fog-bound London where identity is easily obscured, and contains little of Hitchcock's trademark dark humour. The lodger himself is swathed in a scarf; a woman drinking a restorative cup of tea at a late-night kiosk is terrified by a distorted face she sees on the side of a metal tea urn and the lodger is very nearly lynched by a mob that thinks he is the murderer. This was not the London Hitchcock grew up in but one his imagination grew into. Two years later, in his next celluloid outing to the West End, Hitchcock returned to a more sociable, well-lit Piccadilly Circus when he started work on *Blackmail*, a film in which he also turned, arguably for the first time (film experts disagree on this point), to sound. If *The Lodger* concentrated on pricks of light in a gloomy Piccadilly Circus, *Blackmail* gave it a soundtrack – and one that bustled with hectic interruptions, trysts and misunderstandings, just like most people's experience of the real-life Piccadilly Circus.

These early screen versions of Piccadilly Circus were a reminder that the area didn't just belong to revellers when

Mafeking was relieved, or to distant plantation owners taking tiffin and reminiscing about their nights at the Criterion. It wasn't just for angry suffragettes or couples looking for a lodestar in a lonely London. Piccadilly Circus's bright lights themselves highlighted the darkness they pierced: for every backdrop, like the Pavilion, brilliantly illuminated, there was a corner that remained resolutely in the dark. Black-and-white films were perfect for stressing this contrast between good and evil, excitement and danger. Films like *Piccadilly* pointed out the contrast between the onstage glamour of a beautiful Chinese dancer and her previous backstage misery as a scullery maid; it accentuated the easy passage from the bright lights of the West End to the dangerous gloom of the East End. *The Lodger* shows a sinister, foggy Piccadilly Circus and reminds us that it isn't just the place to head to for a good time; its dark alleyways and nightclubs can be a refuge for criminals and gangsters.

11

Friendship and Romance over a Cup of Tea

Theatre- and cinemagoers on their way home after a Saturday night out were in for an unexpected treat in March 1929: Alfred Hitchcock was filming his latest thriller, *Blackmail*, at Lyons Corner House in Coventry Street. The dry, bright weather had persuaded the director to take to the streets after a dull, wet February ruled out filming outside. But as the night-time temperature fell, inquisitive couples pulled their coats more tightly about them and cloche-hatted women stood on Mary Jane tiptoes to catch a glimpse of the famous director and his leading actors: handsome John Longden, playing a harassed Detective Frank Webber, and his impatient girlfriend, Alice White (Czech actor Anny Ondra), her beautiful face framed by a fur collar and blond curls escaping from her black beret. They might also have spotted Cyril Ritchard playing an artist, Mr Crewe. If they had been able to follow the story, the eager crowds would have realised that, especially in a Hitchcock film, leaving the safety of a Lyons Corner House was never going to end well.

Based on the play of the same name, *Blackmail* is about a woman who is blackmailed after killing a man who tries to rape her. Hitchcock's Lyons Corner House is one of chaos and comic confusion. The couple fight their way through the

West End crowds to enter the building and then dupe the door-boy into letting them into a restaurant that has no room for another customer. Once inside, there is a Laurel and Hardy bit of burlesque as Frank and Alice attempt to beat another couple to their table and when Frank tries to summon one of the harassed waitresses with his increasingly frustrated calls of 'Miss, Miss!' It's a noisy room where customers in their smartest clothes eat and drink, smoke and laugh. Like many of their fellow diners, Frank and Alice are on their way to a film, but, at the last minute, Alice decides she doesn't want to go and Frank flounces out. Outside, in Coventry Street, he hums and haws about whether to try to win her over, but just as he turns to rejoin her, he sees her leaving with another man.

When filming was over, the bystanders who had watched *Blackmail* being shot were able to choose between two versions of the film: a wholly silent treatment, filmed in a genuine Corner House, and a version that is often described as the first British 'talkie' and for which a replica restaurant was created in the studio.

If they chose the second option, they might have been surprised that Anny Ondra, playing Alice, was suddenly speaking with a rather clipped middle-class voice that often didn't quite synch with the movement of her lips. The reason for this, as a celebrated audition clip of Hitchcock teasing Ondra demonstrates, was that the actress could not manage to shake off her thick Czech accent and another actress read her lines.

*

Lyons Corner House was an ideal setting for a Hitchcock film. If Piccadilly Circus was the people's meeting place,

Lyons Corner House and Teashop were where those people went for refreshment. The Corner House was full of comings and goings – and interruptions; you could never quite be sure who the door-boy would usher through the highly polished doors or who would leave with whom at the end of the evening. The Coventry Street restaurant was a place for lovers' trysts, a quasi-works canteen for young Jewish dressmakers from Soho, some of whom would be making jackets in the style of Anna May Wong's clothes with silks bought from Berwick Street Market, and a retreat where musicians and performers from the nearby theatres and clubs could eat a hearty meal between performances or engagements.[1]

The fact that anyone was welcome there gave it an anonymity that made it ideal for shady deals and espionage. In January 1914 the Corner House was involved in its own blackmail case when a 26-year-old valet, Albert Wilson, was convicted of stealing an overcoat from the restaurant. He had already been sent to prison and birched for robberies in London and Reading and for being an 'incorrigible rogue', according to *The Times*.[2] The detective who gave evidence in court said Wilson annoyed gentlemen as they left West End clubs and public places. At his lodgings, police found five overcoats and a leather case that contained a woman's wig and make-up. Unfortunately, *The Times* did not go into further detail about the nature of his blackmail.

The Corner House was involved in a much more serious charge – one that threatened national security – when two men were accused of passing on secrets to the fledgeling Soviet government. In 1927, 24-year-old German Georg Hansen, who claimed to be living in London to improve his English,[3] met Dr Odenbach, another German, in the Corner House in Coventry Street. Hansen was later accused of spying for the Soviet government and of obtaining highly secret material about Britain's air and army manoeuvres.[4] Lyons was cited as the scene for a meeting with one of his spy contacts and it's easy to imagine the hustle and bustle of the busy restaurant as a perfect, Hitchcockian setting in which spies could plot. Hansen was sentenced to ten years' penal servitude.[5]

The Corner Houses – others such as one in the Strand (1915) and one on the corner of Oxford Street and Tottenham Court Road (1929) soon joined the original Coventry Street site – were remarkable in that they could make distinct groups of people feel as if the restaurant was their own private club. This was particularly true of the Coventry Street site. Young Jewish couples would congregate there before or after trips to dance halls; gay men felt safe in the 'Lilypond', a name that ostensibly referred to the flowers painted on the walls, but which was also a subtle reference to the queer clientele who gathered there – waitresses knew to seat customers who obviously fell into this category in this part of the restaurant and many felt free to wear make-up. The setting was more domestic than other local haunts that welcomed gay men: the Long Bar at the Trocadero or the Criterion, which could transform at nightfall and earned the nicknames 'Witches' Cauldron' and 'Bargain Basement'.[6]

Perhaps this capacity to make disparate groups feel at home was born of the Corner Houses' vastness. They were, as one historian put it, 'super-restaurants' and 'industrial sites of leisure'.[7] Visiting a Corner House was a noisy experience and the cacophony of diners in the giant emporium often led to mishearings.[8] A man who asked a waitress to recommend a dessert accused her of rudeness because, when she suggested a knickerbocker glory, he heard the retort, 'Buzz off to glory!'

Another customer asked for 'sausage and mash' but the Nippy misheard 'milk and a dash'. Among couples, the noise level was a useful excuse to lean in to catch each other's words.

As well as the opportunity for intimate conversations, customers queued outside so that they could try a wealth of food and drinks inside, from the new American soda fountain to wholesome baked beans on toast. While they queued, they gazed at the famous window displays constructed by a team of six women in the 'studio' at the back of Coventry Street, with mechanical scenes featuring birds, bees, mermaids, rabbits and chickens; the characters were condemned to a perpetual life of running in circles, swinging a hammer or endlessly tossing pancakes. Once inside, they were served in fancy rooms lined with mirrors and mosaics and heavy carpets that helped to muffle some of the noise made by the thousands of diners and a range of live musicians, from gypsy violinists to classical singers, or to take part in tea dances.[9] The Corner House was an all-night refuge that welcomed the flotsam and jetsam that drifted in from Soho and Piccadilly.

At the centre of this maelstrom of emotions and egg mayonnaise (the cheapest dish on the menu[10]) was the 'Nippy', the efficient, perfectly turned-out waitress who 'nipped' around the tables. It was her job to ensure that customers felt like the film star they might, if they were very lucky, spot at a nearby table (most Nippies had a story about the famous person they had once served). The name 'Nippy' was chosen in 1924 from a staff competition held by the company and replaced 'Gladys', which had begun to sound old-fashioned as it had fallen from popular usage. The rejected alternatives included 'Lola of Lyons', 'Lucille of Lyons', 'Lyora of Lyons', 'Sybil-at-your-service', 'Miss Nimble', 'Miss Natty', 'Busy Bertha', 'Speedwell', 'Ganymede' (in Greek mythology a boy who was so beautiful that he was carried off to serve as a cup-bearer for the gods), 'Gaby' and 'Dextrous Dora'.[11]

One of the first waitresses to work in Lyons' very first Teashop at 213 Piccadilly, which opened on 20 September 1894, was Alice Eleanor Bacon. Indeed, Nell, as she was usually known, is often referred to as 'Nippy No. 1'. She grew up in Nayland, a quiet village on the River Stour, close to the Suffolk/Essex border in East Anglia, the youngest of three sisters. When Nell was seventeen, she and her sister Lillian took their first ever train trip and went to London for Queen Victoria's jubilee. They both found temporary positions at Lyons in Piccadilly, where their soft Suffolk accents made them popular with customers. At this stage the waitresses wore high-necked ankle-length dark-grey skirts with a white apron and sweetheart bib that made them look like a nanny or downstairs cook. At first Lyons demanded that only tall, young women with a waist of 17 inches, or slimmer, could apply, but they had to compromise when they found it impossible to retain staff. The Teashop had room for 200 customers and waitresses were paid on commission until a strike in 1895 persuaded Lyons to introduce salaries; although, in reality, this represented a drop in take-home pay. Lillian left when she got married but Nell rose to spend over sixty years with Lyons – the longest period any woman had worked for the company. She became a manageress of a Teashop in 1903 and six years later was chief superintendent of all Teashop staff. She took a close interest in training waitresses and was keen that they should avoid her own experience of accidentally emptying a cup of tea into a customer's upturned top hat, which he had placed next to him, presumably on the table or chair.[12] If she had had her way, she would have staffed the Teashops only with red-headed waitresses; she thought they were more beautiful and efficient.[13] By the end of her life she was living in a company flat above Lyons Teashop in Streatham High Road, south London, and had a chauffeur-driven company car.

By the 1920s the modern Nippy had cast off her Victorian image and donned a fitted, flapper-style alpaca dress. The uniform was neatly chic with thirty pairs of mother-of-pearl buttons sewn on with red cotton on the front and detachable and starched Peter Pan collar and cuffs. The buttons caused extra anxiety for the waitresses because the loss of one could be expensive. A shift started with a 'mad rush' in the dressing room to make sure everyone looked 'spick and span'. Small gas jets, used to heat hair curlers, gave off noxious fumes but allowed Nippies to keep their hair rolled up so that, in line with Lyons' rules, it didn't touch the collar. If a curl unravelled while a Nippy was serving, she would be marched off the floor by the supervisor and given a hair clip with which to contain it. Each waitress wore a black-and-white 'coronet' with the border just above the eyebrow and had to get used to an overeager supervisor tugging it down if she thought it was sitting too high on the forehead. The headdress was capable of accommodating either a bob or a shingle hairstyle, although Lyons warned waitresses against using peroxide. The coronet proved a regal addition and Lyons liked to describe the waitresses as 'Teashop debutantes'.

The cost of the Nippy's uniform came out of her weekly pay packet and she was also obliged to pay for it to be laundered. Waitresses had to make up any shortfall in takings if they forgot to add an item to a bill. This meant that it was not unheard of for a waitress to end the working day out of pocket. Tips were, officially, discouraged, as a way of persuading financially stretched customers to dine at Lyons' Teashops and restaurants, but it was often the tips that kept a waitress going. Sometimes diners gave their favourite Nippy presents and these could be lavish; one Nippy received a record player. The company resisted attempts to unionise their workers and in 1920 a waitress with sixteen years' service was sacked for wearing a union badge.[14] The strike that followed lasted just two days and led to headlines such as 'Storm in a teacup'.[15]

From her very first encounter with J. Lyons, a Nippy's personal appearance was subjected to intense scrutiny. At interview she was often asked to remove her hat so that her hair was visible, and then told to walk up and down and to hold out her hands for inspection. This last detail was part of a daily ritual that many Nippies grew to loathe. One Nippy remembers the manager would make the young waitresses stand on a wooden box so that he could shine a torch through the bottom of their dress to ensure that their petticoat lined up perfectly with their uniform. From today's perspective such attention feels uncomfortably intimate.

Nippies were selected for their pleasant manner, deftness (particularly when handling crockery and cutlery) and memory. The latter was vital if a customer changed their order at the last minute. The Nippy was instilled with the ethos that the customer was always right, and a tiny, oxblood-red notebook held in the London Metropolitan Archives bears witness to this principle. Within its battered covers the neat, pencilled notes remind the owner that 'Sales [probably the sales assistant] must always be polite to customers & address them correctly as Sir or Madam. Always say please and thank you, when asking them to Pay Bill or ordering goods etc Sales are not to remain seated when speaking to customers.'

Kathleen Pittman, who worked in the Coventry Street Lyons

House in the 1930s, remembered that the Nippies had to have immaculate collars and cuffs, which were sewn on before they went on duty, and clean aprons. They weren't allowed lipstick and face power had to be discreet. Shoes had to be one-bar and black and fancy shoes were forbidden; stockings were black, with no ladders and straight seams. The only jewellery they were permitted was a wedding or engagement ring. Kathleen likened the Nippy's status to that of a Bluebell dancer, but the most common description of the waitresses in the press was 'public servants'. In 1928 the *Westminster Gazette* compared their role to that of a policeman or bus driver.[16] Young girls wanted to grow up to be Nippies and the Nippy uniform became a favourite dressing-up present.[17] George V and Queen Mary were believed to have a dog called Nippy,[18] and the name was also given to a racehorse, rose, railway engine and Spitfire (paid for by Lyons staff).[19] In 1928 the *Evening Standard* included a cartoon of a Nippy in its London Life series, though she had higher heels and a shorter hem than a genuine Nippy would be permitted and it's difficult to see how she could physically carry a tray laden with a teapot and cups with just one hand. The caption summed up how customers viewed the waitress: 'The Girl We all Know'. There was even a musical comedy called *Nippy* that ran at the Prince Edward Theatre in 1930, about a waitress who becomes a film star.[20] In May 1935 the Russian-born sculptor Abraham Melnikov, who would eventually settle in Israel, produced a bust of a Nippy; his other commissions would include Winston Churchill – the waitress had become a cornerstone of the British social system.

The Nippy was like a capable, glamorous older sister: she knew how to handle difficult customers and find her own way home at night, and would probably bag a husband (and if she did Lyons would give her a free wedding cake, as long as she'd worked for them for over five years). In 1923 St Dunstan's cigarettes issued a series of special cards that allowed smokers to collect parts of an image that, when all the pieces had been assembled, would reveal a picture of a Nippy.[21] Lyons also produced purse calendars with the slogan 'I'm Glad we went to Lyons!', a reference to the waitresses' earlier nickname Gladys, a photo of a Nippy standing next to two giant Swiss rolls and the caption, 'The symbol of Public Service'.[22]

In 1990 Lyons Company launched a press campaign in which it asked former Nippies to write in with their memories. The thick folder at the London Metropolitan Archives bears witness both to the depth of affection with which waitresses remembered their job and the importance of the Teashops and restaurants for many customers, such as the married couple who wrote in after years of married life with fond memories of how their romance had blossomed over a Lyons tea.

The importance of friendships formed by Nippies in the Teashops and Corner Houses, especially among young women living alone in London for the first time, also echoes through the neatly typed letters and spidery handwriting. Several wrote of friendships that lasted a lifetime and which were forged over the starched tablecloths and silver service. Most never forgot the 'Nippy number' that was clearly displayed on their uniform. There is also a respect for the paternalistic approach the company took towards their charges. One writer describes the job as 'a finishing school for the working-class girl' and many other women, or their descendants, record how the training allowed them to establish their own cafés and businesses once they 'graduated' from Lyons.[23] At the very least it taught the women who worked there how to prepare a good table setting and how to welcome guests with confidence into their own home in a way that would have been unthinkable, and in poorer families unnecessary, for their mothers and grandmothers.

As well as equipping Nippies with the skills to improve their social standing, the job introduced them to a cast of characters they probably wouldn't otherwise have encountered and they learnt to treat everyone with the same level of courtesy, even in the face of unreasonable behaviour, such as the woman who accused one Nippy of giving her baby in its pram a 'black look'. Undercover Lyons employees stalked the restaurants and this could lead to a complaint or a commendation. The waitresses were easily identifiable by their number, which meant that customers could pass on praise or censure. One customer wrote to Lyons to express his gratitude to a Nippy who had reassured him, after he'd spilled ketchup all over the white starched tablecloth, that the previous diner must have loosened the top and that she was changing the cloth anyway. The commendation highlighted the waitress's role in making customers feel at ease in a social setting that might be new to them.

Food was an important part of the Nippy experience. Whatever her shift, a Nippy could expect one hot meal and a snack tea. Many waitresses had their first experience of a banana split or knickerbocker glory at Lyons and many remembered fondly the size and texture of the Teashops' Swiss rolls: a great, spongy wedge, oozing with red jam. Customers, too, were impressed by the standard of food and the servings; some were stunned by the size of the plates. Nippies got to know the orders their regular customers would ask for – whether that was 'milk and a dash [of coffee]' or something more elaborate such as an 'Adam and Eve on a Raft' (two eggs on toast), a 'Baron's Wife' (whose name offers no clue as to its contents) or 'an Airship on a Cloud' (bangers and mash).

For Eveline Taylor, her job at the Coventry Street Lyons Corner House was a family affair that offered the thrills of working at the heart of London's West End. She joined in 1932 when she was fourteen and worked in the dressmaking department, sewing on wayward buttons that popped off the Nippies' uniforms and dashing out to Berwick Street market in Soho to find matching cotton for repairs. Her mother was already serving on the imported American soda fountain, and her father was a 'second chef', working mainly on Indian dishes. Eveline progressed from repairs to become a 'Trippy', a role that put her in charge of a trolley laden with pastries and the knowledge that, if she did well, she would progress to becoming a Nippy. She wore a white uniform and large pancake hat. She remembers the job as 'Great fun . . . My friend and I were considered quite glam girls then.' After a year she was promoted to Nippy. Eveline remembered meeting lots of 'Windmill girls' in the café; they would pop in after a session performing in nearby Great Windmill Street theatre, which became famous during the Second World War for its motto, 'We never close!' The fact that the female performers posed in various stages of undress earned it a variation on that maxim: 'We never clothed!'[24]

Many Nippies spoke of the romance of the orchestra playing in the background and of the excitement of mixing with the musicians. Eveline went out with a drummer, until her mother put a stop to the romance. She left briefly to get married but returned to work on the soda fountain with her mother. She concluded her letter of reminiscences, 'They were great days, hard work, not a big wage, but I'd go back.'

Another Nippy in the Coventry Street Corner House served in the basement for three years from 1929. She worked a six-day week for 12/6, plus tips, and paid 1 1/2d daily for a clean cap and apron and 32/- for the uniform. She joined the Lyons rowing club in Hammersmith and discovered the added advantage that attending training sessions twice a week meant she avoided the chores of laying the tables, cleaning the teapots and wiping the mustard pots. She was also fortunate enough to meet the king and queen when she served at a royal garden party at Buckingham Palace, when the alpaca dress was replaced with a black silk crêpe de Chine version. On another occasion she worked at the Olympia Motor Show, where the tips were higher than at Coventry Street.

The prospect of finding a husband was an important benefit of the job and Lyons was proud to claim that the marriage rate among Nippies was higher than in any other group of working girls. The bridegroom could be a fellow worker, someone the Nippy had met at a staff function or a customer. A *Picture Post* article of March 1939, which told the story of a Nippy's day through images taken by Bill Brandt, reported that between 800 and 900 Nippies married each year. Presumably many of these young women would have found husbands even in other jobs, but the article pointed out that one Nippy had married a Spanish diplomat, another an American 'near-millionaire' and the third a Canadian doctor.

But Lyons didn't just offer a matrimonial escape route; its paternalist approach and the supply of plentiful food provided a lifeline to pull many young women through the economic hardships of the 1920s and 1930s.

Edna Broadbent passed the exam to go to grammar school but knew that, as one of five children and with a father who worked as a miner but could secure only a few days' work a week, her parents simply couldn't afford to buy her the satchel and uniform she needed to continue her education beyond fourteen. Her only option was to go into service, but this was something she wanted to avoid. Her maternal grandmother and two aunts offered to put her up in London until she found work. 'I remember my Dad taking me down, and you can imagine what a different world it was, from a quiet mining village.' At first she looked after three small boys whose father ran a taxi business, and then one of her aunts suggested she applied for a job in the Coventry Street Corner House. She started work on 20 January 1931, when she was seventeen. She was too young to be a Nippy, so she worked as a Trippy, serving hors d'oeuvres from a trolly in the morning and switching to pastries in the afternoon. Her uniform was the reverse of a Nippy's: a white dress with black collar, cuffs and black buttons down the front and a simple headband with a white ribbon. She eventually got a job nearer home, in a café in Bradford, where she met her future husband.

Another young woman who signed herself simply as 'Nippy Barnett' told how, in 1936, she was living in digs with her sister Betty and friends Kitty and Ruby. The sisters were from Durham and the friends from Sheffield. Nippy Barnett stated bluntly that 'we were looking for work where we would be given food because we had no mother'. Kitty returned one day 'all excited about what she had heard' from a friend she had bumped into who was working in Lyons' Marble Arch Corner House. They went for interviews and 'Nippy Barnett', as she would become, secured a position as a Trippy at the

Corner House in Coventry Street, as her age precluded her from joining at a higher level. Betty also got a job there and her cousin Nancy worked as a Nippy near Parliament. She remembered the excitement of her trolley being carried over the heads of diners in a packed restaurant after customers flocked to London to celebrate the coronation of George VI and the future queen mother after the shock of Edward VIII's abdication.

Nippy Barnett was unusual in that she enjoyed being a Trippy so much that promotion came as something of a disappointment. Consolation arrived in the shape of a 'smashing waiter' who helped her to adapt to the increased pressure. He served her customers as well as his own and helped her as she stood crying in the kitchen, trying to decipher the letters on her notepad. She could make out the letter 'c' but was it the start of 'cabbage', 'carrots' or 'cucumber'? Gradually her confidence increased, and she began to enjoy the company of the older staff. She and another waiter and his wife would spend their days off together, sometimes fishing, and sometimes on motor 'bykes' [sic] outings. It was while she was 'larking around' as a Trippy that she fell and broke her arm but, although it meant she couldn't work, the manageress allowed her to come in for her meals because she knew she had no family to support her.

Lyons supported its staff in many ways. When Nancy Meyer, who fulfilled her childhood dream of becoming a Nippy and worked in Coventry Street, was injured by a coffee urn that fell on her head, Lyons paid for her to see a Harley Street specialist. She was offered compensation but told that if she took it, she couldn't keep her job – she decided to carry on as a Nippy. Staff could also join the Lyons 'Sport Club' or take part in art and needlework. There was even a famous outing to France in 1927 that included a visit to the war graves and the Mumm champagne vineyards.

*

Nippies were regularly moved from one Teashop or Corner House to another if one restaurant was short-staffed. This could be within London or to provincial towns such as Cambridge – where one Nippy met the American soldier she would marry – or to a seaside resort, which was popular among Nippies during the summer months. Working in a central Teashop or Corner House like the ones near Piccadilly Circus or Parliament gave Nippies a front window on the world. They witnessed bombs in both wars and hunger marches throughout the 1920s and 1930s; parents worried about how their daughters would find their way home in the blackout, and how they would cope with the crowds of football supporters who descended on the capital for big matches. The Coventry Street Corner House and Teashop were havens for anyone new to London and disorientated by its never-ending activity.

But the Lyons Teashops and Corner Houses weren't just for the lower classes; they were also a refuge for well-to-do customers down on their luck. When, in Agatha Christie's second published novel, *The Secret Adversary* (1922), two schoolfriends, 'Tuppence' (Prudence Cowley) and Tommy (Beresford) bump into one another in Piccadilly after the Great War, they are both 'stony [broke]' and Tommy is embarrassed about where they might eat. Tuppence immediately eases the situation by choosing the Lyons Teashop in Piccadilly. They split the bill and enjoy separate teapots, accompanied by buttered toast for Tuppence and buns for

Tommy. It is in this amicable setting that they hatch their plan to set up a business called Young Adventurers. They decide to meet at Piccadilly Circus Tube station at noon the next day to continue their plotting.

The birth control campaigner, Marie Stopes, author of *Married Love*, was unable to finance the publication of her book until Binnie Dunlop, a doctor and fellow believer in eugenics, arranged a meeting with a prospective backer at Lyons Teashop in Piccadilly in February 1918.[25] Humphrey Roe, an officer in the Royal Flying Corps and an aircraft manufacturer, had not expected to be attracted to Stopes, but found himself falling in love over a Lyons tea. He agreed to help finance her book and they were married a few months later.

*

Hitchcock's *Blackmail*, which begins in a Lyons Corner House buzzing with expectations of a happy night out, soon takes on darker themes, ensuring that the sordid side of Piccadilly remains in the public's imagination. As with so many of his films, the story is steeped in guilt. When Alice abandons her solid, police officer boyfriend to go home with Crewe, someone she barely knows, she finds herself in his apartment. The atmosphere quickly sours and he persuades her to try on a skimpy costume and then attempts to rape her. She manages to save herself by stabbing him to death. Hitchcock then shows a tortured Alice roaming the streets of London grappling with her feelings. She clutches her jacket close to her throat as she wanders, dazed, through the crowds spilling happily out of theatres.

When she reaches Piccadilly Circus she gazes at the familiar, pulsating lights advertising the Café Monico, the flaming torches urging Londoners to 'Read Britannia every day' and the homely brand 'Bovril' picked out in similar lights. As she turns to look at the flashing lights on the corner of Shaftesbury Avenue, next to the Pavilion, the first advert, 'Gordon's White for Purity', seems to taunt her; and then the cocktail shaker pouring liquid into a cocktail glass is transformed before her eyes into a stabbing dagger. She hurries on, terrified by the apparition. Piccadilly Circus seems to know her secret. Her faithful boyfriend steps in to ensure all ends well, and so they escape the blackmailer's plan and justice is done.

Piccadilly Circus was a place of high excitement. For a young couple, or someone enjoying London for the first time, its bright lights could be joyous and celebratory, but for anyone who felt lost, or trapped in mental anguish, the lights could quickly assume the unrelenting harshness of an interrogation cell. However, the warm glow of Lyons Teashop and Corner House provided an unjudgmental bolt-hole for anyone struggling to work out where they fitted in. The venues' quiet acceptance of different customers gave those visitors a reprieve from their status as outsider and played a small, but significant, part in bringing about social change. The possibilities were equally momentous for the staff who worked there. Lyons wasn't just about providing a square meal at affordable prices, it offered a democratisation of dining – no matter what your background or means, you were welcome.

12

The Simpsons Man

For a department store that was to exemplify the Bauhaus ideals of clean-lined utility and elegance, Simpsons had the fustiest of entries into the world. Before Alexander Simpson decided, in 1935, that 203 Piccadilly – now Waterstones flagship bookstore – was an ideal location from which to expand his family tailoring business, the Museum of Practical Geology occupied the long, narrow site. It ushered its visitors in through a quiet entrance on Jermyn Street, traditionally known for its tailoring businesses, and into rooms of vitrines crammed with fossils, rocks and broken pottery. When the Commissioners of Crown Lands decided the collection needed bigger premises, Simpson made his move and paid £11,000 for the site.

The new department store did an about-turn and embraced the hustle and bustle of its Piccadilly entrance, while giving the impression that, although utterly modern in outlook, it was supported by years of tradition and expert workmanship, as exemplified by the tailors and shirtmakers of Jermyn Street. The shop's location was an essential part of its identity and evident in the way the business incorporated 'Piccadilly' into its name: the 'p' in 'Simpsons' formed the start of 'Piccadilly' in the lower deck of adverts. The ultimate accolade came when bus conductors started to call 'Simpsons!' when they approached the store. The shop even cheekily claimed that Eros was directing shoppers in the direction of the department store. Later, in 1951 Eros's help would be enlisted to introduce Simpsons' lavish brochure as part of the Festival of Britain, which was designed to get Britain back on its feet after the Second World War:

> For both sexes this is a propitious spot [Eros wrote]. Not a bowshot from here is a store unsurpassed anywhere in the world. But especially rich in those very goods for which Britain is most famous. And thoughtfully organized to assist the guest from overseas. Let me show you . . .[1]

The business began at the end of the nineteenth century in a rented room in Petticoat Lane, strategically close to both the East End of London and the City. Here a young man named Simeon Simpson made the most of his talent at drawing and cutting straight lines and curves by eye to produce bespoke suits. Industrialisation allowed him to transform his individual labour into a production line, which expanded into factories that made men's and boys' suits, as well as tailored wear for women and girls.

At the start of the twentieth century most provincial towns had at least one tailor's shop and Simeon realised that he could spread his empire beyond London to offer a bespoke service to these shops, or 'agents', as they became known. Like other stores in and around Piccadilly Circus, he was able to harness the new railway network and soon he had established a hectic shuttle of suit parts that commuted up and down the country on the night-train. Simeon's team of expert tailors, who were nearly all male, supplied entire suits made up of shoulders, collars, sleeves and cuffs tacked together; the agent chalked up minor changes after a fitting with the customer and returned it to Simpsons to finish – all within a week. At its height, around 100 parcels a week were leaving London's mainline station. Simeon boasted that orders for weddings and funerals could be turned round in a day. A 1929 photo shows the tailors sitting in an airy, well-lit factory in Stoke Newington, north London; the men, all wearing waistcoats, and many perched on the tables, some cross-legged, look like well-dressed versions of the elves who help the struggling shoemaker in the Grimm fairy tale.

The business's success brought respectability and Simeon's children did well: his daughter married a solicitor, his eldest son became a doctor and his second son, Alexander, or Alec, joined the family firm, where he learnt the trade and travelled around Britain and abroad to see how other tailors ran their businesses. Keenly aware of the changing trends in men's clothing, Alec could see that in most professions the three-piece suit was dying out and that men, particularly in the capital, were taking a more relaxed approach to their clothes. Soft collars started to replace the restriction of starch and jackets were frequently worn without a waistcoat. Sports clothing was becoming increasingly popular and influenced less formal trousers such as the roomy Oxford bags and plus-fours. Men were allowing themselves to choose from a wider range of styles and colours in different materials.

The Prince of Wales, the future Edward VIII, had also helped to popularise golf and set a dandyish example in his choice of plus-fours, flat cap and checked jumper. Alec was a keen golfer but, so the story goes, became frustrated by the way in which his trouser braces inhibited the upward swing as his club struck the golf ball. He solved the problem by drawing on his tailoring heritage to create trousers that fitted neatly at the waist and which were held in place by rubber pads sewn into the waistband. Alec and a friend, Dudley Beck, who ran a gents' outfitters in Chester, talked long into the night to try to find a name for the trousers that was short and punchy. One attempt was an amalgamation of their initials, but they decided that DABS sounded too fishy.

Alec was forward-thinking enough to employ an advertising agent, Crawfords, which had an office in Berlin and was strongly influenced by Bauhaus. Its staff included Ashley Havinden, a talented artist in his own right, who would design Simpsons' distinctive lettering. Crawfords saved the new trousers from their fishy soubriquet by pointing to another name on their list: DAKS. The agency liked the suggestion because it amalgamated 'Dad' (after Simeon) and 'Slacks' (the American term for trousers). Although today this combination represents a sartorial kiss of death, in the 1930s the two words suggested reliability and comfort and the 'dad slacks' proved a bestseller. Eventually, DAKS appeared in forty-one colours and eight materials, and a version was created for women. The trousers featured in a stand Alec took at the British Industries Fair at Earl's Court in February 1934; the set included men taking part in all manner of sports and outdoors pursuits, including playing golf and cricket, riding and sailing.[2]

But, despite the fact that Simpson dressed a large part of the nation and was expanding into 'leisurewear', Alex was frustrated that there was nowhere in central London where customers, particularly overseas visitors, could buy the firm's clothes. This omission was even more irksome because Simpson's rival, Austin Reed, had opened a menswear shop in Regent Street in the 1920s. Alec wanted a store that would make his competitors look fuddy-duddy by comparison and give Simpson's agents a foothold in the West End. When he had visited Chicago Alec had been struck by the work of architect Louis H. Sullivan, creator of the ten-storey Wainwright Building, which was praised for its functionality and described as one of the early skyscrapers, and in Germany Alec had admired the Schocken Department stores in Nuremberg, Stuttgart and Chemnitz, which emphasised glass and sweeping curves.

A few days after Simpson had bought the Piccadilly site, Alec wrote to the architect Joseph Emberton: 'I know that now we have got to work damnably fast, but it is absolutely imperative that we have the ground floor finished for September 1st'.[3] And so began a daily correspondence in which Alec hounded Emberton, treating him like a tailor who has to complete a suit for a special occasion in record time. No doubt, the considerable financial investment added a special urgency to the project: the shop cost £150,000 to build.[4]

Emberton was forty-six when he started work on what was to become his most famous building. Originally from Staffordshire, where his parents had run a drapery store, during the Great War Emberton served in Egypt, where he was influenced by local styles, and he was already familiar with American and European modernism. He had worked on Austin Reed's new shop in Regent Street and secured the commission to build the Royal Corinthian Yacht Club at Burnham-on-Crouch in Essex in 1931, which has since been awarded Grade II Listed Building status. The Yacht Club won him a Bronze award from the Royal Institute of British Architects (RIBA) and the building represented Britain at the International Exhibition of Modern Architecture, held at the Museum of Modern Art in New York City in 1932. Emberton was committed to creating buildings designed for modern life, and he did so with a no-nonsense approach.[5]

From the start, the architectural world was fascinated by the Simpsons building: its materials and ethos. Like the Peter Jones building in Sloane Square, with its sweeping glass curtain wall, Simpsons represented modernity and a new approach to shopping that was as revolutionary as the advent of the paned glass windows at the start of the century. One of the central pillars of that modernity was the fact that the shop had a new customer in mind – the 'Simpsons Man' – and, in theory at least, the shop at 203 Piccadilly allowed him to buy an aeroplane while browsing for handkerchiefs or hats. The new store represented seven floors of masculine fantasies. The shop's advertising campaigns focussed on this male cornucopia and the celebrity chosen to open the shop epitomised speed and adventure.

Sir Malcolm Campbell had led his entire life at full pelt and had moved urgently from one form of evolving transport to the next; as a boy he had raced pushbikes, before progressing to motorcycles, aeroplanes and then racing cars. In his twenties he haunted Brooklands, where he started to call the series of cars he thrashed round the track 'Blue Bird'. During the Great War he served as a motorcycle rider and then switched to the Royal Flying Corps (the precursor of the RAF). In the 1920s he spent his life chasing the world land-speed record, and finally caught it in 1925 when he became the first person to travel in excess of 150 mph. Over the next few years, Campbell chipped away at his land-speed times, finally hitting 301.13 mph in his ninth and last land speed record, on 3 September 1935 at Bonneville Salt Flats, Utah, when he became the first driver to exceed 300 mph.[6]

He was fast in every sense of the word; when he opened Simpsons on 29 April 1936 he was fifty-one and married to the second of his three wives, who shared him with his string of lovers.

Campbell's presence helped Simpsons to attract attention when it opened its doors for the first time, and reporters marvelled at the range of treats and services available within its spacious departments. You could sit in one of sixteen barbers' chairs to have your hair cut, then move on to see a chiropodist and manicurist, have your shoes shined and relax at a licensed snack bar. 'Here a man can buy anything from a pair of socks to a complete tropical outfit,' the *Herald* told its readers.[7] The fifth floor housed aeroplanes in an exhibition space that would change regularly. Transporting the Gipsy Moth and Flying Flea biplanes and Supermarine seaplane through the front door and up the stairs proved troublesome and was probably only achieved by removing the wings and winching the fuselage up the central stairwell.[8] There is no record of any plane having been sold. Catering for the horse owner who wanted to update his wardrobe was more straightforward, though; a customer could sit astride a dummy horse to see how his jodhpurs felt in practice.

The *Tatler* covered the banquet to celebrate the opening in April 1936, held at Grosvenor House, at which four to five hundred 'very distinguished guests' celebrated a shop 'devoted entirely to the needs of mere men'. 'It is comforting to find that someone still loves us and caters for our little wants!' the magazine noted.[9] Parts of the building felt like a gentleman's club where a ticker tape machine spewed out share prices and other financial and sporting news. Individual departments sold guns, fishing tackle, wine and spirits, luggage and saddlery, and cigars and cigarettes in an air-conditioned room where an elderly Russian man rolled the product by hand. But there was a less rugged side to the shop; you could visit the soda fountain, the chemist and travel agents, or buy theatre tickets, dogs (and, for its opening, a marmoset and Siamese cats)[10] and flowers. There was also a scaled-down tailoring workroom, which proved popular among shoppers, eager to see where the magic of tailoring took place.

Simpson's choice of location, which was stressed in the store's name, cleverly capitalised on the area's clubs and shops that sold men's shirts, ties and suits, as well as tobacco. Lyons Teashop, which was next door, also gave it a whiff of popularism. Within this safely masculine domain men could be tempted to experience shopping – a pursuit that had, traditionally, been the preserve of women. But they needed guidance as they ventured into uncharted terrain because, unlike women, so it was thought, men shopped with a definite purchase and price in mind. Men needed clear and frequent signs if they were to find their way around the shop, whereas women were happy to waft through the store, succumbing to temptation at the drop of a silk handkerchief. It was the conviction that male shoppers needed to be able to orientate themselves that led to the installation of a wide, open staircase with chrome light fittings that drew the eye upwards. The Simpsons Man had to be able to see the next floor so that he could heave himself upwards, using the handrail like the mountaineering equipment that was available in the sports section.[11]

The use of lighting and new materials helped to lure the customer off the street in the first place, and glazed doors made it transparent what awaited the hesitant shopper. The banks of non-reflecting windows of 'invisible glass' that climbed from street level upwards encouraged people to look in rather than preen in front of their own reflection. At twenty feet in length, the windows were said to be the largest in the world.[12] As night fell, the spectacular floodlighting and use of neon signs – particularly the Simpsons logo, which could be moved around the frontage – and the lines of windows that could be individually lit up conveyed the drama of a stage or film set, or more accurately, as cultural historian Bronwen Edwards has suggested, the modern cinema or fairground.[13] Even after closing time, the lights continued their promotion.

Lighting was only one aspect of modernist design that got the shop noticed. Fortunately for Simpson, László Moholy-Nagy, the Hungarian-born painter, sculptor, photographer and designer, was in charge of its display department, which decided the most advantageous place to display items in a store and how to make the most of window and in-store displays. Moholy, as he was known, had an infectious grin and his small round glasses and industrial boiler suit made him look like a scientist. He had taught at the Bauhaus School in Berlin under Walter Gropius before fleeing Nazi Germany for Amsterdam in 1934, and then joining Gropius in London, where the artists continued to spread the religion of modernism supported by key figures such as Frank Pick.

Moholy was transfixed by light and how items changed when seen at particular times of day or by electric light. He was particularly skilled in the manipulation of neon light. The red, blue and green tubes held by the bronze reflectors above the windows and down the side of the building allowed the Simpsons windows to mix the colours in a way that flooded the smooth Portland stone frontage with a choice of blazing white lights or, when combined, with a more colourful mantle. The front could be further embellished, for example at Christmas or for national events. During the coronation, on 12 May 1937, the store covered its frontage with an elaborate trellis of roses, and the new king and queen must surely have caught a whiff of the flowers' perfume as they swept past. Though widely praised at the time, photos make the building look as if it had caught some sort of rash.

*

Moholy's remit included window displays at a time when the form was gaining recognition as a specialist field that melded arresting design and visual storytelling. However, it was still a radically new idea for men's stores and one that depended on 'unimpeachable taste, which would quell any objections to cheapness or vulgarity by the quality of presentation', according to Moholy's wife Sibyl, a German former actress and screenwriter.[14] She was soon to discover that the project would take over their lives.

After the two-dimensional work of designing posters, Moholy relished the 'hands-on' challenge of creating a window display that would stop passers-by in their tracks. Like his fellow modernists he was fascinated by the aeroplane, and Imperial Airways commissioned him to design a mobile exhibition to tour the British Empire in a railroad car, promoting the concept of air travel. It was his idea to introduce the Simpsons customer to the new form of transport. He favoured clean, geometric designs in muted colours, and avoided populating the windows with mannequins: the objects spoke for themselves and didn't need to be worn. Instead, he placed plywood screens and free-standing price labels in his displays. One of his earliest window displays has been described as 'a still-life of men's fashion'.[15]

Moholy was known to be dedicated to his job. In the days before the store first opened to the public, his wife had become used to him working sixteen-hour days, but when there was no sign of him late one night she phoned Simpsons. The operator told her the six storeys were bristling with workmen and that there was no chance of finding her husband. Sibyl left their home in Hampstead Garden Suburb and arrived at Piccadilly as dawn was breaking. The windows were shuttered from prying eyes but inside everything was almost ready for the public. Sibyl found her husband standing on a stepladder, his shirt open and his trousers crumpled. He was trying to assemble a sportswear display using fishing wire as he explained the theory of asymmetric advertising to a group of reporters. His bare feet were bleeding. 'The familiar object in an unfamiliar presentation,' Moholy explained, grinning, before adding. 'Just look at my wife's face over there, and you know what I mean.' As they couldn't find his shoes, Moholy walked barefoot until they were able to hail a cab. On the way home he fell into a deep sleep that lasted twenty-four hours.[16]

Once inside the new store, shoppers could wander through rooms filled with elegant, spare furniture in bent ply-wood and chrome: tables and chairs by Finnish designer Alvar Aalto and the British firm Practical Equipment Ltd (Pel); carpets and rugs by the American textile designer Marion Dorn, who also worked for the Savoy and Claridge's, and by Natasha Kroll. Kroll, who was born in Moscow but grew up in Germany, would eventually become display manager for Simpsons, before working in TV and film – which gives an indication of her eye for drama. There were also plans to include work by Eric Gill and Henry Moore in the new shop, though they came to nothing.

Like other modern department stores of the time, Simpsons had done away with the traditional counter; instead customer and sales assistant chatted next to a table or display unit in a democratisation of the retail experience. The assistant was no longer there simply to deliver the goods but to offer advice. This was particularly true in the sports department, where Simpsons boasted that even experienced sportsmen could learn from the salesmen. In 1938 the store employed an Olympic skier to advise customers.

However, although Simpsons stressed its modernist credentials, it wanted to be seen as a store for the everyman – no matter what his shape or the size of this budget. One early plan was to have one floor devoted to each body shape so that, for example, the tall man might find all his needs – from pyjamas and underwear to suits and sportswear – in the same place.[17] Although this plan was never implemented, Simpsons' adverts reminded customers it was there for them no matter what the occasion, and even if that occasion might be unfamiliar to them. Other adverts emphasised the idea that the right clothes could make the difference between promotion or languishing at the bottom of the career ladder, between a dishevelled and harassed man and the Simpsons Man, who was broad-shouldered, strong-jawed and poised.

Simpsons spent an estimated £35,000 on promotion in its first fifteen months, including some of the first adverts to use colour.[18] One of its logos read, 'Sorry I'm late – but look what I got at Simpsons!' followed by a series of scenarios in which the male shopper had succumbed to a range of purchases from a new dressing gown or a bouquet of flowers to the more outlandish Scottie dog. In one the caption is changed to 'Sorry I'm *early* [my italics] – but look what I got at Simpsons!' as a pilot climbs down from his aeroplane.

Simpsons always had an eye for the novel and John Logie Baird demonstrated his TV in the store in 1936. Tragically, Alec died a year after his new shop opened.

*

Moholy was proud of his work for Simpsons and, in a strange echo of Phroso's escapade in the shop window of Swan & Edgar some thirty years earlier, took guests to see the store at the end of an evening when they had dined in Soho. The rest of the party comprised Sibyl, a Swedish architect and his Russian girlfriend, and a young French painter. Moholy was not happy with the colours and arrangement of leather goods displayed in the window. He insisted that the nightwatchman should let him in – which he did after a call to Alec, who was used to Moholy's eccentric ways – and he climbed into the window in his stockinged feet, carrying more leather goods, which he rearranged with help from his friends on the other side of the plate glass. As neither side could hear the other, they had to mime their suggestions. Eventually a crowd formed, at which point two policemen appeared and said the gathering represented a public disturbance. Moholy, engrossed in his work, was oblivious, even when Sibyl pulled one of the officers right up to the window. Her husband only paused once a police officer appeared next to him in the window display. While Phroso couldn't be made to move, Moholy couldn't be made to stop. In their different ways, the two 'performers' showed how Piccadilly Circus could bring out the obsessive in artists from diverse worlds.

13

From Cockpit to Ski Slope

The new flying craze was being felt in other parts of the West End. *Hell's Angels*, one of the first action movies, set in the First World War, still has the ability to shock with its thrilling aerial dogfights that left audiences gasping. It was produced and directed by Howard Hughes, who had himself succumbed to the lure of flight; he would spend much of his business career building aircraft such as the behemoth Spruce Goose, with its huge, ungainly wings.

Nearly fifty aircraft and seventy-five pilots worked on the film, including Hughes, who had only recently gained his pilot's licence and wanted to impress the film's stunt pilots – though he crashed his plane and was lucky to survive. Hughes started working on *Hell's Angels* in 1927, and had intended it to be a silent film, but in the three years it took to produce sound was introduced and the film had to be reshot. It cost $4 million to make. The film provided Jean Harlow's big break; she replaced the original leading lady, Greta Nissen, who was unable to shake off her heavy Norwegian accent.

Hell's Angels premiered in London at the Pavilion in Piccadilly Circus in October 1930 and demonstrated the extent to which celluloid could offer an audience action that was beyond the reach of music hall or musical revue. In 1934 the Pavilion was converted into a cinema.

Aviation was inspiring visual artists too. In 1937 E. McKnight Kauffer, the American whose posters brightened up London's underground, worked on what he described as 'the Aeroplane job',[1] in which he designed the exterior chocolate brown and black colour scheme of the Handy-Heck aircraft for Whitney-Straight (only one was ever made). He also designed a poster for Shell,[2] a company that was fuelling record-breaking flights as a way of promoting its products. Winston Churchill considered asking Kauffer to come up with a logo for the RAF until he discovered he was an American and unwilling to change his nationality.[3]

In the 1930s the aeroplane symbolised escapism, just as the bright lights of Piccadilly Circus promised adventure. In the USA, Africa and Australia the need to transport mail over long distances helped to establish air networks and over time these networks became safer and more comfortable for passengers. Croydon Airport opened in 1920 and it soon became possible to take a scheduled flight to Paris in a 'flying railroad car'. As early as 1928 the *Daily Mail* produced a supplement entitled 'News of the Future' and dated Saturday 1 January 2000, which now seems extraordinarily prescient. On the cover a biplane called *J. Lyons* formed part of a London–Sydney Express, where Nippys served passengers and other customers could arrive using their own aircraft. 'Park your Aerocar', the caption runs.[4] In reality, in the most upmarket air services passengers sat in wicker chairs and some German airlines offered in-flight movies (because they were silent, the deafening noise of the engines didn't interfere with the viewers' enjoyment). By 1930 United Airlines had introduced the 'air hostess' to tend to its passengers' needs on routes to and from San Francisco and to make sure customers didn't throw rubbish out of the plane's windows. British Airways was formed in 1935 and keen air travellers grew used to the indignity of being weighed before boarding a plane. When Neville Chamberlain went looking for peace for our time in 1938 he flew to Germany. The trip marked the prime minister's first ever flight.

*

The aeroplane was an international phenomenon as air routes for passengers, goods and diplomacy were being developed all around the world. Countries were investing in air forces that signified power and, in the mid-1930s, started to carry the threat of aggression, at least in an international arena. In October 1935 Italy attacked Abyssinia (now Ethiopia) in an act of aggression that used aviation as a means to gain the upper hand. It was a stark example of the ruthlessness of Italy's fascist prime minister Benito Mussolini and, although Abyssinia seemed like a long way off to most Britons and not an immediate threat, there were echoes closer to home as the British Union of Fascists (BUF) appeared in force on the streets of London in a show of blatant aggression. The BUF held noisy rallies at the end of April and in early May 1933, and both spilled onto Coventry Street as protesters gathered at Lyons Corner House.

To most people in the 1930s, though, the aeroplane represented a symbol of freedom and glamour. De Havilland designed planes such as the open-cockpit Gipsy Moth as a sort of aerial sports car: there was just enough fuel and luggage space for a weekend away or a trip to Le Touquet. The plane could be towed behind the family car and its wings folded to fit into a garage. As the *Tatler* told its readers, the Gipsy Moth made Baghdad feel as close as Balham and Tunis as near as Tooting. To begin with, manufacturers assumed that pilots would be male, but a small band of women flyers started to make a name for themselves and the press was quick to pick up on their stories. Most female pilots were rich, or had married well, and managed to make flying sound as effortless as a game of tennis. The Duchess of Bedford, for example, took to flying because the noisy open cockpit relieved her tinnitus. To begin with, she hired a pilot to ferry her around as she knitted in the passenger seat, but she quickly became a devoted pilot herself, flying between her homes in East Anglia, Scotland and Cornwall. Lady Heath, an Irish pilot who was nicknamed 'Lady Hell of a Din' because of her talent for self-publicity, became the first woman to fly solo from South Africa to London, and announced that flying was as easy as Charlestoning. Her luggage on that trip included a tennis racquet and evening dress, and she flew in a fur coat that protected her from the sun. When crossing water, she put on an inflated inner tube because she thought it would act as a buoyancy aid – instead it burst as the plane gained height.

Two women who failed to fit into this pattern of wealthy and well-connected female pilots were the tousle-haired American Amelia Earhart, who in 1928 became the first woman to cross the Atlantic, albeit as a passenger; and Amy Johnson, who in 1930 became the first woman to fly solo from England to Australia. Johnson was originally from Hull in East Yorkshire but had, following the end of a painful love affair, moved to London, where she worked briefly as a shop assistant and then as a secretary at a law firm before learning to fly. In the public's mind she became 'the typist from Hull', but she was a young woman who had grown to love London and, like most newcomers to the area, she naturally gravitated to Piccadilly Circus as a place to find her feet. Before she became famous her father, a fish merchant who doted on his eldest daughter, would visit her and take her to West End shows and shopping. On one excursion he treated her to a spree at Swan & Edgar, where he bought her a jumper, suit and gloves. When, a few years later, she wrote to tell him that the second-hand biplane she planned to fly from Croydon Airport to Australia was to be called *Jason*, after the telegraphic address of the family fish business, she did so from a Lyons Corner House.[5] She was determined that the red Gipsy Moth would be repainted to match her bottle-green flying suit, which had been specially designed by Lillywhites of Piccadilly Circus.

The desire for a colour-coordinated outfit seemed wilful, even reckless, amid the careful preparation for the voyage, which, even if she beat the existing record, would take fifteen days and force her to fly over remote jungles and long stretches of water with no radio link and little more than a compass to guide her. Repainting *Jason* would add precious ounces to the weight of the plane and risk reducing her fuel efficiency, when she needed as much petrol as she could carry to ensure that she reached each refuelling point along her journey. Before she set off for Australia, Johnson's longest solo flight had been from Hull to London and her departure, very early on 5 May 1930, was only covered in any detail by a few newspapers. The *Daily Mail*'s headline ran, 'Miss Amy Johnson – Lone Flight to Australia – Off To-day – Cupboard Full of Frocks'. As *Jason* lifted off at the second attempt, she sat at the joystick in a plane that had, indeed, at the last moment, been repainted to match her flying suit.

When Johnson's flight to Australia was successful she was transformed into an international star and her fame increased with every record-breaking flight she achieved. After her marriage to the Scottish pilot Jim Mollison, the couple became the 'king and queen of the air'. This new breed of celebrities led to a craze for anything associated with aviation.

Although of course only an elite few had the means or the time to fly, some of the fashion accessories associated with the pursuit could be saved up for by ordinary people. In Australia, women asked salons to cut their hair in an 'Amy Johnson wave' and, after Charles Lindbergh flew the Atlantic solo in 1927, 'Aviator hats' became popular. Department stores like Swan & Edgar and the sports specialist Lillywhites designed flying clothes for women in much the same way that they had promoted outfits for the new lady motorist. Lillywhites was particularly proud of its 'Lillisport Aviation Suit for Ladies', which Johnson wore on her historic solo flight to Australia, and which was approved (according to its June 1930 catalogue) 'by all leading women aviators'.[6]

Like Simpsons, sportswear specialist Lillywhites was as much about making the customer feel confident they were wearing the right thing, in the right way, as it was about the items it sold. A shop assistant wouldn't bat an eyelid if you admitted it would be your first time on a ski slope or that you had never spent a weekend in the country. The shop inspired such confidence because of its long sporting history. Frederick William Lillywhite had played cricket for Sussex in the early Victorian period and he and his three sons became adept at promoting their brand name – before the term had been invented – by selling cricketing almanacs and other items connected with the game. The original shop, James Lillywhite, opened in 1863 at number 31 Haymarket, after one of

Frederick's three sons had started to offer items connected with cricket from an exhibition stand in Euston Square. In 1925 it moved to the Criterion Building and began trading under new ownership.

In its new home in the Criterion Building, Lillywhites customers climbed oak-panelled staircases to browse under ornate ceilings. Mass production was in the future; Lillywhites' craftsmen produced cricket bats and tennis racquets that were lovingly weighed in the hand or held in the air so that the wood's straightness could be measured by eye. In one photo from the era, women in white coats stack tennis racquets and look more like librarians handling precious manuscripts than manufacturers of sporting goods.

Lillywhites managed to make the clothes and equipment associated with sports feel bespoke and no sport was too obscure to be catered for. Their specialist – perhaps 'elite' would be a more accurate adjective – approach was the antithesis of today's high-tech, high-turnover way of selling leisure. The shop's knowledgeable staff offered advice on specialist equipment and, despite being hundreds of miles from the nearest mountain, the shop became a supplier for winter sports and even built an artificial ski slope. Skiers waited their turn in front of walls depicting snowy mountaintops, although a quick glance through the window would have reminded them that they were in a busy Piccadilly Circus. If a customer couldn't visit the store they could place orders via Lillywhites' 'fully illustrated' winter sports catalogue. As one commentator has said, the shop could 'entirely equip a big-game hunting expedition or supply a ping pong set'.[7]

Lillywhites also took on individual commissions, such as Amy Johnson's flying suit and George VI's coronation slippers, which were handmade.[8] In 1940, Lillywhites also produced a custom-made, white, leather flying helmet for 23-year-old London model and socialite Cecile Tonge Stuart. Cecile, who was only five feet tall, loved cars and planes – and looking good in both. She was friends with photographer Cecil Beaton, and she appeared regularly in the *Sketch* and *Vogue*, often with jewels in her hair (she preferred a turban during the day). She was a licensed pilot and one photo shows her standing on the wing of a plane in a pair of her famous high-heeled shoes, wearing white tailored trousers and with a patterned scarf taming her blond hair. Before she married, Stuart owned a rare chimpanzee, which she later gave to London Zoo. Stuart earned the nickname 'Bat' because of her glamorous lifestyle and because she really only came to life at night. In 1938 she eloped with the rich aeroplane owner Buster Stuart after he had broken off a previous engagement, and later lived with him in the West Indies when he was stationed there in the Second World War. The Lillywhites flying helmet is held at the Victoria and Albert Museum,[9] together with other remnants of a heady lifestyle such as two pairs of lofty shoes, both made in America. Although tiny in size, the cream leather platform shoes have 10-centimetre heels, despite wartime restrictions of 2.5 centimetres in the USA and 5 centimetres in Britain.

On 28 February 1925, the same year that Lillywhites moved to Piccadilly Circus, Boots became its next-but-one neighbour. The chemist opened Store 1000 opposite Boots' current position. The company chose the site for its first 24-hour, seven-days-a-week shop because, according to John Boot, it was 'an address known to all, and convenient for bus and Tube'.

John Boot became chairman in 1926 after his father, Jesse,[10] sold his controlling interest in the business to Louis K. Liggett, chief of the Rexall group of chemists in America, in 1920.

Jesse had founded the company in Nottingham in the second half of the nineteenth century with the aim of making his company 'Chemists to the Nation'. Jesse was ten when his father died and he was forced to help out in the family's small herbalist shop, where the main customers were working class. As the business expanded, Jesse decided the only way to compete with patented medicines was to try, where possible, to introduce proprietary brands and in other areas to drive the business by high sales that produced better margins. His desire to turn the business into a fully-fledged company led to a significant ruling in the House of Lords that allowed limited-liability companies to employ qualified pharmacists, and Jesse appointed Boots' first pharmacist in 1884. The company expanded through joint ventures in the Midlands and then, in 1901, by gobbling up Day's Drugs Stores in London and the south of England – an acquisition that added sixty-five shops and two warehouses to the empire.

Store 1000 in Piccadilly Circus had trained nurses and qualified chemists as well as a sterile room in which to prepare medicines. When it first opened its all-night doors, the company made a great show of the fact that the key used to unlock the shop was put away in a drawer and never used again. (In fact, the shop had to be locked up once during the Blitz, but the spirit of the statement is beyond dispute.) Customers passed two large display windows and walked under a neon sign that announced 'Day & Night Service', to enter the shop through glazed, wooden-framed double doors. After dark the 'Day & Night Service' and cursive 'Boots' brand glowed in the gloom.

Boots had less to put in their shop window than shops

such as Simpsons and Swan & Edgar; a series of medicine bottles that appeared to be floating could never be as arresting as one of Moholy's avant-garde displays, but it did its best. However, the branch did manage to make a song and dance about 'handkerchief puffs', a curious accessory that became popular in 1927 because it combined the look and attributes of a hanky with a powder puff. Applying make-up in public in the 1920s was seen as racy and the handkerchief puff allowed a woman to powder her face with the utmost discretion. It became a popular present and Boots in Piccadilly Circus sold a huge range, helped by the dozens of examples that floated in its windows like baby ghosts. The company's internal newsletter, *The Bee*, claimed that Store 1000's sale of 'handkerchief puffs' showed 'the proof of the value of display', adding that in June the store had taken on average £5 (about £316 in 2019) a day from sales of the product.[11]

Boots also made the most of the new interest in the outdoors. Before the 1920s, a sun-darkened skin had been associated with hard, physical, outdoor labour, but as the workforce moved indoors, to shops, factories and offices, a tan became linked with money and leisure. Coco Chanel led the way in the new fashion for bronzing when she was spotted skipping off a yacht in the Côte d'Azur in 1923 with a tan that she appeared to have caught by accident. The 1920s and 1930s were also decades when people who couldn't afford the south of France used the improved rail network, or their bikes, to indulge in the less expensive outdoor activity of hiking – or 'Knapsackery' as the *Globe* described it in September 1930.[12] Although ramblers had enjoyed walking before the First World War, hikers yomped into the 1920s and 1930s with greater confidence. Hiking could be achieved quite cheaply, as specialist clothing and equipment were not essential; it offered a new freedom for women and allowed them the perfect excuse to wear shorts and to show their knees and bare legs. The Youth Hostel Association, which appeared in 1930, was inspired by a similar organisation in Germany and made it possible to expand a hike into a greater adventure. Hiking and sunbathing were both part of a greater interest in the outdoors and in all types of physical activity. This emphasis on the human form and exertion found a focus at the 1936 Olympics, which received more press coverage than previous Games, and also provided a stage for Nazism to compete with its opponents in a corporeal as well as an ideological way.

Shops such as Boots and Lillywhites made the most of the nation's new passion for the outdoors by selling products that would help the hiker or sunbather in their new-found pursuit, or ease the pain when either went wrong. Soltan, Boots' proprietary brand of suntan lotion, was launched in 1939 at the same time as shops, including Lillywhites, offered 'sunburn suits'. Boots' enduring No7 brand appeared in 1935, in yellow and blue art deco packaging. The range included eight skincare creams and three cosmetics and sales assistants were trained to advise women on 'the modern way to loveliness'. Seven was chosen because, according to the promotional bumf, the number had long signified 'perfection'.

Boots also made the most of Piccadilly Circus's reputation as the centre of the country, if not the empire. When the *British Medical Journal* reported in its 11 July 1936 edition that adders were increasing in number in Epping Forest, the New Forest and the west coast of Scotland,[13] Boots announced that stocks of the Pasteur Institute antivenom serum were being held at the ready at its branches in Piccadilly Circus and Aldgate High Street in London, as well as Edinburgh and Oban in Scotland and Bournemouth and Boots' home town of Nottingham. The image of Boots as a pharmaceutical St George, saving the nation, if not from dragons then at least serpents and other threats, was one that the company did its best to encourage. During the 1919 flu epidemic Boots had kept many of its stores open until midnight[14] and by 1929, four years after opening its Piccadilly Circus store, it had five more 24-hour shops in city centres around the country. The company advertised its new service using stories that stressed how only Boots – and Boots in Piccadilly Circus – could save a dangerously ill patient. In one account, published in 1930, a man lies feverishly ill behind a lighted window in a cold and wet town in Devon. The pre-National Health Service doctor declares grimly, 'I must have anti-anthrax serum. He will die if I don't.' The advert cuts to a welcomingly bright shopfront in Piccadilly Circus where a manager has sent a messenger to catch the 9.50 express train, urging the man, 'A life depends upon you!' For five hours 'the great express thundered across England', helping the serum to be delivered and injected by 4 a.m. 'It is wonderful,' the doctor coos before adding a sentence that became the headline for the entire piece: 'It is almost as if Piccadilly Circus were just round the corner.' The advert then goes on to stress how even a small Boots could call on a vast range of stock from the company's 870 branches and from its huge range of scientific knowledge. Boots also reminded its readers that its size meant it could buy in bulk and that it manufactured many of its own drugs, allowing it to cut out the middle-man and keep prices low. It concluded by urging patients to 'Especially go to Boots for your prescriptions – whether they are from the greatest Harley Street specialist or your family doctor and [made] . . . from fresh, pure drugs.'

There was no comment about how much, in a pre-NHS world, the doctor and the transportation of the serum would have cost the patient. The mention of 'fresh, pure drugs' did, however, play to justifiable worries that there were still plenty of charlatans keener to sell snake oil than genuine antivenom serum.

Obviously, the advert was designed to tell an exciting story of Boots saving the day, but a letter in the Boots archive from the manager of a branch in Hampshire confirmed that the all-night service could be vital. He explained how he had received a night-time telephone call from a local doctor who needed ampoules of Hepatex to inject into a gravely ill patient. It was 9.30 p.m. before the manager called 'our very good friends at Piccadilly Circus', who told him they had two ampoules of the medicine, which is used to treat diseases of the liver, in stock but were doubtful whether they could make the final train from Waterloo station, which left at 9.50 p.m. In the event, the stationmaster ordered the train not to leave until the parcel had arrived and, although it was late leaving, it made up time and the Boots manager delivered the medicine to the hospital by 11.45 p.m. The patient, who had not been expected to last the night, survived and was discharged from hospital.

*

As well as serving office workers and tourists, the Boots Piccadilly Circus branch's position at the hub of London means that, in the century since it first opened its doors, it has seen more than its fair share of famous customers. It is less than a mile from Buckingham Palace and has provided goods for members of the royal family on several occasions.

(They don't typically line up at the counter clutching their Advantage card, although as head of Her Majesty's medical household from 1973 to 1982 Sir Richard Bayliss did, on one occasion, queue for a packet of painkillers in the middle of the night.) Prince Charles is said to have had the temperature of his first ever bath as a baby checked using a thermometer hurriedly bought from Boots in Piccadilly Circus one Sunday afternoon in November 1948. Sportsmen also popped in when they were in the West End: Freddie Mills, world light heavyweight champion in the same year, bought crêpe bandages and cricketer Sir Donald Bradman purchased a packet of aspirins.[15] Every visit gave the shop assistant who served the famous customer a story to take home to their family that night, and added to the shop's glamour. Boots' all-night hours gave the shop a special rhythm that staff became used to but which changed as Piccadilly Circus crept further into the twentieth century and its customers altered as the 1950s gave way to the 1960s and beyond.

Although Piccadilly Circus was at the very heart of the capital, and quintessentially London in its outlook, its role as a driver of social change meant it didn't seem at all odd that it was also the place where you could learn to ski or seek out a serum to protect against adders. It was a location where you could try on different personas for size – whether that was a new sunburn suit, a flying helmet or more affordable No7 cosmetics. You could sit in the stalls at the Pavilion and imagine you were flying a biplane, or leaf through Lillywhites' catalogue and dream that you would one day go on an Alpine holiday. It didn't really matter if none of these reveries came true. Amid the many uncertainties of the 1930s, a decade of international unrest and economic volatility, it was important to have fantasies to cling on to.

Part Five

The Blackout

14

Here We Go Again

It was 24 June 1939, a full two months before war would be declared, when the windows of Vine Street police station, tucked away just south of Regent Street, rattled with the sound of an explosion. A gust of hot air rushed into the office where Detective Inspector Robert Fabian was bent over a wobbly typewriter and ruffled the pages of a report he was working on about an 'immoral club'.[1] The police officer, who would become famous as 'Fabian of the Yard' and whose memoirs would be televised in the 1950s as one of the earliest 'police procedurals', grabbed his gas mask off the hook where it waited in anticipation of war and headed in the direction of the blast.

Glasshouse Street resembled a scene that would become familiar in the Blitz. Fabian pushed through the police cordon, crunching broken glass underfoot and picking his way through the debris from blown-out shop windows. Cigars and cigar boxes from the tobacconists S. Van Raalte, at 2 Glasshouse Street, which was one of the first to add its advertising lights to Piccadilly Circus at the start of the century, had been flung around as if it had been startled in the middle of announcing the arrival of a new baby, and delicate silk lingerie, which had been blown out of another shop, 'shimmered in crumpled little pools'.[2] It was now nearly midnight and darker than usual as the blast had snuffed out many of Piccadilly's illuminated advertisements. The air was thick with the smell of spent explosives. Fabian forced himself to pause so that he could follow the police officer's mantra of 'giving your eyes a chance' and, sure enough, amid the masonry and debris he spotted a brown paper parcel on the ground. It was tied with string but, ominously, also had two pieces of black sticky tape attached. To the touch it was 'as hot as a tea urn'.[3]

Fabian ordered the constables to push the crowd further away and picked up the parcel, which seemed to grow hotter by the minute. He couldn't see a fire bucket, so knelt on the pavement, where he used his pocketknife to unpack the package until he pulled out something that looked like a sausage wrapped in greased paper. This was followed by more 'sausages' until he had lined up ten sticks of four-ounce Polar Ammon gelignite; one had a pencil-fuse protruding from it, which he cut off and put in his pocket. A fire engine arrived but had no fire buckets, so Fabian decided to cut up the sticks. While he was working a notorious pickpocket arrived and said he could help. Fabian declined the offer. Instead, he started to pack the bomb parts into the cigar boxes scattered on the pavement, as if preparing the ultimate exploding cigar trick. These were taken back to the police station, where each was plunged into a red fire bucket of water.

Although Fabian managed to defuse the bomb at Piccadilly Circus, twenty people were injured by the six IRA explosions that rocked London that night.[4] The attacks were part of the 'S [for Sabotage] Plan' designed to show the Nazis that the Republicans were ready to move in when Britain succumbed to Hitler. In reality, their campaign would fizzle out by 1940.

A few days after the incident a group of well-known criminals called Fabian to a billiard room where a gangland leader thanked him for saving the lives of those who had been 'on the Dilly' that night. The gangland leader pressed a bronze medal with a blue silk ribbon into the policeman's hands; the inscription read: 'To Detective Inspector Bob Fabian, For Bravery, 24-6-39. From The Boys.' In February 1940, when the 'real' war was under way, the King presented Fabian with a Medal for Gallantry at Buckingham Palace. Fabian kept both medals in the same drawer.

*

People across the UK heard Neville Chamberlain's declaration of war broadcast from the Cabinet Room at 10 Downing Street on 3 September 1939 in a variety of different settings. Many gathered round their Bakelite wireless sets, where children became uncharacteristically still, perhaps absorbing the gravity of the moment from their parents. The prime minister sounded sad and regretful, rather than defiant, as he told his listeners that the German government had failed to respond to the British ambassador's demand that Hitler should withdraw from Poland. No such undertaking had been received.

Vera Brittain was at home in the New Forest in Hampshire that day, with her son, John, aged eleven, and Shirley, who was nine, and who would grow up to be politician Shirley Williams. Vera spent her time working for the Peace Pledge Union and as she sat on the camp bed in the study between her two young children, listening to the wireless, she started to weep. Although she had been expecting this outcome it was, nevertheless, a horrible reminder that all her efforts at preventing war had failed and that the losses of the Great

War appeared to have been made in vain.[5] Perhaps her mind went back to that happy day at Piccadilly Circus with her fiancé, Roland, in December 1914.

Some heard the news over a cup of tea in a Lyons Corner House or Teashop, or read the 'special late news' on the billboards clutched glumly by the newspaper-sellers in and around Piccadilly Circus. The siren that wailed out immediately after Chamberlain had finished speaking seemed to herald the start of hostilities but was actually a false alarm, and the expected onslaught was slow to materialise; those first few months became known as the Phoney War, the Sitz Krieg or the Bore War.

But, while Nazi bombs failed to rain down and Londoners grew more cavalier about remembering to take their gas masks with them when they left home, the capital quickly turned into a citadel. Trenches lacerated parks to make it harder for invading planes to land and easier for soldiers to defend. Monuments were barricaded against blasts or shipped to remote parts of the country. London lost its most famous statue when Eros was carted off to Cooper's Hill in Egham, Surrey, to live in a building bought by London County Council in 1938 to use as an emergency headquarters. Eros's plinth was boxed in so that it resembled a brutalist piece of art. The curb of the island on which it sat was painted with a chequered white pattern, like an instruction to 'cut along the dots'. The four lampposts nearest the plinth had their glass removed because it would have proved deadly in a blast, leaving oddly ceremonial poles, as if they were guarding the spot where Eros once stood.

The Circus continued to advertise, but the blackout meant it could only be persuasive during the day. Passers-by were still urged to enjoy Schweppes tonic water and Bovril, and reminded that Guinness was good for you, but these messages were joined by urgent government demands. Eros's base offered a convenient, many-sided billboard and the Allies' most talented artists provided cleverly designed, often colourful, propaganda posters that chronicled the progress of the war. In December 1939 the base seemed to have been transformed into a giant Christmas pudding wrapped in a message urging Londoners to have a happy and safe festive break. Posters from 1942 exhorted passers-by to 'spend less on yourself and lend more to your country' while, in 1944, London County Council offered a much less warlike, and more hopeful, reminder that 'you are on your way . . . to evening classes'.

Shops joined in and by 1941 Swan & Edgar sported a banner that urged women to join the Auxiliary Territorial Service (ATS), which had been formed in 1938 and expanded in December 1941 after the introduction of conscription for women. The ATS provided cooks, clerks, orderlies, storekeepers and drivers.[6] Princess Elizabeth, the future queen, trained to be a truck driver and mechanic. Shops such as Lillywhites started to sell gas-mask holders and boxes designed as fashionable accessories. Luminous buttons became popular as a way of being seen on London's blacked-out streets; this was particularly important in 1941 – a year that witnessed the highest ever number of motor deaths in Britain, a record that still stands today.[7]

The war also changed the way Simpsons viewed its clients. Like other stores, its customer base changed from the man about town to the man in uniform, and it transformed its clubroom into the Simpsons' Service Club to accommodate the shift. Membership was free and open to officers of both sexes, although anyone who wanted to join had to be proposed and seconded. At its peak the club had 12,000 members, who came from all over the world seeking a wash, a rest and to phone home. Even before the start of the war, Simpsons had been forced to recognise that women were a key part of its client base. Within a year of opening, it had a women's department and this was quickly followed by a ladies' hairdresser's and, during the war, by two floors of products aimed at women.[8] Adverts showed women being fitted for Land Army clothes and officers' uniforms.

The blackout was introduced on Friday 11 August 1939 and as Big Ben struck 12.30 a.m. the warm glow behind each of its four faces was snuffed out as the gloom crept over the capital. In Piccadilly Circus, as a *Times* reporter noted, it felt almost like rush-hour as a crowd of smokers sat on the steps that would have led up to the Shaftesbury Memorial and nearby sightseers in cars formed long lines of 'unnecessary light'.[9] Since Piccadilly Circus was synonymous with light, it was the obvious place to witness the historic descent into darkness. The *Yorkshire Post* described the atmosphere as like 'boat race night' as crowds flocked to witness the great switch-off – a bit like a reverse Christmas celebration.[10] According to the *Daily Mirror*, by 12.35 a.m. there was only one shop in Piccadilly Circus that still had its lights on. An angry mob swarmed towards it and threatened to smash its windows. Police formed a cordon, but one man broke through, climbed the shopfront and removed the offending bulb, to cries of appreciation from the crowd.[11] High in the sky, red lights showed the observer planes monitoring the effectiveness of the blackout. Simpsons' neon lighting was switched off and staff took to the roof to watch for fires.

Piccadilly Circus's role as a people's place was now so highly developed that the snuffing out of its lights was seen around the country as deeply significant. The *Liverpool Echo* reported:

> Mention the lights of London and all the world thinks of Piccadilly Circus . . . Every few minutes another blob of light went out, but when the radiating streets were blanketed, the ring of street lights at the Circus still shone. Then, on the dot, out they went, and the huge crowd gave sound to something like a cheer. Not a hearty cheer. It was more like a sigh and a cheer mixed up. One electric sign was a minute or two late going out. Only when it did was the darkness really felt. In an instant Piccadilly Circus was as dark, if not as deserted or yet as salubrious, as a country crossroad.[12]

Piccadilly Circus was transformed from a brilliantly lit stage to pinpricks of illumination that felt more medieval than metropolitan. All-night restaurants, milk bars and cafés served customers in an eerie half-light or from behind heavy blinds.[13] Londoners groped their way round the capital using torches, and batteries were suddenly in high demand; dialling a number from a public telephone box became a dark art. Motorists had to fit visors to their headlamps to direct the beam downwards while, by contrast, the bases of trees, such as those in the small park in Leicester Square, were given white stripes to make them stand out in the gloom. The speed limit was cut to 20 mph and ghostly policemen wearing white coats and carrying flashing red torches patrolled the city to try to slow the traffic.[14] Petrol rationing, which was introduced in September 1939, helped to reduce the number of cars and a photo in the *Illustrated London News* showed the only traffic as a horse-drawn vehicle and a man pushing a handcart.[15] Nature took over in unlikely places: sandbags sprouted green roots and the darkness persuaded owls to appear in parts of the capital.

But if the blackout gave Londoners a feeling of protection from bombers, it could make the city itself feel more threatening. Nippies on the late shift faced a hazardous journey home. Nancy Meyer worked at the Lyons Corner House in Coventry Street from the start of the war and remembered 'many adventures' on the last Tube once the bombing started. She also recalled running through the Blitz with her friends, Kit and Win. Nippies were serving more men and women in uniform and their customers now came from around the world, as the conflict widened. Many Nippies left for war work: driving trucks, rather than trolleys, or manoeuvring searchlights, instead of guiding customers to their tables. Servicemen and women moved around the country and for many, J. Lyons represented a safe haven as they got to know the capital. If the siren went in the middle of a meal customers dashed for the shelter and not everyone returned to pay their bill.

For many, the most obvious place of safety was Piccadilly Circus underground. The government hadn't intended to make the Tube stations official shelters, but the public quickly realised that the deepest ones, such as Piccadilly Circus, Mile End and Bank, offered a protection that official sites couldn't always match. It has been estimated that on one night early in the Blitz, which started on 7 September 1940, 177,000 people headed for one of London's Tube stations.[16] High as this figure seems, it pales in comparison with the 300,000 people who sheltered in the capital's underground stations during one night towards the end of the First World War.[17] Their attraction was, in some part, a tribute to Frank Pick's attempts to make the underground appealing – even without bombs – and the government, which often had a low opinion of the public, feared that once the ordinary man and woman descended into the comparative safety of the underground they would never re-emerge. The Tube felt comfortingly safe despite the privations of bedding down on a hard station platform or snuggling up to the steps of a metal escalator. It offered free heating and lighting and usually a cup of tea – sometimes poured from a giant watering can – and a bun delivered by a special train or volunteers. Card schools and chess clubs sprang up for regular users, and some stations even had a piano on the platform. On 25 September 1940 the Storre Brothers, who had been made homeless by the bombing, treated those sheltering at Piccadilly Circus to their music hall act, which was a mixture of comic patter and knockabout acrobatics. A photo captures one brother standing on the platform while the second balances, full-length on his upstretched arms, looking as though he has just dived from the ceiling. The audience is within touching distance and the platform appears to be a few feet away. The brothers' act was still going strong in the 1950s.

People started to arrive at the Tube to secure their patch before they were officially allowed onto the platform (usually at 4 p.m.), carrying bedding and shopping bags filled with food. By the time the evening rush-hour began they'd found their pitch and businessmen on their way home waved to the children as they boarded the Tube.[18] If you were a passing soldier or a member of the ATS caught in Piccadilly Circus, the shelter was a place to sit out the terror of a blast with the help of a distracting crowd. There were the usual complaints about loud snorers, and the rags that were used to dim the lights couldn't counter the much-resented arrival of noisy late-night and early-morning trains. The warm, sweaty bodies also provided an ideal breeding ground for fleas. A photo of Piccadilly Circus Tube in September 1940, at the very start of the Blitz, shows the escalators littered with bodies – as if the men and women are victims of a blast, rather than passers-by sheltering from one. Most seem not to have shed any clothes, even if they've bedded down under blankets, and many of the women are still wearing their hats. One woman appears to be trying to sleep sitting upright, propped against the bottom of the escalator. The uplighters are all blazing on either side of the escalator and it seems incredible that anyone was able to sleep in such conditions.

The platforms themselves were even more crowded, and cluttered with suitcases and people's personal belongings. There were children here, which must have brought its own problems. Their 'bedroom walls' were plastered with posters promoting the government's latest edicts and adverts for clothes, beauty products or plays or other amusements that seem out of place in such tense conditions. Some people – mainly men – read the newspaper, enjoyed a final smoke before bedtime or swigged from a bottle of beer. The women knitted or comforted small children. Although London Underground asked able-bodied men not to use the Tube as a shelter, there were plenty of young males.

The Council for the Encouragement of Music and the Arts,[19] which played classical music on gramophones on the underground, would have been amazed to discover that the ordinary families who bedded down for the night were sharing the shelter with some of Britain's most precious paintings and museum treasures. Plans to evacuate the nation's valuables had started to take shape at about the same time that the government was agonising over the evacuation of children and young families from areas that were expected to feel the brunt of the *blitzkrieg*. Wales and the West Country were popular destinations because, at least in the early months of the war, they were seen as out of range for German bombers. The National Gallery in Trafalgar Square moved paintings to private houses in Wales and Gloucestershire in an evacuation that took eleven days and was only finished the day before war was declared. Churchill vetoed a plan to ship the contents of museums and galleries to Canada, saying he would prefer they were hidden in cellars and caves rather than leave Britain's shores.[20] The Natural History Museum took him at his word and packed up specimen jars full of strange pickled creatures to begin a gloomy life in Surrey caves.

Other treasures were stored in London Underground's hidden passages: at first in Green Park and then, from 1941, in disused tunnels at Piccadilly Circus. As early as 1937 the London Museum (as it was then known) had divided its charges into three groups. In the event of war, the most important items would be moved by handcart to a disused corridor in the former Dover Street Tube station, which could be reached from Green Park underground station. Other objects would stay in a specially strengthened section of the museum's basement at Lancaster House and the third group, mainly costumes, would be evacuated to one of the Rothschild family houses in Buckinghamshire. In March 1941 the artefacts from Dover Street arrived at Piccadilly Circus station, and a few months later the nineteen crates from the Buckinghamshire manor house joined them.

The Tate Gallery's position right next to the River Thames, and close to the Houses of Parliament, made it particularly vulnerable to attack and it closed to the public on 22 August 1939, soon after news of the German–Soviet Pact. Many of its paintings were sent to the countryside and others ended up tucked away in corridors running parallel to the east- and westbound Piccadilly line platforms that could be reached by a set of stairs. The closest the shelterers came to the treasure was if they used the toilets. Had they found their way to the store they would have discovered a range of artworks, from traditional oil paintings and landscapes to the shockingly modern. *Wake*, by Edward Burra, shows faceless, monk-like figures in brown habits, pointing skeletal fingers at an open grave in a crumbling, cloistered setting. The Tate bought the painting in 1940 and it is thought to have been influenced by the destroyed churches that Burra photographed during the Spanish Civil War.[21] It's not the sort of image you would want to come across in a disused Tube station.

The paintings were tended with all the care of exotic plants in a greenhouse that had to be kept at the right temperature and humidity. Civil servants from the Ministry of Works and Buildings sent letters to the National Gallery's representative, who had been evacuated to North Wales, inquiring about the ideal level of humidity and the maximum and minimum degrees beyond which humidity should not rise or fall. In December 1941 there was much relief that newly installed heaters seemed to be controlling the moisture. However, the dry weather in March 1942 forced the team to keep kettles on standby, ready to release their steam in a way that would readjust the humidity. By May 1942 the Piccadilly Tube store was put through a 'sealing experiment' to allow the temperature to remain constant at 60 degrees and the humidity to fluctuate between 52 and 60 degrees. The correspondence doesn't explain how the store was sealed but makes it clear that the custodian was poring over charts as keenly as the man monitoring the arrival and departure of trains on the Piccadilly and Bakerloo lines.

It is strange to think of this Aladdin's Cave of treasures sitting out the war in the very heart of London at a time when many people who could afford to were fleeing to funk holes such as remote hotels far from London, or, like Vera Brittain's daughter Shirley, being sent to the relative safety of America. It is also curious to imagine how, if the precious paintings and artefacts had been buried by a direct hit on the station, they would have made a startling discovery for future archaeologists more used to ossified Roman sandals and prehistoric skeletons.

*

While art galleries and museums around the country were closing their doors and carefully packing oil paintings and marble busts away in crates surrounded by protective straw, Boots the Chemist was preparing an exhibition whose subject was as searingly relevant to the nation's perilous state as old masters and brocaded costumes were incidental. Joseph Flatter was an Austrian-born portraitist who had turned to political satire as a way of highlighting the evils of Hitler's regime. Like 30,000 other 'enemy aliens' from countries now at war with Britain – Germany, Austria and Italy – he was arrested and interned after Churchill's order to 'Collar the lot!' The decision robbed many of Piccadilly Circus's cafés, restaurants and nightclubs, such as the Café de Paris, of their chefs and waiters and explained why so many men like Flatter, who was Jewish and had fled the Nazis, suddenly found themselves in internment camps like the one on the Isle of

Man, where Flatter spent three months. The majority of the internees were men and many had built a life in Britain; some even had sons serving in the British Army. Eventually, public opinion persuaded the government to relax its position. Flatter was released and, with the support of political cartoonist David Low, secured a position in the Ministry of Information, where he worked on leaflets to be dropped over Germany as 'Black' propaganda.

But Flatter's work was probably most effective in Piccadilly Circus, where his series of cartoons, 'Mein Kampf Illustrated' or 'The Life of Hitler', formed a solo exhibition at Boots that opened in the winter of 1940/1941.[22] His ink drawings managed to cheer up visitors by poking fun at the man who was the cause of so much destruction. Flatter said later that 'hatred led my pencil'.[23] In one of his early jokes Hitler has become addicted to the night-time drink Horlicks, and this addiction prompts him to invade Britain as a way of securing supplies. The exhibition was so popular that Flatter had to produce more drawings and the display moved to the top floor of Selfridges, where it helped raise money for 'War Weapons Week', although a direct hit wiped out many of the sketches.

*

The fifth of April 1940 was a day of nostalgic reunions in Piccadilly Circus. For one hour only, and to launch the National Savings scheme, two flower 'girls' returned to Eros's plinth. Mrs Baker, who had been selling flowers at the spot for forty years and whose aunt had worked there before her, and Mrs Agnes Pegg, whose grandmother had spent her entire career at the Circus, posed in front of a cut-out scene showing

Piccadilly Circus in the 'good old days'. Mrs Baker wasn't impressed by the artist's depiction of the flower girls and believed he'd made them look more like the music hall duo Flanagan and Allen. In another nod to the past, theatrical impresario Charles B. Cochran turned up to receive the first bunch of flowers.

But the encounter was not enough to sate the reporter from the *Daily Herald*'s taste for the past and he sought out Angelo Colarossi, who had modelled for Gilbert all those years ago, in a solicitor's office in Charing Cross. 'A dapper, sprightly little man of some 60 years, just such an unmistakable little elfin figure as you would expect him to be' opened the door and the reporter exclaimed, 'Ah, Eros!' 'Angelo Colarossi is the name,' he corrected, and when the reporter reminded him of his former role he replied, 'Why, yes, I had almost forgotten. That was nearly 50 years ago.' He added that he had worked for Alfred Gilbert because he had originally planned to become a sculptor himself, although he had eventually found work as a solicitor's clerk. He acknowledged that Eros was a very good likeness of how he used to be. 'I can recognise my own face in it easily.'[24]

There was a sadness in the exchange, as if the reporter had dragged Colarossi back to a moment when anything was possible and before he had begun his Pooterish existence in the suburbs of west London. After his modelling career ended, Colarossi had served on the district council for fifteen years, eventually becoming its chairman. During that time, this Eros had kept his feet firmly on the ground, debating a range of subjects from whether pigs should be kept on allotments to the price of milk.[25] In January 1932 he was 'unmasked' by the local newspaper, the *Advertiser and Gazette*, but in a very low-key way, towards the bottom of the 'Social & Personal' column, on page 11. 'An interesting secret revealed in connection with the return of the Shaftesbury Memorial Statue . . . is that the people of Feltham have in their midst the one who some 40 years ago, posed as the model for this famous statue.'[26]

*

Autumn 1940 brought with it the start of the Blitz. The regular, nightly bombardments affected people in different ways. Some became 'windy' or 'nervy'; others were fatalistic: if their number was 'up' they would 'get it', so why worry? People were closer and more intimate. It was common to bed down with complete strangers in shelters, or for a bomb blast suddenly to reveal underwear plucked from a chest of drawers floating in the breeze. A direct hit could turn a house inside out and reveal a cross-section of someone's life, from their dressing table to their toilet seat. The war was a great leveller and robbed everyone of their privacy. But most of all, people were tired. Barbara Nixon, an ARP warden from north London, described London at that time:

> Gay and flashy Shaftesbury Avenue was very largely boarded up. Everywhere the dust of 'incidents' lay thickly on top of the usual London grime. Windows were gaping black holes, and gave the houses a mournful and blind appearance. By degrees these wounds were dressed with canvas by the first-aid repairers, but they still looked like lacerated creatures patched up with sticking plaster.[27]

London was under siege, adorned by sandbags, boarded-up buildings and 'Business as usual' signs. A journey by bus or tram usually meant frequent diversions because of unexploded bombs or crews working to make a building safe. At night the sky was illuminated by searchlights and the orange glow of fires; during the day the air was thick with cinder and brick dust. In December 1941 the second National Service Act widened conscription to include all unmarried women and childless widows between the ages of twenty and thirty, who had to choose between the armed forces or helping with farming or industry. They worked in factories, became Land Girls or put on uniforms to serve in the Women's Royal Naval Service (WRNS), ATS or, like Amy Johnson, the Air Transport Auxiliary (ATA). A wave of khaki, navy and slate-blue serge engulfed London; food rationing reached its most stringent levels and, as well as feeling permanently tired, most ordinary people felt a gnawing hunger. At the start of the war the grand hotels had suffered as guests stayed away but, during the early months of the Phoney War, visitors started to return and restaurants and hotels like the Café de Paris and the Savoy bragged about their sturdy structure and basement features that meant they had no panes of glass that needed to be criss-crossed with sticky tape to contain an explosion.

The 1930s had been a good decade for the Café de Paris. The Duke and Duchess of York, who after the abdication of Edward VIII become George VI and Queen Elizabeth, were frequent visitors, and although their dinner and bar bills were modest compared to the Prince of Wales's, they did – unlike the former king – pay their bills. Lord and Lady Mountbatten made regular appearances and, in doing so, attracted foreign dignitaries such as the Aga Khan, the kings of Spain, Denmark, Greece, Portugal, Norway and Siam and other wealthy guests, who insisted on regular tables. The Canadian-British banker Sir Mackay Edgar had a special telephone line installed close to his table so that he could take advantage of the opening hours of the London and New York stock exchanges. Politicians including Winston Churchill and Anthony Eden visited in the 1930s, as did Joseph Kennedy, the American ambassador, who quit London once the Blitz started, prompting a British aristocrat to comment tartly, 'I thought my daffodils were yellow until I met Joseph Kennedy.'[28]

The club seemed to lead a charmed life. The nearest it had come to a bomb was in 1940 when a 'dud' high explosive landed between Rupert and Wardour streets, just after the start of the Blitz at around midnight on 9 September 1940, but it had failed to explode. The close call fooled some people into thinking that the venue had had its brush with danger and, like the rest of Piccadilly Circus, would continue, unscathed, to entertain men and women from all walks of life and from around the world. But it would be only a matter of months before a persistent bomb changed the reputation of the nightclub for ever and showed that nowhere was safe in the London Blitz.

15

The Blitz-Proof Café de Paris

On the evening of Saturday 8 March 1941, 100 German aircraft appeared over London between 8 p.m. and midnight. At 25,000 feet, London was a blacked-out spectre, with only the half-moon painting the River Thames as a silvery pathway to guide the bombers.

Far, far below Londoners huddled together with strangers in public shelters, crouched under stairs at home or tried to sleep on underground railway platforms. Others at the first wail of the air raid siren snatched up a few last-minute comforts before fleeing into their garden and the damp, musty burrow of their Anderson shelter. Londoners had become troglodytes, or 'trogs', as Winston Churchill liked to call them.

But, while most of the capital had gone to ground to try to block out the incessant rat-tat-tat of the ack-ack guns, the crump of bombs and shells and sudden crash of falling masonry, one group of people, twenty feet below street level, was making the most of their night out. Some were dressed in their finest evening clothes or military uniform, others had done their best to gussy up the only clothes they had at their disposal.

Part of the excitement of the Café de Paris, like Piccadilly

Circus itself, was that you could rub shoulders with people from very different backgrounds and, for one night at least, be someone quite different. The comic actor Joyce Grenfell described what it had been like to visit the club sixteen months earlier, when she was acting in the West End:

> I hadn't been out anywhere since war started and it *would* happen that I'd get asked out on the one night when I was wearing an old reddy-brown skirt, a striped blue lined shirt and sweater and shoes with rubber soles! So helpful for dancing, of course. Anyway there it was and off I went in this costume de sport to see life at the Café de P. Of course the 'no-dress' rule has gone and people wear just what they want to. There were a very few evening dresses, several tea gowns with high necks and long sleeves and more afternoon dresses with feminine white touches! All the girls have gone womanly since war broke out and have wafted themselves on to pedestals, complete with natural nails, un-curled hair and light make-ups. I must say they are quite right. The contrast to the manly figure in uniform is as it should be. The boys, they were there in dozens, looking about fifteen each, broke one's heart. We sat in the gallery, feeling quite the next generation. Down below, on a space measuring little more than eight feet by twelve, they danced and danced. The place was jammed. Looking down from the gallery one felt pleasantly remote and I must say I was glad to be. There was a sort of homesick feeling about it all to me. It was ugly; it was touching; it was dreadfully earthly and it seemed so wasteful to see these babies dancing and drinking in the Noël Coward era manner with a 'let's-eat-drink-be-merry-for-tomorrow-we-die' look on their faces.[1]

Although the war had chipped away at the nightclub's glamorous enamel, in 1941 it was still the place, if you could afford it, to impress a girl or army friend, or simply to forget about the six months of nearly continuous night-time bombardment that had left Londoners in a fug of tiredness.

The 50 kg (110-pound) high-explosive bomb, which was about to be released into the chilly night sky, was the smallest of the German HE bombs and just under four feet long and eight inches in diameter. It was bullet-shaped with fins to make it more aerodynamic and, while it was no 'Hermann' or 'Satan' (the two biggest German bombs – the second of which could produce a crater big enough to swallow two double-decker buses), it was deadly – especially when dropped in a confined space, near glass.

As the German crew took aim, guests checked their appearance in the mirrored walls as they negotiated the twenty-one steps onto the oval dance floor, which was said to have been modelled on either the Palm Court of the *Lusitania* –the passenger liner sunk by a German U-boat in 1915 with the loss of over a thousand lives – or a room on the *Titanic*. Dancers caught sight of their own image endlessly refracted, or observed the scene over a cocktail or glass of champagne. A slim, elegant bandleader named 'Snakehips' Johnson, leading a rendition of the swing number 'Oh, Johnny', stood in front of a discreetly hidden ventilation shaft, installed only two years earlier.

Customers in uniform or 'mufti' (civilian clothes) were making the life-changing decision, in that split second, about whether to take to the dance floor or to leave it to slake their thirst, to head to the powder room or to make a phone call. Diners leant forward expectantly over the mezzanine balcony, scanning the dance floor for famous faces and signs of gossip.

Waiters, who had no say in their own fate, tapped dancers on the shoulder to tell them their food was ready and, in encouraging them to return to their table, unwittingly saved their lives. Beautiful young women shifted in their seats and those who turned their backs on the room's wall of glass unknowingly shielded their faces from the deadly shards that were about to pierce the revellers.

At that moment – 9.55 p.m. – a bomb bounced through the ventilation shaft and, like a silver ball in a pinball machine, hurtled through several floors, through the Rialto cinema, and onto the dance floor of the Café de Paris.

*

Ken 'Snakehips' Johnson cut a surprising figure in London's Blitz. He was six feet four inches tall, and lean.[2] Like Fred Astaire, whom he resembled in so many ways, he had an effortless elegance about him. By 1941, when he was twenty-seven and at the height of his powers as a dancer and bandleader, he had assumed a stylish confidence. The neatly tailored white jacket he wore when he was leading his band or, when he was off duty, the pinstriped suit set off with a striped tie, discreet wristwatch and signet ring on a manicured pinkie, highlighted his taut frame. His nickname followed a tradition set by American dancer Earl 'Snakehips' Tucker, who had perfected a dance that involved an eccentric, almost contortionist, movement of his legs. Snakehips Johnson, by comparison, had a much more fluid and urgent impetus to his dancing, no doubt influenced by his time in New York in early 1935 when he was contracted to make short films and used the opportunity to take dance lessons in Harlem.

Britain's Black population had started to increase at the

beginning of the twentieth century as West Indian and African seamen arrived, particularly during the First World War.[3] But the population was still overwhelmingly white, especially before American GIs arrived. In the 1920s and 1930s Black performers had played mainly small clubs, private parties and halls on the variety circuit. The Second World War offered a once-in-a-lifetime opportunity: the introduction of conscription hit a profession dominated by young men under thirty but, while British musicians were being drafted into the armed services, performers from the West Indies were generally not called up, especially if they had only recently arrived in Britain.

Although British jazz bands were generally technically proficient, they sometimes lacked the verve of a performer like Snakehips, who brought to his act the authenticity of his Caribbean roots (he was born in British Guiana) and his experience in New York. He was also fiercely ambitious. In 1936, when he was still in his early twenties, he joined forces with the Jamaican trumpeter Leslie Thompson to form the Jamaican Aristocrats (or Emperors) of Jazz. Thompson had lived in Britain since 1929 and had risen to prominence by playing with Louis Armstrong on his European tour in 1934. The Jamaican Aristocrats attracted other Black musicians, many living in London, others from Cardiff (where the port's influx of sailors created the foundations for a thriving Black music scene), and recent arrivals from the West Indies (particularly Jamaica and Trinidad). But Snakehips usually stole the show, especially when he tapped his way up a set of glass steps in an act made famous by the American dancer Bill 'Bojangles' Robinson.

Snakehips led the band dressed in white tie and tails and eventually the sophistication of his outfit started to match his surroundings when they were booked by the Florida Club in Mayfair. However, the partnership ended abruptly when Snakehips renewed his contract with the Florida in a deal that excluded Thompson. Instead, Snakehips recruited four musicians he had met during his time abroad and re-formed as the Emperors of Swing. They appeared on early television and broadcast regularly on radio with Cardiff-born Don Johnson as the main singer; some of these sessions were recorded in the Café de Paris, where they appeared for the first time in October 1939. They started to secure bookings at more London clubs, eventually changing their name to Ken Johnson & His West Indian Dance Orchestra. Fan mail poured in and critics acknowledged their ability to 'swing', perhaps the first ever British band to do so. There were twelve band members, including the Trinidadian saxophonist Dave 'Baba' Williams and Jamaican pianist Yorke de Souza.

Like any commercial performer, Snakehips' repertoire had to include songs that were easy to dance to and one such catchy tune, which their band became famous for, was, 'Oh, Johnny'. But he was keen to introduce music that was less well known in London and in 1939, with horrible prescience, he told a reporter for the music newspaper *Melody Maker*: 'I determined to play swing at the Café or die – and boy, I nearly died!'[4]

Snakehips' accent and delivery were surprising. His origins in Georgetown and his fascination with jazz prepared the listener for a relaxed, American accent but, instead, he spoke with the received pronunciation of someone who had spent all his life in the English Establishment. This was no doubt due to his two years at Sir William Borlase's School in Marlow, Buckinghamshire.[5] His father, a doctor, and his mother, a nurse, had both hoped he would pursue a career in medicine, but their son studied law after leaving school, before succumbing to the lure of show business.

At around 9 p.m. Snakehips was enjoying a drink at the Embassy Club in Mayfair with Leon Cassel-Gerard, a theatrical agent who booked acts for the Café de Paris.[6] Snakehips was due on at around 9.30 p.m. and had been planning to jump into a cab, but the West End, which had started the evening quietly, sprang to attention as air raid sirens picked up their mournful wail at 7.48 p.m. and ack-ack guns announced the start of what would become the heaviest attack on the capital since December. As Londoners scurried to take cover in air raid shelters, underground stations or doorways, Snakehips, unable to find a taxi, decided to sprint the half-mile across Regent Street and Piccadilly Circus to Coventry Street. At a brisk walking pace this should have taken about ten minutes; at a dash, Snakehips would have made it in half that time and must have felt relieved to catch sight of the Rialto cinema, its three giant arches still impressive despite the blacked-out windows. He avoided the cinema's main entrance and, instead, lifted back the blackout curtain to duck into the small doorway that led to the safety of the subterranean dance club. Although he must have been slightly out of breath, his trademark carnation was almost certainly still in his buttonhole.[7]

Much of the Café de Paris's wartime success was founded on its reputation as a glamorous bunker. Its manager, Martin Poulsen, bragged that it was 'Blitz-proof' and demonstrated his confidence in the venue by ordering 25,000 bottles of champagne for its cellars.[8] The war had a democratising effect and, while actors, debutantes and members of minor European royal families still came, they were joined by those who spent most of their lives in uniform, including British and Canadian airmen and representatives of the Free French 'army' who had been flung out of their country after the arrival of the Germans and were looking for a way to fight back. Often they couldn't resist gossiping to eager listeners, and sometimes their drinking companions turned out to be German spies.[9]

Many off-duty soldiers and airmen grumbled about the exorbitant prices they paid to impress their girl. Others found compensation in watching from tables illuminated by little shaded lights or craning their necks from the gallery as silk gowns, dinner jackets and pressed uniforms shuffled past on the small dance floor beneath. The club's atmosphere had shifted from an effortless hedonism to a more concentrated desire to enjoy the moment.

Among the guests that night was 25-year-old Group Captain John 'Jackie' Darwen.[10] He was a career airman whose father had served in the early years of the RAF. It seems likely that he met his future wife, Marjorie, in India, where her father, Brigadier H. S. Gordon, OBE, had been based in Lahore. Jackie had, apparently, sent Marjorie to a 'bolt-hole' in the country for safety but had suggested she returned to London for a special reunion on one of his rare nights off. She was just twenty.[11]

Helen Bamber would always remember the night of the bombing because her beloved Aunt Mina planned to go to the Café de Paris with her boyfriend – a soldier who had survived the evacuation of Dunkirk.[12] Mina had taken her to a Lyons Corner House in the 1930s to initiate her into the secrets of the adult world and she recalls her aunt as 'full of fun and outrageous clothes, platinum blonde hair with a social conscience'.[13] She was a communist, ran her own hairdressing business and frequently acted as a go-between for Helen's unhappily married parents.[14] She taught

When it opened in 1915 the Regent Palace was the largest hotel in Europe and had 1,028 bedrooms. At its height it employed over 1,000 staff who prepared meals for guests who enjoyed staying in the centre of London for an affordable price.

The Lyons Nippy was instantly recognisable from her uniform. This waitress, from around 1935, is wearing mother-of-pearl buttons sewn on with red cotton and starched Peter Pan collar and cuffs. The coronet had to be positioned just above the eyebrow.

Simpsons used floodlighting, neon lights and non-reflecting 'invisible glass' to create the atmosphere of a film set. The department store employed the Hungarian-born artist László Moholy-Nagy to design intriguing window displays that lured passers-by into the shop.

Lillywhites' craftsmen produced cricket bats and tennis racquets that were lovingly weighed in the hand or held in the air so that the wood's straightness could be measured by eye. A. D. Somers (pictured) followed his father into the trade and started making sports equipment in 1900.

Women stacking tennis racquets for Lillywhites look more like librarians handling precious manuscripts than manufacturers of sporting goods.

Although shoppers at Lillywhites were several hundred miles from the nearest mountain, they could try out their ski wear on an artificial slope, high above Piccadilly Circus. Sportswear in the 1930s was still unsophisticated and one skier refused to relinquish his pipe.

A passenger appears oblivious as workmen deliver paintings and other works of art from the Tate and London Museum to Piccadilly Circus Tube as part of a scheme to protect them from aerial bombardment. The humidity eighty feet below ground level proved a constant concern.

The Café de Paris on 12 September 1933. The nightclub became a favourite haunt for Europe's royalty, British politicians and Hollywood stars such as Fred and Adele Astaire. The future Edward VIII brought his friends and would practise the Charleston when the club was deserted.

During the Blitz many families found refuge from the raids in Piccadilly Circus Tube station. On 25 September 1940 the Storre Brothers, who had themselves been made homeless by the bombing, entertained shelterers with their music hall act of comic patter and knockabout acrobatics.

Ken 'Snakehips' Johnson was a jazz band leader and dancer at the height of his popularity in 1941. He and his band, the West Indian Dance Orchestra, were regulars at the Café de Paris and performed popular swing numbers such as 'Oh, Johnny'.

Clearing up in the bombed Café de Paris on 9 March 1941. The club's manager Martin Poulsen boasted that the venue's subterranean setting made it 'Blitz-proof' He was one of over thirty people who died that night.

A man holds an undamaged guitar on his shoulder as he helps to clear up after the bombing of the Café de Paris. Injuries were made worse by the glass-lined walls and in many cases securing the best seat in the room had proved fatal.

Angelo Colarossi, model for Eros, with his wife and daughter. He never grew beyond five feet and lived a quiet life as a solicitor's clerk and councillor in West London. A journalist who met him in his sixties described him as a 'little elfin figure'.

A postcard shows Rainbow Corner which aimed to be a 'home from home' for American GIs. Thousands of men visited during the war and the club claimed to have thrown away its key because its doors never closed.

Sergeant Karen Hermeston, Canadian Army Film and Photo Unit, on VJ Day, 15 August 1945. Behind her the Pavilion has restored letters from *Blood on the Sun* (a film about Japanese plans for world domination) which a sailor had removed and hurled to the crowd below.

Helen how to swim and dance and took her to plays that were probably inappropriate for her age. Afterwards they would dine at the Corner House, where Helen would always have the same: Welsh rarebit (savoury, melted cheese on toast) and an ice cream sundae. Mina was slim and energetic but not beautiful; however, she had lots of boyfriends and talked to Helen about sex, offering advice such as 'Always remember that the shoes come off last.'[15] Mina was keen to see Snakehips Johnson, but after she set off Helen could hear the bombs landing in town from her home at Stamford Hill in north London.

The list of people there that night shows the international mix of those who were dancing – or serving – at the Café de Paris.[16] Christos Costi, a thirty-year-old waiter from Cyprus who lived near St Pancras. Epaminondas Cominos, who grew up in Athens but left enough money (over £646) to suggest that he was there as a guest. Hanna Duszynska was twenty-eight and from Hampstead, but her name hints at an eastern European heritage. Ulf Erik Larsen was twenty and born in north London. He was in the Home Guard and had a twin brother; their father was a stockbroker who, like his wife, originated from Denmark. Spros (also known as 'Spyros') Joannis Frangos was a 37-year-old captain in the Merchant Navy. Angelo Rezzani was forty-eight and lived in Marylebone; his name sounds Italian and one wonders whether he had, like many Italian waiters and chefs (if that was what he was), been interned the previous year when Italy entered the war on Hitler's side.

Not everyone relished the international flavour. Charles Graves, a journalist and brother of novelist Robert who knew the venue well, wrote in his diary for 9 March 1941, 'Anyway, it was full of aliens, and if any restaurant had to be hit that was the one to catch it.' The diary was published later that same year.[17]

At 9.30 p.m. it was still relatively early for those looking for a good time. Howard 'Boogie' Barnes represented the new type of customer that Poulsen would now welcome through the blackout curtains. He was thirty-one and worked in advertising, although he had experienced a Roy of the Rovers few years in his early twenties as an amateur footballer for Wimbledon Football Club before Crystal Palace signed him as a striker. He had an athlete's square jaw and the slightly quizzical look of a music hall performer, his piercing eyes framed by eyebrows that resembled quotation marks.[18]

That morning Boogie had been best man at the wedding of his brother, Mickey. Boogie was particularly close to Mickey and had helped him find a job in advertising. He did his best to persuade his brother and new sister-in-law to join him and his girlfriend for a night out. Not surprisingly, they decided to enjoy their honeymoon alone. When Boogie arrived at the Café de Paris he tipped the head waiter to secure one of the best seats in the house, at a table in the balcony overlooking the dance floor. The couple's arrival coincided with a change of artists as Snakehips joined his band on the small dais embraced by the twin staircases that led to the balcony. When the band started to play 'Oh, Johnny', Boogie's girlfriend led him away from their coveted spot on the balcony and onto the dance floor. Neither could have known just how significant the decision to take to their feet would be.

Boogie was unlikely to have felt as comfortable on the dance floor as Mary Honer, who was a member of Sadler's Wells Ballet Company. Less than a year before, she had been on a tour of Holland and had managed to leave the country just as the Germans were arriving. She was on the second from last ship to leave the Netherlands – the Dutch royal family was on the last.

Honer may well have brushed shoulders with a young couple who were celebrating their recent wedding. The husband, Jim, was in the RAF and they were there with his mother, Kathleen ('Kat') Humphreys. Kat was fifty and a wealthy divorcée from Canada who, in her younger days, had lost a fortune in Hollywood. She had moved to London at the outbreak of war to live with her son.[19] She decided to sit this dance out, preferring to watch her son and his young wife on the dance floor. She was one of several Canadians at the Café de Paris that night: Helen Stevens, a physiotherapy assistant with the Canadian Military Hospital, was visiting London on her weekend off. She took the train with a friend, determined to find 'cookies'[20] in London and to go dancing with a group of fellow Canadians. 'As we drove through the blacked-out streets in one of those funny London cabs we could hear German bombers going over the city,' she said later. 'They seemed quite a piece away from Piccadilly, though, and there was distant gunfire and flashes in the dark sky. The restaurant looked like a safe place for it was below the street level . . .'[21]

Lady Betty Baldwin was also enjoying a night off – in her case from ARP duties with Ambulance Station 41 in Bruton Mews, near Berkeley Square. Unlike many of the other guests, she cut a rather frumpy figure and was stout with a round face. Nevertheless, she often caused a ripple of whispers when she entered a room because her father, Stanley, had been Conservative prime minister three times between the world wars. He had come to realise that rearmament was necessary and was famous for the line, 'the bomber will always get through'. Betty was there with a female friend and two Dutch officers but was peeved to be told that they could not sit at one of the sought-after banquettes in the gallery; instead, they occupied tables clustered on the periphery of the dance floor. It was a setback that had life-altering consequences.

Showgirls, bathroom attendants, cooks and coat-checks all played their part in ensuring that guests enjoyed the best possible night out. Carefully vetted hostesses hinted at more than a turn around the dance floor, and sometimes received what became known as 'service stripes' in the form of lavish gifts of diamond bracelets and even marriage proposals, if the night continued in a nearby hotel or private apartment.[22]

Outside, the rescue services were settling in. Ballard Berkeley, who grew up in Margate, was thirty-seven and already an established screen and theatre actor.[23] His most famous role, as the bumbling Major Gowen in the BBC comedy *Fawlty Towers*, was still thirty-four years in the future. During the Blitz Ballard worked as a reserve police officer based at West End Centre, a beat he knew well from his acting career. During the Phoney War he was able to carry on working in theatres, which opened at five in the afternoon and closed before dark. He was outside the Comedy Theatre in Panton Street when he heard the blast. His role that night would be to protect the injured, not from German bombers but from their own side.

There were people who should have been there but weren't – due to illness, a change of heart or a quirk of fate – and people who shouldn't have been there but were.

Nineteen-year-old Jean Campbell-Harris had already spent a year working as a Land Girl on David Lloyd George's estate (the former prime minister was a close family friend).[24] Later, she became a cipher clerk at Bletchley Park, where she helped to crack the German U-boat codes. Her mother scraped together enough clothing coupons to buy her a dress for the 1941 debutantes' ball, but Jean attended only briefly before sneaking off to the Café de Paris. She arrived after the bomb had dropped, and survived to become the celebrated Tory politician Lady Trumpington. Richard Todd, a future actor,[25] was also turned away earlier that evening when he was told there was no room and another actor, John Mills, cancelled his booking for no apparent reason.[26] The club had earned a reputation as a place to explore extramarital affairs and Poulsen had been known to hide a man in his office if a wife turned up unexpectedly. Pamela Jackes, twenty-five, was in the ATS and had been invited out by one of the officers she drove around London as part of her job. 'It was gay. You wouldn't have known there was a war on,' she later remembered. 'It was underground and one felt perfectly safe and you went down two lots of staircases to get to the dance floor and it was a marvellous evening up until ten minutes to ten.'[27]

At 9.30 p.m. the Café de Paris was still filling up and there was an air of expectant excitement, like the moment before the curtain lifts at the theatre. Snakehips and his band chose to kick off with a sure-fire hit. The choice prompted Boogie Barnes' girlfriend to turn to him to suggest they take to the dance floor. They walked down the famous steps.

*

The music and the Café's subterranean setting probably meant dancers could not hear the commotion that was going on above their heads; or perhaps the same bravura that persuaded them to venture out in the Blitz meant they were good at ignoring it. Certainly, the war had taught band members to block out the rumbles and reverberation that juddered through their instruments and the floor whenever they were performing. As one musician said, 'It's only when you stop playing, and your mind returns to its surroundings, that you become aware of the banging and whistling overhead. But somehow, even then . . . I find myself staggering a little as the floor rocks from a nearby explosion, the lights and the people dancing . . . seem to relegate the danger and inhumanity of it all to a secondary consideration.'[28]

The showgirls who were due to go on after the West Indian Dance Orchestra were getting ready in their dressing rooms, making last-minute adjustments to their costumes, hair and make-up, probably catching up on gossip and wondering what that night's crowd would be like. Their position on the bill turned out to be life-saving.

Poulsen was almost certainly clucking over guests and making sure the waiters paid the right attention to the most significant diners. One young woman chose that minute to leave the dance floor to call her mother and remind her to take shelter in their hall. The telephones were situated near the ladies' powder rooms and one of the safest places in the building. The pennies clattered into the slot just as the bomb fell; she had the presence of mind that often appears in moments of extreme stress to press the 'B' button to retrieve the coins, find her tin hat and head for the foyer.[29]

Helen Stevens and her Canadian friends had been forced to sit in the balcony because the Café de Paris was so busy, although they would have preferred to have been nearer the dance floor. At about quarter to ten the waiter brought their desserts – pink ice cream served with a dainty silver spoon.

Bussetti, one of the head waiters, pulled a table away from

the wall to prepare it for a new set of guests and thought he must, somehow, have short-circuited the power supply.[30] Pianist Yorke de Souza had been studying the dance floor, taking in the guests and how they were responding to the music, trying to gauge the mood of the evening. Boogie's girlfriend stepped away from him, raised her right hand, executed a neat 'hep step' dance move and, in time with the music, cried 'Wow, Johnnie!'[31] At that exact moment, just as Helen Stevens dipped a spoon into her ice cream and Betty Baldwin and her dance partner neared the band, there was a blinding flash. The bomb dropped.

16

The Bomb Drops

Three other HE bombs dropped close to the Café de Paris just before ten o'clock that night, adding extra strain to a rescue service that was already under immense pressure.[1] There remains controversy over whether there were one or two bombs, and how they penetrated the Café de Paris, but it seems most likely that there was one and that it slalomed down the ventilation shaft to land close to where the West Indian Dance Orchestra was performing.

Immediately after the explosion there was an eerie silence and then a few people tried to use their cigarette lighters to illuminate the darkness, until a Canadian voice shouted for them to stop in case leaking gas sparked a further explosion. In the darkness, the injured cried and groaned. The air was thick with brick dust, plaster and cordite, which many thought was poison gas. The survivors pressed handkerchiefs to their mouths.

One of the injured guests likened the atmosphere to 'swimming through cotton wool'.[2] When she came to, she found she was sitting on an officer wearing a kilt. She tried to stand but her leg was broken and her back wet with blood. The room was covered with dust and there were flares burning. When she looked up at the balcony, she was shocked to see a line of crossed arms but no heads. As she lay on the floor a very large Dutch officer dressed in gold braid, peak cap and overcoat, who had been passing the Café de Paris, picked her up and carried her to the kitchen, where he chose the unused hotplate to act as a temporary operating table and laid her out. He washed her wounds with champagne – the only liquid available – and set her leg with a wooden spoon. While he was doing this an agitated waiter tried to clean her face with a napkin, but as her skin was bristling with tiny particles of glass the small act of kindness proved agonising.[3]

Yorke de Souza, despite his position exactly between the bomb and Snakehips, survived. He found a man lying face down and, with another band member, tried to lift him, but the torso came away in their hands. They realised the corpse was saxophonist Baba Williams. Yorke vomited and then stumbled up to street level.[4]

Another woman staggered to a nearby hotel. She was wearing a black dress that was ripped and white with dust; the dust had also powdered her complexion with a Regency-thick whiteness, making her look prematurely old, and her face was covered with blood. She didn't recognise the Miss Havisham who stared back at her from the mirror.[5] Other guests had had their clothes ripped from them so that they lurched about in an undignified state of undress that added to their shock.

Journalist Mollie Panter-Downes, who was reporting for American newspapers, recorded the event:

> One of the West End night haunts got it, and those who sat enjoying a quiet bedtime Scotch on the balcony there had a terrifying experience of seeing the ceiling come down on the dancers below while they themselves were left

perched intact on the edge of chaos, their glasses freakishly unspoilt in front of them.[6]

During the Second World War most people who died in raids were killed by falling masonry or wooden beams; it was common to be buried and suffocated by rubble or brick dust. If you were trapped under a pile of debris you also risked dying from a fire started by an incendiary bomb or from escaping gas. Other victims were killed by bomb fragments, shrapnel or splinters of glass. The risk of deadly shards flying through the air explains the advice to criss-cross windows with sticky tape, and is why the Café de Paris's mirrored walls proved so deadly.

Death from the blast itself was far less common, but the special circumstances of the Café de Paris made the location ideal for this type of tragedy. An exploding bomb sends out shock waves that travel with as much as 600 times the force of a hurricane.[7] This means that anyone unlucky enough to be close to the point of detonation is affected by its high pressure. Witnesses report feeling their eyes being sucked from their sockets, or as if they are being held down by a giant hand. The effect is exacerbated if the bomb explodes in a small space such as the Café de Paris. The pressure pulls at the body's cavities – ears, lungs, stomach and intestines. The victim appears unscathed but has, in fact, died within seconds.

Luck played a large part in whether you lived or died that night. Snakehips Johnson's head was severed and Kat Humphreys was killed, although her son and daughter-in-law survived. Poulsen died but Bussetti, the waiter who thought he had fused the lights, suffered only a wound to his back. Boogie Barnes woke to find his girlfriend alive but covered in blood. His leg was causing him agony and two strangers stood over him to stop survivors trampling on him in the dark. Betty Baldwin's eye was damaged by shrapnel and one of her Dutch officer friends lost all the fingers on one hand. Other diners sat, like waxworks, apparently unscathed but, in reality, killed by the blast. Others walked away without a scratch.

One of the patients who was fighting for her life was Marjorie, the young wife of Group Captain Jackie Darwen. They had hugged one another as the masonry fell around them and, initially, they both seemed uninjured. However, as he clasped his wife he realised that she had been pierced by a shard of glass. She died from her wounds in Charing Cross Hospital three days later.

Yorke de Souza, obviously in shock, found himself round the corner in Rupert Street, where he walked to the nearest bus stop. He eventually got home, where he noticed that the £60 he had had in his pocket at the start of the evening had disappeared. He suspected looters. The next day he went to Middlesex Hospital, where doctors found a splinter of glass in his eye. It was too close to the pupil for an operation.[8]

A dustman who happened to be passing the Café de Paris wept at the sight of 'young men in uniform carrying out their dead girlfriends'.[9]

*

The bombing turned out to be the largest raid on London since 8 December 1940 and the rescue services spent the night rushing from one pile of rubble to the next in an area that stretched across the city, from the docks in the east to homes in Kensington, the Schweppes factory in Lambeth, St Thomas's paediatric ward and Guy's surgical unit, and a pub in Islington. Major railways stations, including Waterloo and Liverpool Street, were hit.

Later, there was an inquiry into whether ambulances had been given the right information, especially as they took an hour to arrive, and whether they had transported casualties to the most appropriate hospitals. Some patients went to Charing Cross where, such was the demand for medical assistance, ambulances had to queue in the Strand. Others were rushed to the more modern Westminster Hospital, which was a mile away in Horseferry Road, just south of Westminster Abbey, but under less pressure. Boogie Barnes was lying waiting on a stretcher on the steps of the Rialto cinema when a religious fanatic bawled in his face, 'Are you prepared to meet your God?'[10] He swore back and his girlfriend recognised his voice and knew he was alive. She was taken to Charing Cross Hospital, while he ended up at Westminster Hospital after the ambulance driver realised the queue was too great and that he needed an immediate blood transfusion. Surgeons at Charing Cross operated on a range of patients for the next forty-eight hours as they struggled to remove shrapnel and fragments of wood, glass and crockery.

Nurses who had been working in nearby air raid shelters hurried to the scene. One said later: 'Moving among the dead and injured in the debris, with only the dim light of our torches to guide us, was a ghastly, and really a ghostly, experience. It was difficult to sort out the dead from the living.'[11] Nurses tore up strips from once-beautiful ball gowns to dress the injuries and, in the absence of tap water, a matron from Charing Cross Hospital told the nurses to use the soda siphons that had so recently been filling the crystal glasses to make compresses for burns.

Some of the injured who were still waiting to be treated fell victim to looters, who took rings, watches, cigarette cases and other jewellery. One woman assumed a stranger was checking her pulse until she realised she had lost all her valuables. When the nurses saw what was going on one ran to St Martin's Crypt, where she knew Scots Guards were sheltering, and returned with a group who formed a protective cordon in front of the Café de Paris.[12]

Ballard Berkeley was called in to help deal with the looting and was shocked by what he found, 'to see these people sitting at tables quite naturally – dead – all dressed beautifully, dead, not a mark on them, some of them, some of them with arms blown off or head blown off. It was like watching wax works.'[13]

The woman who had had her leg set in a makeshift splint was carried up the stairs of the Café de Paris on a stretcher made from screens, as the regular stretchers had all been used. She was taken to Leicester Square and lay there listening to human screams and German planes. She wasn't in much pain and felt quite calm about her predicament. Several times she was carried to an ambulance but other, more pressing cases, always took precedence. By the time it was her turn she was rigid with cold and shock and the person in the bunk above her in the ambulance was dripping blood through the wire mesh onto her.

A temporary first aid post was set up at the Mapleton Hotel, at 30–36 Coventry Street,[14] and a temporary mortuary at the Honey Dew Restaurant, also in Coventry Street, with an overflow at the nearby private shelter at Stagg & Russell ladies' department store, on the site of today's Swiss Centre. Mr A. Weaver, who ran the restaurant and shop, was praised in the subsequent ARP report.

Perhaps the most gruesome task of a rescue crew in the Second World War was to gather up the body parts and personal belongings that survived a bombing. Their work of going carefully through remains to place them in baskets for identification and burial was compared to that of archaeologists. One of the most poignant items discovered in the wreckage of the Café de Paris was a square, silver metal evening bag that was all that remained of a young woman known for her exuberance and love of dancing.[15]

Helen Bamber was alone in the house when her uncle rang on Sunday morning to say that Mina had failed to return. Her boyfriend was also missing. Helen went with her mother to see if they could identify the metal evening bag found at the scene but, while her mother was convinced it was Mina's, they could never be sure she had reached the club that night. There is no official record of her passing: no death certificate, nor does she appear on the list of civilian dead, although she is remembered on an inscription on her father's grave in Willesden United Synagogue Cemetery.

The London diarist Anthony Heap recorded in his diary on Sunday 9 March:

> The most sensational occurrence was a direct hit on the Café de Paris in Coventry St – one of the West End's most fashionable night haunts. It was crowded at the time and dancing in progress. Several were killed, many celebrities being among the casualties.
>
> The news must have spread round London like wildfire today; for when I passed it this afternoon crowds were standing outside gaping there at [?]. Though there was nothing to be seen externally. All the damage must have been confined to the interior a gruesome sight, I should imagine.[16]

The bombing of the Café de Paris represented much more than a tragic episode in the Blitz. The war had, to some extent, democratised the Café de Paris so that, like Piccadilly Circus itself, the club had become a people's meeting place. But the tragedy also came to symbolise the randomness of the war years – how a small decision like where you chose to sit, or the moment you decided to take to the dance floor or to powder your nose, could change your life for ever. Just as a chance encounter at Piccadilly Circus might force you to re-assess your life, so the night of 8 March 1941 made everyone who was there – or who was *almost* there – take stock.

17

Rainbow Corner

As she approached the busy front door of Rainbow Corner for the first time, Fred Astaire's sister, Adele, may have paused to reflect on just how far she had come since her first stage appearance in the West End twenty years earlier. The building faced one of the busiest thoroughfares in London: 23 Shaftesbury Avenue, on the corner of Denman Street and just a block from Piccadilly Circus. As well as the usual parade of men in suits and female office workers going about their daily business, thousands of American servicemen,[1] like worker bees on a crowded road to and from their hive, streamed in and out of the club, some picking up travel brochures, postcards and free tickets from a stand outside the building.[2] They were more relaxed than the Europeans in uniform and had obviously not been brought up to believe that putting your hands in your pockets was sinful. One Mass-Observation diarist commented, in March 1944, on the contrast between the image the USA had 'assiduously' built up of its soldiers as 'civilised, smart and at the same time full of high resolve' and the 'slouching sullen men in uniform who fill Piccadilly Circus – the gorilla-like Military Police, in white helmets and leggings . . . They do not look like soldiers, and make a pretty poor showing by the side of our own straight-backed soldierly troops.'[3] Other Britons, however, were entranced by the GIs, many of whom wore stylish shades and leant casually against the building as they chatted and glanced at the passing traffic. They looked like they owned the place and, in this corner of London, it was probably fair to say that they did.

Rainbow Corner was a five-storey, ornate edifice that occupied two buildings: the site of the former Maison Lyons (yet another offshoot of the giant empire) and an extension to the famous Café Monico. Stars and stripes fluttered in the wind, six flags on the ground floor and two larger ones on the next level, and, together with the blue awnings above the windows, they offered a splash of red, white and blue in a part of London whose colour palette had dimmed as the war progressed.

Like the branch of Boots at Piccadilly Circus, which boasted that it had no need for a key because it was open twenty-four hours a day, Rainbow Corner claimed it never closed and it had, therefore, thrown away its key. The club took its name from the 42nd Infantry Division, part of the United States Army National Guard, which was mobilised at great speed to fight in the First World War and, like the arc of a rainbow, stretched across the USA to scoop up soldiers to serve their country. The club aimed to create a home from home for American soldiers who, after their country joined the war in 1942, started to appear on London's streets, often in a state of bemusement or with a reckless desire to have the time of their life in the full knowledge that their next mission might be their last. A scheme in which 4,000 English families offered to host GIs on their days off proved a flop because soldiers wanted to be at *the* meeting place in London and to experience all that it had to offer. The invitation was well meant but far too wholesome, as Corporal Maurice Sellers from Bellingham, Washington said: 'The English are grand people, and we certainly appreciate their kindness. But on our 48 hours' leave we'd rather grab a girl and go out dancing.'[4] Ralph Hammond, a GI and reporter from Alabama, wrote of his experience:

> London was the great furlough melting pot for all United States soldiers in Britain . . . And for the GIs, everything in London focused towards Piccadilly Circus . . . and to them Piccadilly Circus meant Rainbow Corner.[5]

The club opened for the first time on 11 November 1942 and the *Illustrated London News* made the astonishing claim that between that day and 11 p.m. on 8 January 1946, when it closed for the last time, some 18 million GIs and their friends had passed through its doors.[6] The American Red Cross ran the building with the help of 314 British workers and 241 volunteers. American newspapers boasted that the club had better facilities than its stuffier counterparts on the other side of Piccadilly Circus and that Rainbow Corner's members had a lot more fun. Adele Astaire, or 'Dellie' as she was known, helped to provide that fun.

*

Adele wasn't beautiful in the conventional sense of the word and if a passer-by gave her a second glance in the street it was because of the way she carried herself, her nimbleness and neatness, rather than her prettiness. The American Red Cross uniform sat well on her spare frame and accentuated her tiny waist. She knew how to make the most of make-up to define her sculpted eyebrows, eyes and lips, and how to pose for a photograph. Her expensive and tasteful jewellery set her apart from the other volunteers.

Until she married Lord Charles Cavendish, the second son of the 9th Duke of Devonshire, in 1932, she had been her brother Fred's dancing partner. They graduated from American vaudeville to star in the 1920s in a range of musical comedies,[7] which often started in New York before transferring to London. The siblings, who were genuinely close and managed to avoid showbiz rivalry, injected whimsy and effervescence into their performances. They charmed London in *Stop Flirting* at the Shaftesbury Theatre in 1923, when they sang the wonderfully daft song 'The Whichness of the Whatness', accompanied by a ludicrous runaround routine, and in two Gershwin pieces: *Lady Be Good*, at the Empire, Leicester Square in 1926, and *Funny Face*, at the Prince's Theatre in 1928. The Prince of Wales and other members of the royal family, particularly the Prince's younger brother and George V's fourth son, Prince George, took a shine to them and they were frequently seen at clubs such as the Café de Paris, the Kit-Kat and the Embassy. On one occasion, Fred was spotted dancing a rather too intimate Charleston with Lady Mountbatten.

According to their biographer, Kathleen Riley, it was London that truly made stars of them.[8] Dellie endorsed products from toothpaste to Pond's Cold Cream, shampoo and bronchial pastilles, and was friends with writers including J. M. Barrie (who wanted her to play Peter Pan), George Bernard Shaw, Somerset Maugham and A. A. Milne. P. G. Wodehouse was smitten, commenting: 'Such words as enchanting, delicious, captivating did not seem like tired adjectives from a Hollywood pressbook when applied to her.'[9]

Dellie's husband, Lord Charles Cavendish, or 'Charlie', by comparison, was tall and thin with a long face and slightly bemused expression that made him look like one of P. G. Wodehouse's most famous characters, Bertie Wooster. He was also a 'hopeless alcoholic'[10] and had been sent by his concerned family to New York to learn about finances from J. P. Morgan in the belief that the prohibition laws would cure him of his addiction.[11] Instead, Charlie engaged a boot-legger and had his suits adjusted to accommodate a hip flask. Although he was shy, he managed to persuade Dellie to marry him, despite his mother's disapproval and Dellie's reluctance to abandon her brother. The wedding took place, after a hasty Church of England baptism once it was discovered that she was a Catholic, in the private chapel at Chatsworth in 1932, when she was thirty-four. The bride won over her new in-laws with her *joie de vivre*, which, on one occasion, involved pepping up a stuffy family gathering by turning cartwheels.[12]

The couple then retired to Lismore Castle in County Waterford, Ireland, a grey, fairy-tale building that their in-laws had given them as a wedding present, and which jutted out of the rocks above the River Blackwater. Dellie moved into a home with 200 rooms, although, she joked, just one bath-room. One of her first tasks was to remedy the imbalance, and this activity explains why the travel writer Patrick Leigh Fermor would later describe the castle as 'Built by King John, lived in by Sir Walter Raleigh and plumbed by Dellie Astaire.'[13] Deborah Mitford, who, as wife of the Duke of Devonshire's younger son Andrew, later lived at Lismore, remembered Dellie as a 'fascinating creature of irrepressible vitality but . . . also capricious and [someone who] used a torrent of bad language'.[14] When she succumbed to these outbursts her mother, Ann, would reproach from one end of the long dining room table, 'Oh Dellie, oh Dellie, oh *Dellie*'.[15]

It wasn't easy being the mistress of such a beautiful, if remote, castle, especially when the master was an alcoholic unable to kick his addiction despite several trips to German spas and London hospitals. Dellie also lost a baby girl and then faced the tragedy of stillborn twin boys in 1935. In 1939, when she was forty-two, she suffered a miscarriage. Charlie's ill health meant he was not fit for active service and, instead, they paid for two fighter planes known as 'Dellie Astaire' and 'Cavendish', but it was only when she met Colonel Kingman Douglass on a trip to London in late 1942 that she finally found her vocation and was able to use all that Piccadilly Circus could offer to establish a new identity.

Douglass was a Yale-educated American who had won the Distinguished Service Cross and Croix de Guerre with Palm for his service as a pilot during the First World War. In peacetime he worked in finance before joining the Eighth Air Force and serving as chief of air force intelligence and liaison officer with the RAF in London. He would go on to help set up the forerunner of the CIA. He was in his mid-forties and married with three sons when he started to pursue Dellie, persuading her to become involved with the American Red Cross in a ploy to keep her in London.[16]

*

The atmosphere inside Rainbow Corner was a mixture of hedonism and practical assistance. The GIs who strode through its doors included fresh-faced recruits who were still getting used to fog so thick that London's landmarks disappeared before their very eyes, the endless queueing, the bewildering underground system, the rationing, the way that bread and other goods were handed over unwrapped, and the fact that you could be on a bus all day and never reach London's limits. Staff at Rainbow Corner had to answer questions about where a soldier could catch a salmon, visit a castle or go for a bike ride.[17] They also had to translate words such as 'torch', 'frock' and 'pavement', and British servicemen's slang like 'brolly hop' ('parachute jump'), 'ace gen' ('important information' and the opposite of 'duff gen') and 'bus driver' ('bomber pilot').[18]

As the war progressed, more seasoned servicemen made their way to the club. By then many had fought in North Africa and Italy, and airmen were flying regular missions over Germany. They had witnessed terrible sights and might also be dealing with personal tragedies of failed romances, pregnancies and disintegrating marriages. When its director, Verbon F. Gay, described the club 'as a place to come clean',[19] he was probably thinking of somewhere that offered a barber and soap and hot water, but the building also provided the chance for a soldier to unburden himself of nagging worries.

The GIs entered through a grand, high-ceilinged lobby with elegant columns and lights that felt like a busy, continental railway station. The room was teeming with jostling soldiers and a few military police, who helped to keep order. The first thing they saw was a cashier's desk on their right, where they could leave valuables during their stay in London, cash cheques for American banks or swap their foreign currency for sterling. If they were really down on their luck the Red Cross field director might lend them money from a room at the back. They could also take advantage of the enquiry desk,[20] where female members of the American Red Cross greeted them with a familiar accent or would chalk up a message on the huge blackboard that hung on the wall to help them find their buddies. At its busiest about ten young women, their hair neatly rolled in the wartime fashion, answered queries from GIs who leant anxiously over the counter to hear what they were saying or to listen in to the telephone calls made on their behalf. As Rainbow Corner had few beds, the most pressing request was for accommodation in one of London's other Red Cross centres. Above their head a sign reminded them, 'New York – 3271 miles [sic]',[21] but the overriding aim of the club was to make them feel closer to home.

One of the most popular parts of the club was Dunker's Den in the basement, where a jukebox played until 3 a.m. Anyone was welcome to play the piano, which sat on a small, raised platform, and songs such as 'Deep in the Heart of Texas' and 'Pistol Packin' Mama' were popular to sing along to, usually accompanied by raucous banging on the tables as the soldiers lounged around in their drab greatcoats and khaki caps, many drinking Coke or smoking. Others sat down to study the newspaper or indulged in American staples such as doughnuts, coffee and ice cream. If the drawings in the *Illustrated London News* and a photo in the *Sketch* are representative,[22] there were also a few Black GIs among the servicemen,[23] who took advantage of the club and the absence of the segregation they would have experienced at home. However, clubs such as the Bouillabaisse in New Compton Street[24] and Frisco's International in Soho[25] were far more inclined to welcome Black GIs and white partners. In other clubs where white GIs were in the majority, the presence of such couples could prove incendiary. One suspects that some white GIs at Rainbow Corner would have found it difficult to adjust to the freedom their Black counterparts enjoyed in Britain.

The British Red Cross ran a nursing station in Dunker's Den where soldiers could go to have a dressing changed or new ones applied. Presumably most of these injuries were the result of official combat, but there may have been some caused by scuffles among other GIs or local men. American soldiers weren't universally popular – particularly with British men, who often resented their easy charm, relatively high pay and access to luxuries such as silk stockings, chewing gum and chocolate bars. There was also a small room where soldiers could go if they were desperate for a sleep, or too drunk to stay awake. The cubicle became known as the 'Where am I?' room, after the first words usually uttered by the occupant when they woke up.[26]

Captain Glenn Miller, looking oddly scholarly in his rimless glasses, and his band, whose trombones and saxophones appeared to come to life as their owners rose from their seats at carefully choreographed moments in their swing routine, performed five times at Rainbow Corner in 1944. British child protégée Petula Clark offered a poignant reminder of families back home. 'The GIs were so lovely with children and visited my street afterwards in Jeeps with Hershey bars and oranges which I shared with the other children,' she later remembered. Many years after the war, when songs like 'Downtown' had turned her into an international star, veterans would approach her at concerts to reminisce about Rainbow Corner.[27]

In the Games Room GIs played pool or grappled with the noisy pinball machines that were free to use; top scorers won a packet of cigarettes.[28] Another game offered the chance to take a potshot at a cartoon Hitler, who stared back with a toothy grimace, hands in the air. The Amusement Catering Association supplied forty machines free of charge and turned the room into what the *Daily Mirror* described as a 'Coney

Island in Piccadilly Circus'.[29] At Christmas a massive tree stretched to the ceiling and competed for attention with the chandeliers. A sign, 'It's worth the climb', pointed to the Quiet Room, which had been a private dining room during the building's time as a restaurant, and which now housed easy chairs, writing desks and a piano. In the nearby Arts and Crafts Room female volunteers took photos of GIs (three for a shilling) to send to their friends, and in 'Dabbler's Den' servicemen tried their hand at sculpting, painting and sketching. The whole building quickly became pebble-dashed with chewing gum as the GIs left knobbly reminders of their visits on the floors, chairs and tables that hardened into crustaceans that had to be chipped off.

Tuesday night was fight night. The topless caryatids that supported the vaulted ceiling in what had once been the banqueting hall looked down on the sweaty bodies of boxers and wrestlers sparring in a roped-off ring. These fight nights could attract as many as 600 men to cheer on the fighters in what became known as the 'Madison Square Garden of the ETO' (European Theater of Operations).[30] To add to the tension, organisers sometimes pitted Americans against Britons.

The dances and parties led to many romances and several marriages – some of them quite rushed due to unplanned pregnancy. The new brides had so many questions about what to expect when they joined their new husbands in the USA that in 1943 staff organised a meeting on Christmas Day, and this blossomed into a monthly Sunday 'marriage class'. By 1944 some of the women were bringing their babies with them. The most common questions were about recipes for dishes such as doughnuts, clambakes and pumpkin pie, and whether Americans really did eat something called 'fruit salad'.[31] The anxious women wanted to know how likely it was that they would be bumped off by gangsters and how many cotton dresses they would need. They were curious about sewing bees, barbecues, drugstores and whether they could expect to own a marble swimming pool like the ones they saw in the movies.[32] They watched films about life in the USA and heard lectures on topics such as clothes and make-up to help them adapt to fashions in their new home.[33] Although Americans also faced rationing, it was not as severe as in the UK and they found different ways of adapting to wartime strictures by using materials such as denim, seer-sucker and jersey and even unrationed sequins. Stockings were notoriously hard to come by in Britain and many women resorted to drawing a seam down the backs of their naked legs to give the impression they were wearing stockings. American women tended to wear more make-up, while their British counterparts were encouraged to be more subtle when in uniform; on their days off they often had to be inventive in the face of shortages. If the press is to be believed, GIs said they preferred the more natural look of British women, compared to the heavy 'pancake' foundation worn by Americans at home.

When she entered Rainbow Corner, Dellie returned to her vaudeville roots. She flirted, cajoled and responded to cheekiness as if she were taming a heckler as in her early days on the stage. Like the other volunteers, her main task was to ensure the men had a good time, and that usually meant dancing beneath the glitter ball in the same room that was used for boxing. Her girl-next-door looks, and the fact that her heyday was a decade in the past, meant that she wasn't always recognised. When a soldier said, 'If you're Fred's sister, then let us see you dance,' she rose to the challenge, though, like most of the English volunteers, she struggled to master the energetic jitterbug dance that was popular in the USA and which American soldiers had imported to Europe. As she watched an enthusiastic GI throw a slim English girl across the dance floor she gasped: 'When I left the States in thirty-two nobody danced like that outside of Harlem,' before accepting a request from a young private who asked, 'Hey, how about our dance, Adele?' and who found himself locked in a foxtrotting clinch. If she was introduced as Lady Cavendish she would convert it to a more approachable 'Lady Dish-a-hash'.[34] More than one airman was shocked to discover that his dance chit, which promised a repeat dance next time he was in London, had been signed by one half of the famous Broadway partnership.[35] The scrap of paper created a sustaining memory for those Americans who became prisoners of war.

Dellie worked at the front desk, went shopping for the men (often taking them with her) and helped them write about 300 letters a month home to their mothers, wives and sweethearts, sometimes signing off, 'Adele Astaire, Fred's sister'.[36] By the end of the war, she had written thousands of letters. Dellie was a good sport and 'up' for most things if they offered a distraction from the war. She was happy to tap Private Walter Milewski from Milwaukee on the chest and to feel his shoulders as part of her effort to 'Guess the weight of a GI' at a carnival in March 1943 (she was twelve pounds off).[37] She judged the 'best legs' competition and found a wisecrack for each pair, telling one beefy servicemen, 'My word, that leg doesn't belong here – it should be holding up the Steinway.'[38] But she could also stand her ground; when a young soldier bounced up to her writing desk, which was decorated with a huge bunch of flowers, and yelled, 'Where you been the last coupla days?' she gently rebuffed him with, 'You're going to get hay fever, Tootsie.'[39]

Rainbow Corner allowed Dellie Astaire to escape from her troubled marriage and gave her the chance to feel useful again in a vibrant home from home: a building filled with young Americans who wanted to dance and remember what waited for them on the other side of the Atlantic. She worked seven days a week at the club while her mother looked after her husband Charlie, who was now an invalid, at Lismore Castle. Dellie was granted compassionate leave when he died, aged thirty-eight, in March 1944.

In addition to Dellie, about seventy-five hostesses, who had been interviewed for their suitability and given an ID card to allow them to enter the building, provided additional dance partners. They also inducted GIs into English customs and offered advice such as not to apply English mustard on their hot dogs so thickly that it made them yelp with pain.[40] Apart from the opportunity for romance, the main appeal for these young women was the chance to enjoy American food and to experience the thrill of seeing a well-known face – such as actors James Stewart and Bebe Daniels, and composer Irving Berlin – who popped in to Rainbow Corner when they were passing through London.

*

Irene Whittaker was another woman who, like Dellie Astaire, pushed through the swing doors of the club to discover another identity for herself. In her early fifties when she decided to volunteer in the canteen, Irene helped serve around 500 lunches a day, all prepared by a Swiss chef who used to work at Claridge's, and costing just a shilling.[41] Irene was a small, bird-like figure who barely reached the shoulders of many of the GIs. Little was known about her, although an air of tragedy clung to her – perhaps because her husband had died recently, although nothing was known about his passing or if it had been heroic. Neither did she appear to have had any close family. Americans who were still getting used to English accents assumed that she came from an aristocratic background, and she was often referred to as 'Lady Whittaker', but this was a courtesy title that didn't carry the ballast of an entry in *Debrett's*. In fact Irene's father ran a stable in Limehouse, in the East End of London, from where he rented horses and carriages. Though Irene had no children of her own, at Rainbow Corner she was also referred to as 'Ma Whittaker'[42] and her role was widely covered by American newspapers, who described her as 'Mother to the AEF [American Expeditionary Forces] in England'.[43]

Irene was elevated to the status of GI mother after setting up a sewing corner in Dunker's Den. She had very little experience of sewing but, after being repeatedly asked for a needle and thread, spotted a need. As clothing was rationed, the service was vital. GIs came to Irene to have their uniform mended, socks darned (often, to save time, they wore them as she worked), new stripes added after a promotion, a piece of parachute material that had saved their life transformed into a scarf and, most importantly, to chat to someone who reminded them of their mother. She sewed on hundreds of shoulder patches and slipped in little handwritten notes and farthings for good luck; favourite airmen received a silver half-crown for added good fortune.

Her table was surrounded with uniforms waiting to be mended and she was well known for her store of various buttons and scraps of material that would meet most emergencies, whether that was mending a cap or a glove or repairing a New York sergeant's trousers after they had been devoured by mice (he took cover behind a modesty shield of fellow soldiers while Irene set to work).[44] Her two tablecloths and a lampshade were assembled from a colourful array of badges and insignia from all divisions and each theatre of war or major assault, including North Africa, Italy, the Tokyo Raid and the Battle of Britain, given to her by the men she had helped. On the wall behind her sewing table, Irene kept a gallery of photos sent by grateful servicemen.

*

Irene arrived at noon and worked a six-hour shift, including Sundays, most Christmases and New Year's Days. Like Dellie, she wrote letters home, reassuring mothers that their boys had found a surrogate in London. The GIs became her family and she kept in touch with many of them for the rest of her life. Eleven thousand of her customers filled six books with their signatures and the names of their home towns. Her appeal was that she was motherly and sympathetic, and also that she knew the United States and other parts of the world well because she had travelled widely before the war. The GIs assumed this indicated an aristocratic lifestyle, but in fact she had married a wealthy dentist, who was nearly thirty years her senior, and they had taken two round-the-world trips together in their twenty-seven years of married life. Irene brought a True View portable slide show to Rainbow Corner and encouraged her customers to squint through it at pictures of Yosemite National Park and other tourist spots.[45]

Aircrew in particular regarded Irene as a talisman, and named two planes after her. The crew of one, a Fortress bomber, took a St Christopher medal she'd given them on every mission. Sadly, their plane crashed over Germany in mid-January 1944. Airmen went with her to restaurants and the cinema when they came to London and visited her at home in Kensington, where she cooked or waited anxiously with them for news of missing crew. On another occasion she received a note from an airman on the day he was reported missing. She bought a wreath of carnations and took it to Brookwood Military Cemetery, where she placed it on the first grave she came to; it happened to belong to a 'George', the name of her deceased husband.[46]

The *Lady Irene*, a B-26 Marauder called after her, had a happier life and managed seventy successful bombing missions. Its pilot, Second Lieutenant Clarence J. Smith, from Pennsylvania, won the Distinguished Flying Cross and Air Medal with three oak leaf clusters.[47] Irene was invited to the base to see the plane and brought the crew a cake with 'Happy landings' iced on it. She gave each man a slice and a miniature horseshoe, which they pinned next to their wings.[48]

Rainbow Corner transformed Irene's life. It is difficult to think of any other place that could have offered her the chance to meet so many different people and to indulge her motherly instincts. She, in turn, touched the lives of countless GIs, who flocked to Piccadilly Circus because it was *the* place to meet and because it provided a home from home in a sea of uncertainty.

18

'Hello Yank, Looking for a Good Time?'

One aspect of Rainbow Corner that didn't attract attention in the US press was the warm welcome the area's prostitutes, who became known as 'Piccadilly Commandoes', offered GIs, many of whom were innocent and who had grown up in a country that took a much stricter official line on prostitution. In a letter home one American lieutenant described Piccadilly Circus as a 'madhouse after dark',[1] saying it was impossible to venture out without being attacked by dozens of women.

The blackout provided opportunities for impromptu fumbles in shop doorways and within a serviceman's greatcoat (one naïve chaplain couldn't understand why soldiers persisted in wearing this item of clothing in the summer), and the long-term women of the night were joined by less seasoned females who drifted into sex work to earn extra money.[2] If a serviceman could afford it, the nearest bed was the Regent Palace Hotel, and it was said that receptionists would procure a prostitute if a guest posed the coded request for an extra pillow.[3] Prostitutes crowded the pavements outside Rainbow Corner, picked off soldiers queuing at Lyons Corner House in Coventry Street or loitered near the entrances to Piccadilly Circus's Tube.[4] Often, they 'advertised' by directing a torch beam at their ankles, or approached with the opening line, 'Hello Yank, looking for a good time?' – a catchphrase that found its way into many wartime jokes.[5] The seasoned professionals were adept at weighing up their customers in the dark and quickly sought out a customer's insignia on their shoulders and sleeves to allow them to judge how much to charge: 10 shillings ($2) for an enlisted man and a pound ($4) for an officer. Clients weren't always equally astute, and on one occasion a drunken American sailor accosted the teetotal and upright Lady Astor, who promptly marched him into Rainbow Corner, where he laughed and grabbed her round the waist, saying, 'Come on, toots, let's dance.' Apparently, she obliged.[6]

Once Japan overran Malaya in 1942, rubber became scarce, and the shortage of condoms was exacerbated by the British government's decision to favour production of babies' feeding teats over prophylactics.[7] The American Red Cross was acutely aware of the risk to GIs of unprotected sex, and set up discreet posts near Rainbow Corner where servicemen could obtain condoms. Those in the know could also buy them from newspaper vendors.[8] But this did little to stop the rise of venereal diseases in Britain, which had started to increase at the beginning of the war, and which leapt when GIs arrived. Rates tripled among US troops in the UK from twenty cases after their arrival in 1942 to nearly sixty per thousand in early 1943 – a rate that was three times higher than among US troops based at home, and six times higher than the average among British soldiers in the UK.[9]

In the US, prostitution was a criminal offence in most states, whereas the British authorities took a more relaxed stance. This differing attitude gave the Americans the perception that their troops were under attack and led to tension between the two governments. The Americans couldn't understand the police's *laissez-faire* attitude and were frustrated that, while they had jurisdiction over GIs in the UK, they could do nothing to stop what they viewed as predatory prostitutes. At a Home Office meeting in 1943 the provost marshal of the US Army, Major General W. S. Key, singled out Rainbow Corner as a particularly acute example of an area where sexual transactions were sealed. The commissioner of the Metropolitan Police denied that the prostitutes targeted American clubs, and insisted that the pavement could not be kept clear because it was 'thronged with ordinary people on their lawful business'.[10]

But the general public was in no doubt about the attraction of the GIs, as this joke from 1944 suggests: A kindly man comes across a little boy who is wandering around Piccadilly Circus, crying his eyes out. The man establishes that the boy has lost his mother and says, 'Never mind, my little man . . . We'll soon find her. What's she like?' 'Double gins and American soldiers,' wails the little boy.[11]

The influx of GIs, and Rainbow Corner's proximity to Soho, also fuelled the black market. Prostitutes were willing to be paid in cigarettes, stockings or chocolate, and spivs gathered in the evenings to press GIs for hard-to-come-by or rationed items; perfume, pens, cameras and watches were particularly popular to sell or barter.[12] Berwick Street market in Soho provided a convenient place in which to trade these goods, as well as guns and ammunition. It was possible to buy a handgun at Rainbow Corner for £25 and a German Luger could fetch as much as £60, although its price dwindled to a few shillings once German troops started to be captured in large numbers.[13] The emergence of shifty characters from the shadows ready to do business, combined with the thick fog that added another layer of density to the blackout, and the constant threat that an air raid siren might at any moment wail, transformed night-time Piccadilly Circus into an area that fizzed with danger and anticipation.

That danger seeped into daylight hours, too, as the Nazis became more desperate to cause destruction once the Allied invasion of mainland Europe began on 6 June 1944. When Lorelle Hearst, a reporter from the *San Francisco Examiner*, was sent to record the mood among GIs in Rainbow Corner's canteen, she found the place deserted and Dellie Astaire unable to eat because she was suffering from 'invasion stomach'. London had been emptied of uniforms and replaced by civilians trying to distract themselves by keeping busy. People walked faster and, Hearst noted, 'One has the feeling everyone has a terrific job to do and [is] in a hurry to get it done as soon as possible or perhaps is being chased by some one [sic].'[14] American women were noticeably tense; many chain-smoked or doodled furiously. In Rainbow Corner they pored over newspapers for clues as to how the invasion was going. It was now possible to saunter past the club without having to step into the road to avoid the crush; taxis drove by with no one hailing them and some cinemas reported their audiences had halved. Hotels once more had plenty of available bedrooms and diners didn't have to queue for as long outside restaurants.[15] Aeroplanes droned constantly overhead, and it was impossible to reach anyone by telephone.

The Germans reacted to the invasion by hurling a new weapon at London: the V-1 flying bomb (also known as the 'doodlebug' or 'buzz bomb' because of the noise it made). At 12.40 p.m. on 30 June 1944 a V-1 hit the staff annexe of the Regent Palace Hotel instantly killing a chambermaid as she rested in her bed between shifts and fatally injuring a man. A young nurse, Joanne Shipway, who was walking through the area at the time, saw his body blown through the top-floor window. She and a doctor, who had his medical bag with him, rushed to help. Shipway dashed into the hotel to collect copies of the *Evening Standard* to use as a splint, but there was no hope for him. A few streets away, between the hotel and Rainbow Corner, the famous Windmill Theatre continued with its *tableaux vivants* of nude models; the Lord Chamberlain had allowed the displays on the condition that the naked women didn't move.[16] According to one version of events, the blast prompted the performers to momentarily break the immobility rule when a dislodged dead rat fell from the rafters onto the stage. In another story a performer, who was dressed only in a sombrero, turned and thumbed her nose in the direction of the explosion; the audience rewarded her with a standing ovation.

Piccadilly Circus's reputation as a meeting place, and Rainbow Corner's role as an open-house for every GI new to London, made it the obvious space for the start of a sexual adventure. The blackout added opportunity and the last desperate attacks by V-1 rockets gave those encounters a further sense of jeopardy. The final days of the war brought together much of what Piccadilly stood for: a mixture of race and nationalities, the opportunity for thrills and danger and the chance to experiment. The next stage of its history would reinforce its position as a people's place and one that specialised in celebration.

19

The Light Returns

The capital was slow to acknowledge that the war was drawing to a close. It was as if Londoners didn't want to release their joy until they were convinced it was absolutely safe to do so. Hitler took his own life on 30 April 1945 and the news reached Britain the next day. Monday 7 May was warm and sunny, and people queued for ice cream; most of all, though, people were hungry for news, which trickled through in newspaper headlines such as 'Dönitz orders submarines cease-fire'. Street vendors did a brisk trade in British and American flags, and sold a few hammer and sickles too. Crowds hung around Piccadilly Circus aimlessly eyeing up one another. Three young women perched on the back of an RAF van parked outside Swan & Edgar's main entrance and an American soldier photographed the scene from the top of an air raid shelter.[1] Everyone was waiting and watching.

Germany surrendered at 7 a.m. on Monday, but no official announcement was made until 7.40 that evening, after squabbling between Churchill and Stalin about the timing. The British PM also needed to check with the Board of Supply that the capital had sufficient beer to stage London's biggest party. Finally, the headline everyone had been waiting for appeared in giant letters and in special editions rushed out to capture the moment: 'Germany Quits'. The good news was exhaled in one long sigh of relief.

At Rainbow Corner an American band was warming up for a dance on the second floor when they heard a commotion outside. They could see crowds gathering below and one musician heard shouts of 'V-E, V-E!' although the band members couldn't understand what it meant until they listened carefully and realised the war was over. They leant out of windows to play their instruments as the crowds waved back until they joined the swarm below. The BBC interrupted its scheduled programme with a newsflash that Tuesday 8 May had been designated Victory in Europe Day and would be treated as a holiday. Thousands rushed onto the streets to start celebrating immediately, until heavy rains forced them to pause their revelry at around midnight.[2]

VE Day was a gloriously warm summer day and families ventured out to taste the atmosphere. People wore red, white and blue and buildings were decorated with Allied flags and Victory streamers. Hawkers in Trafalgar Square sold rosettes, party blowers, hats and flags. The Board of Trade announced that it was permissible to buy cotton bunting without coupons, so long as the material was in patriotic colours, and bonfires were allowed, though they had to be fuelled by material that couldn't be salvaged. Restaurants offered special 'Victory menus' and a few commemorative mugs were rushed out. The protective boards around the Shaftesbury Memorial were torn down.[3]

The day had a strange, dreamlike quality to it. Bumping into matinee idol David Niven in the West End, handsome and neat in his commando uniform, didn't feel as unusual as it should have and, in film footage, Niven appears happy to chat to the fans who had recognised him among the swirling crowds. The encounter appeared symbolic of a new freedom. London red buses ground to a halt, stuck in a mud of humanity. Churchill made a radio broadcast at 3 p.m. and the King followed at 9 p.m.; both appeared on balconies to wave: Churchill in Whitehall, the royal family at Buckingham Palace.

High spirits soared over the course of the day. Licensing hours were extended and dance halls stayed open until midnight. A young pilot was thrown out of a restaurant for singing an improper version of 'Roll Me Over in the Clover'. A sailor, naked but for a placard announcing 'Sold Out', climbed to the top of Eros's pedestal. An American soldier followed him and tried to plant a flag (the Mass-Observation observer didn't record whether it was the Stars and Stripes, but that seems probable in the general atmosphere of friendly rivalry) but the sailor took it from him and wrapped it around his bare body so that he could put the 'Sold Out' sign at the top of the pedestal. In Coventry Street another GI was performing a striptease while hanging from a lamp-post; he started with his wristwatch and gradually threw every item to the crowd, until he was left with only a 'teeny' pair of pants.[4] Women lost their inhibitions and their clothing, although observers noted that there were few prostitutes about. Nineteen-year-old Brian Abel-Smith, who would go on to be an influential economist, had taken the bus into town with a few friends from his home in Kensington and was shocked to witness 'one of the most sordid sights' he had ever seen when a very drunk girl displayed her private parts outside Piccadilly Circus Tube and invited everyone to look at her.[5] A searchlight, which would normally have been trained on the skies, was sniffing its way through the crowd until it found another young woman, who had lost her skirt altogether and was clutching her coat around her lower half. The crowds cheered as the beam lingered on her embarrassment.

The sharpest indication that peace had arrived shone out as night fell and the lights stayed on. Simpsons and the Regent Palace Hotel were floodlit for the first time in nearly six years and a bonfire burned at the Leicester Square end of Coventry Street. Mass-Observation observers noted how people gathered around it in intense silence, their faces smudged, a few eyebrows scorched. Piccadilly Circus congealed into a mass of bodies that made it difficult to move and easy to lose the friend you had come with. Songs like, 'She'll be Coming Round the Mountain' and 'Knees up Mother Brown' rose and then, just as quickly, faded away again. In side streets, young people formed conga lines and set off in a chaotic start–stop progression, happy in their lack of direction. American sailors and laughing girls conga-ed down the middle of Piccadilly, while others surged into the crowd in a rush of hokey-cokey energy. The Union flag was everywhere. The congestion was worst at the gates to Piccadilly Circus Tube, which closed at 11.30 p.m., forcing some people to walk home. It was estimated that by midnight around 50,000 people were crammed into the Circus; the excitement was such that it is rare to find a photograph of the crowds that doesn't contain a hand or face blurred by movement. Observers also noted how few people smoked; perhaps the celebrations were so encompassing that there was no room for distraction, or perhaps people were no longer bored or anxious.

Amid these scenes of jubilation there were plenty of people for whom the end of the war was a painful reminder of what they had lost or what was still at risk. For those with relatives fighting in the Far East, or held in Japanese prisoner of war camps, the future seemed horribly uncertain.

Though Japan did not formally surrender until 2 September 1945, VJ Day was celebrated on 15 August 1945, when Japan publicly announced the end of hostilities. The parties that accompanied this second victory day felt well practised rather than spontaneous, and, as before, the joy seeped onto the streets as soon as the enemy announced its intention to stop fighting. The crowd at Piccadilly Circus that day was younger, many wore paper hats and whirled football rattles; some let fireworks off in the swarm of people, who scattered to avoid them; policemen stood around looking bored.[6] A few days earlier sailors had scaled the front of the Pavilion at midnight and picked their way between the lights to prise off the wooden lettering that spelt out the name of the film being shown and the actors starring in it (*Blood on the Sun*, a thriller in which James Cagney plays a journalist who thwarts Japan's plans for world domination). They hurled the letters to the crowd, who either called out for the souvenirs or complained that they didn't want to be hit on the head. A Scottish officer provided a sideshow by climbing to the top of the Guinness Is Good for You sign in his kilt. GIs hung out of the windows of Rainbow Corner and when a young woman spotted them, she shouted out the American forces' catchphrase, 'Got any gum, chum?' In response, packets of chewing gum rained down on the crowds.[7]

A woman is captured on film standing at the base of traffic lights in front of the Pavilion's advertising-bedecked frontage, where Wrigley's chewing gum, Gordon's Gin and Bile's Beans scream out their marketing messages. She wears a red sweater with a newspaper on top, like a tabard. Its headline reads 'Japan surrenders' and her fingers make a V for Victory sign. But the atmosphere is slightly different at this Victory celebration. The sun still shines but people stride through the pavement litter without pausing; there are still conga lines but not with the same urgency or abandon; still women sitting on car roofs, bumpers and mudguards, but now they speed through traffic that is keen to get moving again, and no one seems to notice the man clinging, like a lemur, to the very top of a lamppost in Piccadilly Circus. A woman, unable to shed the mindset of shortages, grumbles about the profligacy as streamers and ticker tape float down from buildings.

Celebrations surrounding the end of the war must have been particularly painful for those who had lost loved ones, including Angelo Colarossi and his wife Elsie and daughter Phyllis. The couple's son, Lucien, had been killed on 4 April 1942 while serving in the RAF Auxiliary Air Force, 413 (RCAF Squadron) when he was patrolling the Indian Ocean south of Ceylon (modern-day Sri Lanka).[8] His fate is recorded, with 24,319 others, on a wall of remembrance at Kranji Cemetery in Singapore. It seems ironic that, unlike his father, Lucien literally took to the skies, rather than simply representing an airborne god, although with tragic results. It's difficult not to see the tragedy as a symbol for what Piccadilly Circus can offer: the chance to dream but the danger of seeing those dreams fulfilled.

On 28 June 1947 Angelo was interviewed for a *Picture Post* feature, 'The Man Who Was Eros', to mark the statue's return to Piccadilly Circus. He was seventy-two and had given up his job as a solicitor's clerk to work in a similar role at an aircraft factory in Feltham, Middlesex. The contrast between the muscular young god and the bespectacled old man in his tie and jacket, a handkerchief in his breast pocket and a tank top keeping out the cold, could not be sharper. He's captured with his mouth open as if he's about to correct the photographer. His death aged seventy-three, in 1949, was widely reported, particularly in the USA.

Amy Johnson, whose father had treated her to a shopping trip at Swan & Edgar when she was a humble typist and who had flown solo to Australia in a bottle-green suit especially designed for her by Lillywhites, was denied a grave when her plane disappeared over the Thames Estuary in January 1941. At the time she was working for the Air Transport Auxiliary (ATA), an organisation that ferried planes around the country so that the RAF could use them for training. She had been at first reluctant to join the organisation because at her interview she had met another candidate whom she described disparagingly as a 'Lyons waitress type'.[9]

Those who had been fortunate enough to survive the war still saw their lives transformed by their experience of it. The Café de Paris was so badly damaged that it lay derelict for two years until it was converted into a club for injured servicemen known as the 'Café de Khaki'. Comedians such as Jimmy Edwards, Michael Bentine, Frank Muir, Peter Sellers, Tony Hancock and Harry Secombe would cut their teeth in the final years of the wars. Betty Baldwin – whose eye had been damaged by shrapnel in the blast, and who was treated by the famous plastic surgeon Archibald McIndoe, who helped so many RAF airmen to recover from terrible burns – had had a stammer for a month after the explosion, and remained reluctant to go to the cinema, theatre or nightclubs for the rest of her life. She never returned to the Café de Paris and never married, ending her days in a genteel village in Sussex where neighbours rather cruelly referred to her as 'batty Baldwin'.[10] 'Boogie' Barnes, the former footballer, had his leg amputated and spent a year convalescing. During that time he wrote what became a bestselling song, 'Chewing a Piece of Straw', and went on to become a successful advertising executive, writing jingles such as 'Murray mints, Murray mints, too good to hurry mints'.

Captain Jackie Darwen, who had cradled his young wife in the wreckage of the Café de Paris only to discover she had been fatally wounded by a shard of glass, continued to serve in the RAF but with an added fury. His fellow pilots commented on how he undertook every possible operation and ran more and more risks, flying nearer and nearer the ground. When, in October 1942, he was awarded a 'bar' to his original Distinguished Flying Cross, the citation noted that during the attack for which he had won the award he had flown so low that his propeller struck the ground. In 1943 he helped to create a bridgehead for Allied troops to move north in Italy. The weather that month was particularly wet, and on 7 October he managed to get airborne but was shot down later that afternoon. He was twenty-seven and is buried at the Commonwealth War Graves site at Sangro River, close to the Adriatic Sea and south of Chieti. His grave is one of 2,617 white headstones, gleaming in the Italian sunshine and overlooked by snow-topped mountains and olive trees. It is a thousand miles from his widow Marjorie's final resting place in Lyme Regis, Dorset. A fellow pilot who survived the war wrote of him: 'I always felt that when Johnnie [Jackie] finally saw Old Man Death moving in, he already on the down-swing, he would have stepped into the sweep of the murderous blade with a welcoming smile.'[11]

The Café de Paris became a gruesome cause célèbre. The

contents of its wine cellars were sold for extortionate sums of money and many people claimed that they had been there that night or had *nearly* been there. Much like modern terrorist attacks, there was a cachet, if not a comfort, in feeling fate had prompted the person to turn away from disaster.

One genuine survivor who returned was so traumatised by revisiting the dance floor that he had to retreat to the toilet to splash cold water on his face. When he told the cloakroom attendant why he was upset the attendant replied in disbelief: 'You were really here the night the bomb fell? Well, sir, I can assure you that if everybody who said that they were here, or on their way here, or intending to come here [were added together], the Café de Paris would have been able to hold at least fifty thousand people.'[12]

Children's author Noel Streatfeild, who was adamant she was not there that night but who knew the Café de Paris intimately, wrote a convincing, and bestselling, account of the bombing of a West End nightclub, the Porte Verte, in a novel published the following year called *I Ordered a Table for Six*. Reviewers assumed the book was based on the Café de Paris and highlighted the element of fate in the story. 'Which will be spared? – that is the whole theme, and a very good one Miss Streatfeild makes of it as, by describing their lives and thoughts, she leads them together through the restaurant doors to the fatal dinner,' one reviewer wrote.[13] The book was the first of six novels over the next seventy years in which different authors featured the events of Saturday 8 March 1941.[14]

Snakehips Johnson's death had repercussions beyond his friends and family. Although the West Indian Dance Orchestra was not the first all-Black band to appear in Britain, it still left an important legacy for British jazz and Black musicians who followed. Frank Deniz, who played briefly with Johnson's band as a second guitarist, said, 'He elevated the colour question — people thought something of him . . . It made me think and that's why I tried to model my band on his.'[15] The West Indian Dance Orchestra performed on two further occasions, but the surviving musicians were reluctant to discuss the Café de Paris and would not play Johnson's theme tune, 'Dear Old Southland'. The members were quickly absorbed into London's white dance bands, creating a remarkable number of racially integrated groups.

The disaster provided a strange forewarning for Al Bowlly, the white South African singer, famous in the 1930s for songs such as 'Goodnight, Sweetheart'. It is believed Snakehips may have borrowed a book of music with his name on it and it was this remnant that confused teams of rescuers scouring the rubble. The rumour spread, and still persists, that he had been killed in the raid. However, Bowlly was to live a few more weeks, until 16 April, when he was killed by a bomb while reading in bed. He had performed in High Wycombe that day but declined to stay over, preferring the comfort of his own home. The last song he recorded was 'When That Man Is Dead and Gone'.

Tension between white American forces, many of whom were used to Jim Crow segregation laws, persisted to the end of the war and erupted into an ugly scene near Piccadilly Circus in August 1945. At about 1 a.m. on Saturday 18 August, American military police came to the assistance of two Black GIs who were cornered by a mob of about thirty white American soldiers. The military police fired shots in the air to try to bring the crowd to its senses and to stop it following the Black GIs into the Coloured Colonial Social Club in

Gerrard Street, Soho, which was soon besieged by Americans with bottles and truncheons. In a foreshadowing of what would become a sadly all too familiar white-on-Black racist taunt, a Black Briton had told a white American GI, 'Why don't you get back to your own damned country?' The comment fanned an already tense situation and two US marines, a white GI and a white woman were stabbed in a 'race brawl'[16] and taken to hospital. The crowd continued to hurl rocks at the building and demanded that the two men come out. Military police in jeeps arrived and, together with London police, tried to cordon off the club by linking arms. When one man made a break for it, he was chased by the crowd to Rainbow Corner. A police sergeant later told a newspaper, 'He was nearly lynched. Police beat off his attackers in the nick of time. Even so, he had a serious head wound.'[17] Twenty-three Black GIs, two white soldiers and three white women were arrested before the matter was quietly dropped.

The violent face of the 'friendly' invasion was forgotten when Rainbow Corner closed its doors for the final time on Tuesday 8 January 1946, having been open continuously, day and night, since 11 November 1942. Anthony Eden, former minister for war, and Mrs Eleanor Roosevelt, wife of the president who had manoeuvred the USA into the conflict, broadcast to America from the club. She later told 1,000 GI brides: 'You will understand men who have been in the war more than many American women will.' Eden and Roosevelt already looked as though they belonged to a different era. The end was marked by a farewell dance and at 11 p.m., while the band played 'Auld Lang Syne', the club's director Mrs Hamilton locked the door for the first and last time.[18] As the original key had been deliberately thrown away, a new one had to be made especially for the occasion. Colonel Kingman Douglass's ploy had paid off and he finally married Dellie in 1947. A plaque was unveiled in February 1949 to mark the building's original use and the site demolished in 1959.

Postscript: The Digital Screen

Britain's blackout officially ended in 1945 but, as a way of saving electricity, 'display lights' on shopfronts as well as theatres, cinemas and other entertainment venues remained turned off until Saturday 2 April 1949 when Piccadilly Circus, and other public places throughout the country, flicked the switch on their red, green, gold and white illuminations and floodlights after nearly ten long years in the dark. The transformation was most thrilling for children who had never experienced pulsating advertising signs or glowing neon lights, who'd never been window-shopping and emerged, blinking, from the darkness of an underground station to a blaze of light. Youngsters on the top decks of London buses gasped and whooped as shops in Regent and Oxford streets switched on their lights long before dark. In Piccadilly Circus, as night fell, an estimated ten thousand people gathered to stare up into the sky, as if waiting for a UFO to land. Toddlers, bonneted against the cold, sat on their fathers' shoulders, while adults in heavy coats and scarfs reminisced about the crowds they had witnessed on VE Day.

Zoe Gail, a South African-born musical comedy star, was chosen to switch on the lights and did so wearing her trademark white tie and tails and a top hat that tamed her long, blond, curly hair. At 7.10 p.m. a spotlight from the Pavilion picked her out as she sang her hit 'I'm Going to Get Lit up When the Lights Go Up in London' from the balcony of the Criterion restaurant. White-capped chefs watched the spectacle from the roof above her. Gail had first sung the song in *Strike a New Note* at the Prince of Wales Theatre in 1943 but she was, nevertheless, a controversial choice. Back then, J. B. Priestley, the Yorkshire writer whose fireside chats were nearly as popular as Churchill's broadcasts, had disapproved of a woman in men's clothing and of lyrics that promised the singer would be 'pickled and positively pie-eyed'. Gail's husband, Hubert Gregg, who wrote the words, later quipped, 'Mr Priestley apparently wishes I'd written a song called "I'm Going to Get Down to Some Real Postwar Reconstruction on Armistice Night"'.[1]

But Gail's cross-dressing, joyful persona was exactly right for the occasion and for Piccadilly Circus. After she'd delivered her famous song, she declared, 'Abracadabra, hey presto,' and flicked a switch, tossing her top hat into the crowd and breaking open a jeroboam of champagne. The famous Bovril sign spluttered into life first, closely followed by the 'Guinness is Good for You' clock, but the Schweppes Tonic sign remained in darkness, as did many of the other advertising mainstays. Boots was unable to illuminate its trademark name, but 'Dispensing Chemist' glowed above it. The crowds looked slightly cowed by the semi-darkness and kept their distance from the shop windows, as if they were radioactive. When the rain started it only served to intensify the impression of a bright, shiny city.

A week later, it took 30,000 Scottish football fans – plus quite a few bagpipe players – to remind London how to celebrate in true style. They crowded, 'Tartan-scarved, red-tammied', into Piccadilly Circus and danced reels around Eros in celebration at their 3–1 victory over England. Late into the night and early morning Boots did a brisk trade in aspirin.[2]

As the century wore on, Piccadilly Circus's lights would also be used to denote respect. When Britain's wartime prime minister, Winston Churchill died on 24 January 1965, aged ninety, the lights in Piccadilly Circus were dimmed. London was lowering its eyes in grief, as it would again when cranes on the River Thames dipped their heads as the boat carrying Churchill's coffin passed by six days later.[3] Piccadilly Circus's lights would dim, once again, to mark the passing of Diana, Princess of Wales in 1997, and in March 2016 they were switched off for sixty minutes at 8.30 p.m. as part of Earth Hour, an initiative organised by the World Wildlife Fund (WWF) to highlight climate change. In January 2017 the electrical billboard went dark for ten months to allow developers to instal a single, live video-streaming display. The new, hyper-real billboard marked the final transformation for Piccadilly Circus.

*

Long after the suffragettes' demands had been met, Piccadilly Circus continued to act as a driver of social change and, in one important case, its position as *the* place to meet played a key part in bringing about that change. Perhaps surprisingly, it was Churchill's Conservative government who, in February 1954, started to debate the need to reform the laws relating to homosexuality. They did this in great part due to a chance encounter in the subway of Piccadilly Circus's underground station on a rainy night in June 1952 when Peter Wildeblood, a 29-year-old, Oxford-educated diplomatic journalist on the *Daily Mail*,[4] bumped into Corporal Edward McNally. 'Eddie' was twenty-three and on leave from the RAF hospital where he worked in Ely, a quiet cathedral city in the Cambridgeshire Fens. He had a broad Scottish accent, wore civilian clothes and carried a cardboard suitcase. According to the later, sensational court case, they exchanged glances and then Wildeblood asked McNally what he was doing, to which the RAF man replied, with a smile, 'I am looking for a bed.'[5]

On 24 March 1954 Wildeblood was convicted of conspiracy to incite acts of gross indecency – significantly, the first use of the charge since the trials of Oscar Wilde. At the time, the crime was deemed so serious that the judge could have sentenced Wildeblood to fifteen years. He was 'fortunate' to serve 'only' a year of his eighteen-month sentence and wrote about his experience in a witty, moving and highly readable memoir, *Against the Law*.[6] The book was also notable as one of the first times that anyone in the English-speaking world had identified themselves as homosexual rather than simply confessing to having practised homosexual acts. The four words 'I am a homosexual' were hugely significant; the memoir and the trial together led to a reassessment of homosexuality and contributed to a more sympathetic public attitude towards gay men. The government commissioned the Wolfenden Committee and, in 1957, its findings recommended the decriminalisation of homosexuality.

The relaxation of the law allowed gay men to come out of the shadows. By the 1970s young men were draping themselves over the black-and-gold painted railings under the arches on Regent Street, in a part of the Circus that became known as 'The Meat Rack', to advertise their availability, or gazing out of the window seats of the Wimpy Bar next to Boots. But this freedom was short-lived: the AIDs pandemic of the 1980s and 1990s made casual encounters potentially life-threatening for the men whose sexuality had only recently been accepted by society. The risk of predatory men added another level of danger. Between 1978 and 1983, Piccadilly Circus Tube became a hunting ground for Dennis Nilsen, who killed at least twelve young men, and following his arrest police set up an interview room at the station.[7] One of London's most famous meeting places had never been so dangerous.

When the journalist Nicholas Tomalin spent twenty-four hours in Piccadilly Circus in 1971 it was surely ironic that the newspaper decided to publish the account on Valentine's Day; the Piccadilly Circus he observed was now a long way from the concept of romantic love. His portrayal depicted a part of London that had become drenched in sleaze, and the reporter, most famous as a foreign correspondent, described a sad stage setting populated by a cast of characters it would be difficult to find anywhere other than Piccadilly Circus. At 8.30 a.m. the 'jaunty' ticket collector at the Tube station pointed out young women who'd been indulging in all-night revelling and were retreating down the escalator in long evening dresses. By 11.40 a.m. Tomalin had encountered his first junkie, stumbling along Haymarket and bumping into walls. At the Tube station he observed drug pushers and police loitering near Smith's newsagents. By 3.45 p.m. he had worked out the social niceties and territories of Piccadilly Circus: drug addicts and drunks haunted the south pavement; the western pavement near Swan & Edgar, where young women waited for their boyfriends near the police telephone and London map stand, was more middle class; the County Fire Office belonged to gay men; and the London Pavilion pavement was for what Tomalin called 'transients, tat, popcorn and soft drugs' (marijuana sellers were identified by the green overcoat they wore or carried over one arm).[8] A queue started to form outside Boots as heroin prescriptions become due at midnight.

Tomalin's Piccadilly Circus was balancing on a knife-edge between respectability and sleaze. As the reporter pointed out, Swan & Edgar and Lillywhites enjoyed 'one of the finest sales positions in the world; [but] both resolutely refuse to exploit it. Why do Swan and Edgar's not make something of that frontage on the pavement where everyone arranges to meet everyone else? And why do Lillywhite's [sic] fill their windows with golf clubs and underwater tugs for aqua-lungers? Scarcely impulse buys for Piccadilly strollers.' His comments show that by the 1970s and 1980s the cast of people who frequented the area had changed dramatically and it was as if the traditional establishments like Swan & Edgar refused to acknowledge that times had moved on.

*

The Beatles' association with Piccadilly Circus exemplifies many of the technological influences that would propel the area into the second half of the twentieth century. The arrival of film and then TV, with its emphasis on global news, transformed the group into an international brand, and on 6 July 1964 the London Pavilion was 'besieged' by fans desperate to see the world premiere of the Beatles' film, *A Hard Day's Night*, and its stars. Police linked arms to hold back the screaming mob of about a thousand teenagers (the *Daily Mirror* thought as many as 10,000); a thirteen-year-old-girl fainted and an ambulance had to be called, while other young women tried to slip inside through a door that had been left ajar. When the band's limousine arrived, John

Lennon was reported to have suggested that Paul McCartney should be pushed out to bear the brunt of the fans' adoration because he was the 'prettiest',[9] but George Harrison's door was opened first and a young woman lunged in to tear frantically at his hair. Programme sellers wore black-and-white dresses with the Beatles' faces cascading down the front, which they asked the singers to sign. Department store C&A sold versions for 39s 11d and offered it in additional pink and blue versions.

Five years later, the Beatles were still causing the policemen whose beat included Piccadilly Circus problems – but this time it was as noisy neighbours. Police Constable Ken Wharfe, who was then a nineteen-year-old probationary officer, first knew about the disturbance when he spotted the blue light flashing on top of the Metropolitan Police phone box on the south-west corner of Piccadilly Circus. The phone box, a shorter, narrower version of *Doctor Who*'s Tardis, similar to a sentry box, is still in place, although mobile phones and two-way radios have made it redundant. Wharfe took the call from his duty sergeant, who told him to go and investigate the loud music coming from somewhere near Regent Street. Wharfe and another policeman, Ray Shayler, followed crowds of women and ended up at 3 Savile Row, the Beatles' headquarters, where the band were playing on the roof. When he was let in, Wharfe discovered that he wasn't the first policeman on the scene, but no one wanted to be the spoilsport to end this unique moment in musical history. The police officers joined the Beatles on the roof while a traffic jam was forming in the street below and office workers from other buildings were taking to their own rooftops to watch the spectacle. The police, who were clearly starstruck, didn't know which offence to charge the Beatles with and agreed to allow them to play one last track to complete the album. 'Get Back' was their final live performance as a band.[10]

*

Piccadilly Circus is willing to embrace change while, at the same time, preserving its identify. It is remarkable just how little the area has changed since the Second World War. There were attempts to redevelop it in the 1960s, which would have reduced the site to a motorway flyover surrounded by cereal-box-style buildings. The first plans emerged in 1961 when a Pathé news clip urged viewers to take a good look at Piccadilly Circus because it was about to disappear for ever. London County Council asked Sir William Holford to update the interchange and he proposed blocking Coventry Street with a giant cinema and diverting traffic underneath the building. There was bitter opposition to the plans from many quarters, and they were finally thrown out because the proposal failed to increase traffic to the extent called for in the first place. The notion of rebuilding the Circus returned in the 1970s when it was mooted that it could be a second Centre Point, the 33-storey tower block that glowers down at shoppers from the corner of Oxford Street and Charing Cross Road, but the Greater London Council (GLC) elections of 1973 saw the London Conservatives voted out of office and the plan permanently shelved.[11]

Other buildings managed to move with the times, although some took longer than others to adapt to their new clientele. In 1971, Tomalin noted the 'merry middle-aged' men and women preparing to go out for dinner dances from the Regent Palace Hotel, remarking, 'The overall effect, because of the ladies' mink stoles, is of a furry belt about three feet from the ground, supported by hundreds of sturdy, stockinged legs. A sort of giant, hairy centipede.' A few decades later, visitors were being warned about a different kind of insect and reviewers left lurid accounts of being bitten by bedbugs. English Heritage designated the Regent Palace Hotel a Grade II listed building in 2004 and it closed as a hotel at the end of 2006, although Brasserie Zédel carries the spirit of the place in its art deco-style elegance. I spent a happy evening in the noisy dining room before the UK's second lockdown, feeling like a reckless civilian taking a last supper in full knowledge that the enemy was only a matter of hours away.

The Criterion, at whose bar in 1887 Arthur Conan Doyle's Dr Watson met the man who would introduce him to Sherlock Holmes, has managed to preserve some of its former glamour through its golden mosaic ceiling and marble columns, although it has had its ups and downs and now trades under a different name.[12] Incredibly, despite its old-fashioned approach, Simpsons staggered on in its own time warp until 1999, when Waterstones bought the building and converted it into a temple to books rather than comfy clothing. Swan & Edgar closed in 1982 and the site has since became associated with a range of names: Tower Records, Virgin Megastore, Zavvi and The Sting. Today the windows, which long ago showcased Phroso, are frosted out and the name Swan & Edgar lives on only as a luxury watch brand.

Even in the most brutal reimaginings of Piccadilly Circus, Eros was usually to be found tucked away in the architect's concrete towers and motorway flyovers, and it has never stopped being a 'third pole' or ley line. When the *London Evening Standard* dropped the capital's name from its title it kept Eros on its masthead, knowing that the statue would sum up the metropolitan image it hoped to convey. The paper had already tried to trademark the likeness of the Grade I-listed statue but London County Council refused, saying it was a monument of 'national importance and is recognised worldwide as a symbol of London'.

During the Queen's coronation in 1953 he was trapped in a gilded cage created by Sir Hugh Casson (who designed enclosures for the elephant and rhino houses at London Zoo). The cage was lit up at night and transformed Eros into a burlesque performer who, it was easy to imagine, might at any moment settle onto a swing that took him out across the London crowds. In the 1980s he was whisked away for cleaning and repairs to his knee and ankle. When he was put back in March 1986 it was in a pedestrian piazza that made it impossible for traffic to swirl round him. In December 2013 he was trapped in a heavy-duty PVC bubble measuring thirty feet (nine metres) in diameter, which was believed to make him the biggest snow globe in the world.[13]

It can no longer be claimed, even with an obvious sense of hyperbole, that anyone lingering at Piccadilly Circus will, eventually, meet up with everyone they have ever known in the world. However, the name still represents perpetual comings and goings, albeit in a way that, despite appearances, is not completely out of control; it remains in the public imagination a place of constant activity. British soldiers have long used the name to superimpose an English familiarity on a foreign land: in a trench facing Gaza in 1917; as a title for a junction where several paths crossed in a Second World War POW camp; for a busy roundabout in post-war Hamburg, where a photo caption describes two soldiers from London looking at the Piccadilly Circus sign as one asks, 'Where's blinkin' Eros?' When troop convoys set out in preparation for the invasion of France in 1944, they met at a zone, south of the Isle of Wight, called 'Piccadilly Circus'.

The area's association with habitual activity provided an obvious motif for bleak isolation when the pandemic struck in 2020. If a TV reporter wanted to demonstrate how desolate London had become, a shot of a barren Piccadilly Circus did the trick; if a newspaper sub-editor needed to stress how our lives had been changed by the virus, a photo of Eros wearing a surgical mask spoke volumes. When the Queen reminded us, like a latter-day Vera Lynn, that, while we had much still to endure, better days would return, she did so on the now famous, vast digital screen to an empty arena, a giant monarch addressing a void.

Although it will always be a port of call for tourists, we no longer come to Piccadilly Circus in our droves – rather we summon Piccadilly Circus to our lives through our own screens. In 2002 Yoko Ono spent an estimated £150,000 on an old-fashioned banner of her late husband's lyrics, 'Imagine all the people living life in peace', which was displayed for three months. Forty years earlier she and John Lennon had paid for a poster declaring 'War is over!' on the wall that had once abutted Rainbow Corner. In both cases, the impact came from the wider media coverage rather than the immediacy of the pedestrians who glanced up, as they would have done, at Schweppes Tonic Water, Bovril or Gordon's Gin, decades before. At a time during the pandemic when galleries were closed, visual artist Ai Weiwei, musician and poet Patti Smith and photographer James Barnor shared their work on the giant screen and those who couldn't be there in person watched the live streaming.

Just as Hitchcock enlisted Piccadilly Circus to conjure up the heartbeat of London, so modern film-makers have used it to tell viewers that they are at the very centre of the capital, whether that's in *Harry Potter and the Deathly Hallows*, *Bend It Like Beckham* or *Bridget Jones's Diary*. In the computer game *Call of Duty*, Piccadilly Circus becomes a nightmarish stage set where heavily armed police officers battle their way through a terrorist attack against a backdrop of blocked roads and flying grenades. Eros remains untouched throughout.

Piccadilly Circus is no longer the hub of empire, but it still has a magnetic pull, and it is still the place to be ticked off on a tourist's checklist. Eros's steps, which have accommodated everyone from flower girls selling their wares from giant wicker baskets to hippies in floral dresses and floppy hats, to befuddled drug addicts and excited tourists, still offer the best vantage point from which to view London and, generally, to take stock of life.

Acknowledgements

Like Piccadilly Circus itself, this book has been influenced by a range of very talented people. I am hugely grateful to my original publisher Lisa Highton, at Two Roads, for the gift of the original, wonderful idea for a book. Lisa guided me to the first draft and sustained me with images of Piccadilly Circus, past and present, and took me to Brasserie Zédel at regular points in the process. She then handed the baton to my patient, clever and meticulous editor, Kate Craigie. I am very grateful to all at Two Roads, including Publishing Director, Kate Hewson, Assistant Editor, Charlotte Robathan and copy-editor Jacqui Lewis. Thanks, too, to my tenacious agent, Eleanor Birne at PEW Literary Agency.

This book was researched and written during a peculiar and, I hope, never-to-be-repeated period in history. The pandemic was hard for most people; it would have been even harder for researchers without the support of so many librarians and archivists. I am deeply grateful to the following individuals and institutions: Alabama University; British Library; Judith Wright, Archivist at Boots; Peter Charlton and Alison Young of the British Music Hall Society; Jessica Gardner and the staff of Cambridge University Library (collecting books in plastic bags has never been so thrilling); Simon Offord, Curator (Archivist), and the staff of the Imperial War Museum; Richard Bull at Lyme Regis Museum; London Metropolitan Archives; Ruth Thomson, Museum Archivist and Records Manager, Museum of London; the

National Archives; Chris Bastock, Tate Archives; Victoria and Albert Museum, Westminster Archives. As ever, I am very grateful to the Society of Authors.

I am also grateful to the many scholars who shared their expertise and enthusiasm: Kellie K. Bradshaw for allowing me to read her dissertation, 'Reality, Expectations and Fears: Women Shop Assistants in London, 1890–1914'; Jo Turner for putting me in touch with football historian Ian King; Paul Millett for his encouragement and for his knowledge about the 1940s. I first came across the Café de Paris in Joshua Levine's book, *Forgotten Voices of the Blitz and the Battle for Britain*.

Many people shared their memories of Piccadilly Circus and of the friends and relatives who frequented it. Thank you to Jill Weekes and Jonathan Kydd and to Kim Porter Sands for extra information about Bat. I was unashamedly thrilled to talk to Petula Clark.

*

I wrote this book while teaching creative writing at the University of Cambridge Institute of Continuing Education and am grateful to the students and fellow tutors who have kept asking me, 'How's it going?'. I am particularly grateful to Jenny Bavidge for introducing me to the film, *Piccadilly* and Anna May Wong, to Lizzie Speller and Derek Niemann for their support and good humour (and, in the case of Derek, a jigsaw of Piccadilly Circus – a writer who knows a good metaphor when he sees one in a charity shop). Thank you to Rupert Wallis and Lucy Durneen for reminding me of the value of a good story.

Writing is a solitary business, but I've been fortunate to

have had many friends who've entertained me and encouraged me while writing this book: Andrew Balmford and Sarah Blakeman (particularly for buying us *The London County Council Bomb Damage Maps, 1939–1945*, and for the gourmet new year's isolation dinner), Roger Browning, Sarah Mnatzaganian, Katherine Roddwell and Veronica Forwood. My trips to London would have been so much duller without regular dinners out with Kathryn Hughes.

Lastly, I thank my daughter, Rosa Gillies Kelly, and my husband, Jim Kelly. I can't imagine writing books without your support and, Jim, though it pains me to say it, you were right (for the wrong reasons) when, in early 2020, you urged me not to delay my visit to the Café de Paris.

Notes

Abbreviations:

C&C: *Champagne and Chandeliers* by Charles Graves
ILN: *Illustrated London News*
IWM: Imperial War Museum
LMA: London Metropolitan Archives
MO: Mass-Observation
ODNB: *Oxford Dictionary of National Biography*
TNA: The National Archives

Introduction

1 Eros was moved during both world wars, in the period 1925–1931 (while the new underground station was being built; it resurfaced in a different spot), 1932 (when it was damaged by a New Year's Eve reveller) and in 1984; it reappeared two years later on a new site to the south meant traffic could no longer go round it.
2 Thomas Burke, *London in My Time* (London: Rich & Cowan, 1934), 22.
3 Annual General Meeting, reported in *The Times*, 11 June 1925.
4 W. MacQueen-Pope, *Goodbye Piccadilly* (Newton Abbot: David & Charles, 1960), 309.
5 Robert Fabian, *London after Dark: An Intimate Record of Night Life in London, and a Selection of Crime Stories*

from the Case Book of Ex-Superintendent Robert Fabian (London: Naldrett Press, 1954), 60.

6 H. V. Morton, *The Nights of London* (London: Methuen, 1948), 21.

1. Eros: Piccadilly Circus Takes Shape

1 *Evening Standard*, 24 December 1931, 6.

2 Ibid.

3 *ODNB*.

4 Ibid.

5 The account by Isabel McAllister, *Alfred Gilbert* (London: A&C Black, 1929), 120, includes quotes from Gilbert, who remembers being there with Toole and Irving, but doesn't mention Hicks, who later described the night in 'Londoner's Diary', *Evening Standard*, 24 December 1931, 6.

6 Cecil Gilbert (ed.), 'Study Diary, 13 March 1893', *The Studio Diaries of Alfred Gilbert between 1890 and 1897, Volume One, 1890–1894* (Newcastle upon Tyne: C. Gilbert, 1987).

7 Richard Dorment, *Alfred Gilbert* (New Haven and London: Paul Mellon Centre for Studies in British Art by Yale University Press, 1985), 112–113.

8 The most recent biographical accounts of Alfred Gilbert's life are by the art historian Richard Dorment: see his biography, *Alfred Gilbert*, and the catalogue to the Royal Academy exhibition in 1986. Isabel McAllister had the benefit of knowing Gilbert personally, but her devotion to him and the biographical conventions of the time meant her life of 1929 teeters on the edge of hagiography. Joseph Hatton's interview of 1903 (*The Easter Art Annual*) offers

a contemporary insight, as do the fascinating studio diaries of 1890–1901, edited by his grandson Cecil Gilbert. Jason Edwards's *Alfred Gilbert's Aestheticism* (2006) provides context to his life and times. *Shadow of Eros*, by Gilbert's nephew, artist Adrian Bury, appeared in 1954 and is slightly more balanced than McAllister, but hazy on sources. London County Council, *Survey of London: Volumes 31 & 32, St James Westminster, Part 2* (London: London County Council, 1963) is also invaluable (see *British History Online*, http://www.british-history.ac.uk/survey-london/vols31-2/pt2).

9 Cecil Gilbert (ed.), *The Studio Diaries*.
10 Ibid.
11 Joseph Hatton, 'The Life and Work of Alfred Gilbert', *The Easter Art Annual* (unknown publisher, 1903), 13–17.
12 Isabel McAllister, *Alfred Gilbert*, 107.
13 London County Council, *Survey of London*.
14 Richard Dorment, *Alfred Gilbert*, 138.
15 Matt Cook, *London and the Culture of Homosexuality, 1885–1914* (Cambridge: Cambridge University Press, 2003), 24; London County Council, *Survey of London*, 101–10.
16 *The Times*, 30 June 1893.
17 Joseph Hatton, *The Easter Art Annual*, 13–17.
18 *The Times*, 13 October 1893.
19 *The Times*, 23 September 1893.
20 *The Times*, 17 July 1893.

2. A People's Place

1 *The Times*, 30 June 1893.
2 *The Times*, 19 May 1900.

3 Peter Bird, *The First Food Empire: A History of J. Lyons & Co.* (London: Phillimore, 2000), 51.
4 *New York Times*, 19 May 1900.
5 Richard Dorment, *Alfred Gilbert*, 245.
6 London County Council, *Survey of London*.
7 *The Times*, 7 August 1923.

3. Shopkeepers Take on the World

1 *Bolton Evening News*, 25 August 1904.
2 Ibid.
3 *The Times*, 3 September 1902.
4 *ILN*, 28 March 1903.
5 *Millom Gazette*, 26 August 1904.
6 *Preston Herald*, 27 August 1904.
7 *London Daily News*, 25 August 1904.
8 *Preston Herald*, 27 August 1904.
9 *Bolton Evening News*, 25 August 1904.
10 *ODNB*.
11 Amy Henderson, 'Why the Department Store Brought Freedom for the Turn of the Century Woman', *Smithsonian Magazine*, 13 March 2013, https://www.smithsonianmag.com/Smithsonian-institution/why-the-department-store-brought-freedom-for-the-turn-of-the-century-woman-2078832
12 Lindy Woodhead, *Shopping, Seduction & Mr Selfridge* (London: Profile Books, 2008), 5.
13 For the origins of the word 'Piccadilly' see *The London Encyclopaedia* (3rd edition, London: Macmillan, 2003), by Christopher Hibbert, Ben Weinreb, John Keay, Julia Keay and Matthew Weinreb, and the *Oxford English Dictionary*. The word crops up in two other references,

both of which reflect the area's reputation as a place where dressing up was encouraged: Victorians coined the terms 'Piccadilly weeper' for a long side-whiskers worn without a beard – and 'Piccadilly window' for a monocle.

14 *Bucks Examiner*, 22 October 1915.

15 *Tewkesbury Register*, 25 December 1909.

16 Quoted in Madeleine Ginsburg, 'The Making and Distribution of Clothes', *Costume*, (London: Costume Society by the Dept of Textiles, V&A Museum), vol. 1, supplement 1 (1967), 14–22.

17 *Morning Post*, 1 January 1909, quoted in Thomas Harding, *Legacy* (London: William Heinemann, 2019), 175.

18 Quoted in Jerry White, *London in the 20th Century* (London: Bodley Head, 2016), 312.

19 The *OED* cites the *New York Daily Tribune*, 19 September 1890, as one of the earliest examples: 'I Met Him "Window-shopping" in Broadway . . .'

20 Quoted in Matt Houlbrook, *Queer London* (Chicago: University of Chicago Press, 2005), 47.

21 Simon Bradley and Nikolaus Pevsner, *London 6: Westminster* (Pevsner Architectural Guides: Buildings of England) (New Haven; London: Yale University Press, 2003), 452.

22 Ibid., 155.

23 *The Builder*, 27 April 1907, 497.

24 Quoted in London County Council, *Survey of London*, 85–100.

25 *The Times*, 3 October 1912.

26 *New York Times*, 3 February 1924.

27 Andrew Martin, *Underground, Overground: A Passenger's History of the Tube* (London: Profile Books, 2012), 12.

28 *ODNB*.

29 Ibid.
30 Douglas Rose, *Tiles of the Unexpected Underground* (London: Capital Transport Publishing, 2007), 3.
31 'Conquistador of Metroland', *The Economist*, 17 December 2014, https://www.economist.com/christmas-specials/2014/12/17/conquistador-of-metroland.
32 *ODNB*.
33 Andrew Martin, *Underground, Overground*, 142.

4. Suffragettes and Shop Girls

1 *The Times*, 2 March 1912.
2 Ibid.
3 *Leicester Daily Post*, 7 March 1912; Elizabeth Crawford, *The Women's Suffrage Movement: A Reference Guide, 1866–1928* (London: UCL Press, 1999), 74–5.
4 *The Times*, 2 March 1912.
5 *The Times*, 7 March 1912.
6 Richard Dorment, *Alfred Gilbert*, 270–1.
7 Peter Gurney, *The Making of Consumer Culture in Modern Britain* (London: Bloomsbury Academic, 2019), 106.
8 Ibid.
9 *The Times*, 14 December 1911.
10 Quoted in Fern Riddell, *Death in Ten Minutes: The Forgotten Life of Radical Suffragette Kitty Marion* (London: Hodder & Stoughton, 2018), 128.
11 Christine Woodworth, 'The Company She Kept: The Radical Activism of Actress Kitty Marion from Piccadilly Circus to Times Square', *Theatre History Studies* (Pleasant Hill, California) vol. 32 (2012), 80–92, 252. See also Viv Gardner and Diane Atkinson, *Kitty Marion: Actor and*

Activist (Manchester, Manchester University Press, 2019) [online access].

12 H. Leslie, *More Ha'pence than Kicks: Being Some Things Remembered* (London: Macdonald, 1943), 99. Quoted in Naomi Paxton, *Stage Rights!: The Actresses' Franchise League, Activism and Politics 1908* (Manchester: Manchester University Press, 2018).

13 'Taking Tea and Talking Politics: The Role of Tearooms', *Historic England*, https://historicengland.org.uk/research/inclusive-heritage/womens-history/suffrage/taking-tea-and-talking-politics

14 Elizabeth Crawford, 'WALKS/Suffrage Stories: Suffragettes and Tea Rooms: The Criterion Restaurant, Kate Frye, and the Actresses' Franchise League', *Woman and Her Sphere*, 5 September 2012, https://womanandhersphere.com/2012/09/05/suffrage-stories-suffragettes-and-tea-rooms-the-criterion-restaurant-kate-frye-and-the-actresses-franchise-league

15 Naomi Paxton, *Stage Rights!*, 108.

16 *Votes for Women*, 23 April 1909.

17 *The Times*, 25 May 1914.

18 *The Times*, 6 & 7 June 1913.

19 Jerry White, *London in the Twentieth Century*, 184.

20 Kellie K. Bradshaw, 'Reality, Expectations and Fears: Women Shop Assistants in London, 1890–1914', D. Phil. Dissertation (George Mason University, 2019), 26.

21 Somerset Maugham, *Of Human Bondage* (London: Vintage, 2000; originally published William Heinemann, 1915), 569.

22 Alison Adburgham, *Shops and Shopping, 1800–1914: Where, and in What Manner the Well-Dressed English Woman Bought Her Clothes* (London: George Allen & Unwin, 1981; first published 1964), 243.

23 See, for example, Lise Shapiro Sanders, *Consuming Fantasies: Labor, Leisure and the London Shopgirl, 1880–1920* (Columbus: Ohio State University Press, 2006).
24 Robert Fabian, *London after Dark*, 5.
25 Lindy Woodhead, *Shopping, Seduction & Mr Selfridge*, 5.
26 Kellie K. Bradshaw, 'Reality, Expectations and Fears', 73.
27 *The Londonderry Sentinel*, 13 February 1908.
28 Ibid.
29 11 February 1907.
30 Elizabeth Ewing and Alice Mackrell, *History of 20th Century Fashion* (London: Batsford, 1992), 36.

5. 'Now You've Got Yer Khaki On'

Jerry White's *Zeppelin Nights: London in the First World War*, Vintage, 2015, and Ian Castle's *The First Blitz: Bombing London in the First World War*, Osprey Publishing, 2015, are both excellent on this period.

1 Vera Brittain, *Testament of Youth* (London: Virago, 1978), 82.
2 Ibid., 211.
3 Ibid., 115.
4 Ibid.
5 Ibid., 116.
6 Ibid., 118–19.
7 Christoph Ribbat, *Flickering Light: A History of Neon* (London: Reaktion Books, 2011), 8.
8 'Former Rialto Cinema and Cafe de Paris', list entry, *Historic England*, https://historicengland.org.uk/listing/the-list/list-entry/1264006
9 Midge Gillies, *Marie Lloyd: The One and Only* (London: Victor Gollancz, 1999), 250.

10 W. MacQueen-Pope, *Goodbye Piccadilly*, 151–2.
11 Jerry White, *Zeppelin Nights*, chapter 2.
12 Ibid.
13 Helen Brown, 'How "It's a Long Way to Tipperary" Became the Hit of the First World War', *Financial Times*, 29 May 2017.
14 Matt Houlbrook, *Queer London*, 57.
15 Jerry White, *Zeppelin Nights*.
16 Ibid.
17 Daniel Farson, *Marie Lloyd and the Music Hall* (London: Tom Stacey, 1972), 84.
18 *ODNB*.
19 Lyn Gardner, 'Ladies as Gentlemen: The Cross-Dressing Women of Edwardian Musical Theatre', *Guardian*, 13 May 2010, https://www.theguardian.com/music/2010/may/13/cross-dressing-women-musical-theatre
20 *Bioscope*, 21 August 1916.
21 'Vesta Tilley', *National Fairground and Circus Archive*, University of Sheffield, https://www.sheffield.ac.uk/nfca/researchandarticles/vestatilley

6. 'The Wickedest Pavement in England'

1 See trial reports in *The Times*: 25 May & 1 June 1917.
2 Robert Fabian, *London after Dark*, 10.
3 See also 'Historical Glory of the Regent Palace Hotel, London', *Regent Palace Hotel*, http://www.regentpalace-hotel.co.uk/history.htm and LMA.
4 David Dean, *The Thirties: Recalling the English Architectural Scene* (London: Trefoil, 1983), quoted in 'Regent Palace Hotel (Main Building and Bridge)' list entry,

Historic England, https://historicengland.org.uk/listing/the-list/list-entry/1391115

5 *Building,* May 1935, quoted in https://www.telegraph.co.uk/travel/destinations/europe/united-kingdom/england/london/articles/london-regent-palace-hotel

6 Quentin Crisp, *The Naked Civil Servant* (London: Flamingo, 1985), 84.

7 A. E. Richardson, 'London Architecture in 1916', *The Burlington Magazine for Connoisseurs* (London), vol. 30, no. 167 (February 1917), 82–3.

8 The Regent Palace Hotel list entry, J. Lyons & Co., https://www.kzwp.com/lyons1/regent.htm

9 Hotel prices from the *Scotsman*, 29 November 1917.

10 Oliver Smith, 'London's Lost "Palace for the People" That Was once the Biggest Hotel in Europe', *Telegraph*, 26 February 2019, https://www.telegraph.co.uk/travel/destinations/europe/united-kingdom/england/london/articles/london-regent-palace-hotel

11 *Ballymena Observer*, 27 August 1915.

12 Laura Ugolini, 'The Illicit Consumption of Military Uniforms in Britain, 1914–1918', *Journal of Design History*, vol. 24, no. 2, Uniforms in Design History, edited by Artemis Yagou (2011), 125–38.

13 Robert Fabian, *London after Dark*, 109.

14 Rob Baker, 'Neon-lit Debauchery and the Wrong God – the Fascinating History of Piccadilly Circus', *Telegraph*, 19 February 2019, https://www.telegraph.co.uk/travel/destinations/europe/united-kingdom/england/london/articles/the-fascinating-history-of-piccadilly-circus

15 Jerry White, *Zeppelin Nights*, chapter 9.

16 Ibid.

17 'The Women Police Service', *UK Parliament*, https://www.

parliament.uk/about/living-heritage/transformingsociety/electionsvoting/womenvote/case-studies-women-parliament/what-difference/seizing-the-initiative/the-women-police-service

18 *The People,* 18 February 1917; Norinne married for a second time, in July 1918. Her new husband was a used-car salesman from Shepherd's Bush who was a sergeant in the Army Services Corps. They separated and Richard married for the second of four times in 1925. Norinne died in 1934, aged forty.

19 Jerry White, *Zeppelin Nights.*

20 This changed in 1917 but there was still no warning during the night. See *Zeppelin Nights* on maroons.

21 Jerry White, *Zeppelin Nights*; Wendy Moore, *Endell Street* (London: Atlantic, 2020), 140.

22 James Fox, '"Traitor Painters": Artists and Espionage in the First World War, 1914–18', *British Art Journal*, vol. 9, no. 3 (Spring 2009), 62–8.

23 Jerry White, *Zeppelin Nights.*

24 Ian Castle, *The First Blitz*, 96–9.

25 Ibid.

26 Virginia Woolf diary, 20 October 1917, in Anne Olivier Bell (ed.), *The Diary of Virginia Woolf, Volume I: 1915–1919* (London: Hogarth Press, 1977), 63.

27 Ibid.

28 Ibid., 22 October 1917, 65.

29 *Western Gazette,* 31 May 1918.

30 *Sheffield Daily Telegraph*, 14 November 1918.

31 Guy Cuthbertson, *Peace at Last: A Portrait of Armistice Day, 11 November 1918* (New Haven: Yale University Press, 2018), 51.

32 Alwyn W. Turner, *The Last Post: Music, Remembrance*

and the Great War (London: Aurum, 2014), xvi. As Turner points out, there were no bugles at the Cenotaph that morning but the 'Last Post' was sounded at several other points in the West End.

7. Under Ground in the Jazz Age

1 *ODNB*; Alison Child, *Tell Me I'm Forgiven: The Story of Forgotten Stars Gwen Farrar and Norah Blaney* (Machynlleth: Tollington Press, 2019).
2 *C&C*, 70.
3 Ibid.
4 D. J. Taylor, *Bright Young People*: *The Rise and Fall of a Generation 1918–1940* (London: Chatto & Windus, 2007), 96; 'Cecil Beaton's Bright Young Things', *You Magazine*, 8 March 2020, https://www.you.co.uk/cecil-beatons-bright-young-things
5 Nancy Mitford to Mark Ogilvie-Grant, April [the exact date isn't given], c1932 quoted in Selina Hastings, *Nancy Mitford* (London: Hamish Hamilton, 1985), 75.
6 Richard Rayner, 'Some Foggy Nights in London Town', *LA Times*, 4 January 2009, https://www.latimes.com/archives/la-xpm-2009-jan-04-ca-dj-taylor4-story.html
7 *Sheffield Daily Telegraph*, 25 January 1929.
8 Ibid.
9 Ibid.
10 *Graphic,* 2 February 1929.
11 *Daily Mirror*, 30 January 1929.
12 *Western Daily Press* (Bristol), 26 January 1929.
13 Robert Fabian, *London after Dark*, 119.
14 Ibid., 120. See also Rose Collis, *Colonel Barker's Monstrous Regiment: A Tale of Female Husbandry* (London: Virago, 2001).

8. The Moving World of the Underground Railway

1 *ILN*, 12 March 1927.

2 *ODNB*; 'Frank Pick: The Man Behind London Transport's Identity', London Transport Museum, https://www.ltmuseum.co.uk/collections/projects-partnerships/frank-pick

3 Pick's vision is remembered in the 2016 installation at Piccadilly Circus Tube's concourse. Artists Ben Langlands and Nikki Bell conceived their artwork after rootling through Pick's personal papers, where they discovered two columns of four words that he had scribbled down before he was about to deliver a speech. The two-metre-high bronze words, linked by 'less than' signs (Beauty < Immortality, Utility < Perfection, Goodness < Righteousness and Truth < Wisdom), in Johnston typeface, sit on a marble wall, lit by LED lights, next to the Tube roundel he invented showing the destination 'Frank Pick'.

4 Christian Barman, *The Man Who Built London Transport: A Biography of Frank Pick* (Newton Abbot: David & Charles, 1979), 121.

5 *The Times*, 8 March 1927.

6 *ILN*, 31 July 1926.

7 According to *The Times*, 10 December 1928, the 25 million passengers it handled a year was 17 times the figure it welcomed in its first year of operation.

8 *The Times*, 10 December 1928.

9 Christian Barman, *The Man Who Built London Transport*, 122.

10 Ibid., 124.

11 *The Times*, 6 September 1928.

12 *ILN*, 27 September 1919.

13 *Daily Graphic*, 13 May 1925.
14 Ibid.
15 *The Times*, 28 December 1931.
16 Richard Dorment, *Alfred Gilbert*, 304.
17 *Evening Standard*, 12 October 1928.
18 *ILN*, 7 February 1925.
19 Isabel McAllister, *Alfred Gilbert*, 110.
20 *The Times*, 13 February 1925.
21 *The Times*, 16 February 1925.
22 *The Times*, 8 March 1928.
23 *The Times*, 6 September 1928.
24 *The Times*, 29 September 1928
25 Ibid.
26 Bill Lancaster, *The Department Store: A Social History* (Leicester: Leicester University Press, 1995), 50.
27 It is a convention that took hold, despite the established etiquette in other parts of the world, that those riding an escalator should stand on the same side as the side on which they drive their car. In Australia and New Zealand, where motorists drive on the left, users of escalators stand on the left; the fact that the slow lane is on the *left* on British motorways adds a further ambiguity. The habit of standing on the right when using the underground still produces clusters of bemused tourists who can bring a hurrying passenger to a frustrated halt.
28 Annie Mole, 'Bumper Harris Was My Great, Great, Grandfather', *Going Underground*, 10 September 2007, https://london-underground.blogspot.com/2007/09/bumper-harris-was-my-great-great.html
29 *ILN*, 14 October 1911.
30 Sam Selvon, *The Lonely Londoners* (London: Penguin Modern Classics, 2006), 72–3.

31 *ILN*, 15 December 1928.
32 Ibid.
33 'Piccadilly Circus Underground Station Booking Hall Concourse and Bronzework to Pavement Subway Entrances' list entry, *Historic England*, https://historicengland.org.uk/listing/the-list/list-entry/1226877
34 See 'Renzo Picasso' archive entry, http://www.renzopicasso.com/renzo-picasso

9. Private Passions behind Closed Doors

1 *The Times*, 1 November 1932.
2 *Lancashire Daily Post*, 22 November 1932; *Yorkshire Post*, 11 November 1932.
3 *Lancashire Daily Post*, 22 November 1932.
4 *Lincolnshire Echo*, 13 December 1932..
5 *The Times*, 5 November 1932.
6 *The Times*, 11 November 1932.
7 *Citizen*, 2 November 1932.
8 *Western Daily Press*, 3 March 1930; *Birmingham Gazette*, 5 March 1930.
9 For reports of the inquest see *Liverpool Echo*, 4 November 1932.
10 *Lincolnshire Echo*, 13 December 1932.
11 Alexa Neale, 'Murder at the "Love Hut": At Home With Elvira Barney', in Marianela Barrios Aquino, Eduard Campillo-Funollet, Naomi Daw, Ketan Jha, Myles Logan Miller, Alexa Neale and Tom Ottway (eds), *Beyond the Boundaries of Home: Interdisciplinary Approaches* (Brighton: University of Sussex Library, 2017), 10–23.
12 Douglas G. Browne and E. V. Tullett, *Bernard Spilsbury: His Life and Cases* (London: The Companion Book Club, 1952), 405.

13 *Daily Mirror*, 4 June 1932.
14 *Daily Mirror*, 5 July 1932.
15 *The Times*, Law Section, 23 December 2003, 13.
16 Rob Baker, 'The Café de Paris and How the Socialite Elvira Barney Got Away With Murder', *Flashbak*, 25 July 2019, https://flashbak.com/the-café-de-paris-and-how-the-socialite-elvira-barney-got-away-with-murder-417788
17 Ibid.

10. A 'British Hollywood'

1 For current research into Anna May Wong see https://halfcastewoman.substack.com
2 A character based on Anna May Wong features in the Netflix mini-series *Hollywood,* set in the 1950s. A young director tries to give her a leading part, but the studio executive warns him against this casting decision.
3 Paul Matthew St Pierre, *E. A. Dupont and His Contribution to British Film* (Madison: Farleigh Dickinson University Press, 2010), 82.
4 Graham Hodges, *Anna May Wong: From Laundryman's Daughter to Hollywood Legend* (Hong Kong: Hong Kong University Press, 2012), 17.
5 Robbie Aitken, 'Embracing Germany: Interwar German Society and Black Germans through the Eyes of African-American Reporters', *Journal of American Studies*, vol. 52, no. 2 (2018), 447–73, http://shura.shu.ac.uk/14021
6 Paul Matthew St Pierre, *E. A. Dupont*, 83.
7 *Sketch*, 26 December 1928.
8 *Citizen,* 31 May 1933.
9 Graham Hodges, *Anna May Wong,* 117.
10 *Staffordshire Sentinel*, 9 January 1929.

11 Graham Hodges, *Anna May Wong*, 72.
12 *Sphere*, 14 July 1928; *Sketch*, 8 August 1928.
13 *Leven Advertiser & Wemyss Gazette*, 15 September 1928.
14 Graham Hodges, *Anna May Wong*, 45.
15 *Sketch*, 5 June 1929.
16 Ibid.
17 Graham Hodges, *Anna May Wong*, 82.
18 His character would later appear in season five of the BBC's *Peaky Blinders*.
19 Marek Kohn, *Dope Girls: The Birth of the British Drug Underground* (London: Granta, 1992), 128.
20 Ibid., 32.
21 Ibid., 33.
22 Ibid., 144.
23 Anne Witchard, 'Thomas Burke' list entry, *London Fictions*, https://www.londonfictions.com/thomas-burke-limehouse-nights.html
24 Quoted in notes to remastering of film, Milestone Film & Video and the British Film Institute, 2003.
25 *Tatler*, 13 February 1929.
26 *ILN*, 16 February 1929.
27 *Illustrated Sporting News*, 15 December 1928.
28 *Evening Telegraph*, 25 September 1928.
29 Ibid.
30 Ibid.
31 *ILN*, 24 November 1928.
32 Quoted in notes to *The Lodger* by Professor Neil Sinyard.
33 Patrick McGillian, *Alfred Hitchcock: A Life in Darkness and Light* (London: John Wiley, 2003), 82.

11. Friendship and Romance over a Cup of Tea

1 LMA has an extensive collection of items connected to the Lyons Teashops. Letters of Reminiscence from former Nippies (ACC/3527/235), created in 1990, is particularly useful.
2 *The Times*, 7 January 1914.
3 *The Times*, 18 January 1928.
4 Ibid.
5 *Nottingham Journal*, 19 January 1928.
6 Matt Houlbrook, *Queer London*, 72.
7 Judith Walkowitz, *Nights Out: Life in Cosmopolitan London* (New Haven: Yale University Press, 2012), 195.
8 LMA, ACC/3527/235.
9 Peter Bird, *The First Food Empire*, 118.
10 Judith Walkowitz, *Nights Out*, 10.
11 *Picture Post*, 4 March 1939.
12 Peter Bird, *The First Food Empire*, 116.
13 Dr Kate Law, '"The Sister Found Romance. Nell Found Her Adventure and Fortune as the Uncrowned Queen of the Nippys": Nell Bacon, J. Lyons & Co.'s "Nippy No. 1" by Leila Kassir', *Women's History Network*, 20 June 2020, https://womenshistorynetwork.org/the-sister-found-romance-nell-found-her-adventure-and-fortune-as-the-uncrowned-queen-of-the-nippys-nell-bacon-j-lyons-co-s-nippy-no-1-by-leila-kas
14 Judith Walkowitz, *Nights Out*, 206.
15 Peter Bird, *The First Food Empire*, 111.
16 Judith Walkowitz, *Nights Out*, 204.
17 LMA.
18 LMA, letter from Suzanne Howe.
19 Peter Bird, *The First Food Empire*, 119 & 179.

20 *ILN*, 15 November 1930.
21 LMA.
22 LMA.
23 Camac, LMA.
24 David Wiff, 'Saucy Secrets of Britain's First Nude Show-Girls', *Mail Online*, 12 February 2016, https://www.dailymail.co.uk/femail/article-3444007/Saucy-secrets-Britain-s-nude-showgirls-six-performers-reveal-thrilling-appear-legendary-Windmill-Theatre.html
25 See June Rose, *Marie Stopes and the Sexual Revolution* (London: Faber, 1992), 132.

12. The Simpsons Man

1 Quoted in David Wainwright, *The British Tradition: Simpson – a World of Style* (London: Quiller Press, 1996), 63.
2 Ibid., 4 & 7.
3 Quoted ibid., 7.
4 Bronwen Edwards, *Making the West End Modern: Space, Architecture and Shopping in 1930s London*, PhD thesis, November 2004, UAL, 115.
5 See Joseph Emberton Archive, Archives Hub, https://archiveshub.jisc.ac.uk/designarchives/archives/c26a2dec-4236-34a6-8763-c6d58a3d6171
6 *ODNB*.
7 *Daily Herald*, 30 April 1936.
8 David Wainwright, *The British Tradition*, 17.
9 *Tatler*, 6 May 1936.
10 Ibid.
11 For a fascinating discussion on this see Bronwen Edwards, 'Making the West End Modern'.
12 Advert in *Store*, December 1936, 73, ibid., 430.

13 Ibid., 217.
14 Sibyl Moholy, *Moholy-Nagy: Experiment in Totality* (Cambridge, Massachusetts & London: MIT Press, 1969), 120. For further details of Moholy and the influence of modernism see Caroline Maclean, *Circles and Squares: The Lives and Art of the Hampstead Modernists* (London: Bloomsbury, 2021).
15 David Wainwright, *The British Tradition*, 27.
16 Sibyl Moholy, *Moholy-Nagy*, 121–2.
17 Bronwen Edwards, 'Making the West End Modern', 180.
18 David Wainwright, *The British Tradition*, 34.

13. From Cockpit to Ski Slope

1 Mark Haworth-Booth, *E. McKnight Kauffer: A Designer and His Public* (London: Gordon Fraser, 1979), 74.
2 Ibid.
3 Ibid., 25.
4 Peter Bird, *The First Food Empire*, 121.
5 Midge Gillies, *Amy Johnson: Queen of the Air* (London: Weidenfeld & Nicolson, 2003), 117.
6 *The London Encyclopaedia*, 483.
7 Thelma H. Benjamin, 'London: Shops & Shopping', 102, quoted in Geraldine Biddle-Perry, 'The Rise of "The World's Largest Sport and Athletic Outfitter": A Study of Gamage's of Holborn, 1878–1913', *Sport in History* (Abingdon), vol. 34, no. 2 (2014), 295–317.
8 'What's Happened to Lillywhites?', 2 April 2006, *Telegraph*, https://www.telegraph.co.uk/finance/2935802/Whats-happened-to-Lillywhites.html
9 See V&A Museum Collection, Museum No. T.85–2009.
10 *ODNB*.

11 *The Bee*, August 1927.
12 Rose Staveley-Wadham, 'Hiking in the 1930s', *British Newspaper Archive*, 1 June 2021, https://blog.britishnewspaperarchive.co.uk/2021/06/01/hiking-in-the-1930s
13 *BMJ*, 11 May 2006.
14 Boots Archives, *A History of Boots the Chemists*, (Nottingham, 2007), 12.
15 *The Bee*, March 1949.

14. Here We Go Again

1 Robert Fabian, *Fabian of the Yard*, 64.
2 Ibid.
3 Ibid., 65.
4 The IRA, a few weeks later, was believed to be behind cutting the wires in four telephone boxes in the Piccadilly Circus area, according to the *Nottingham Journal*, 16 August 1939.
5 Penelope Middelboe, Donald Fry and Christopher Grace (eds), *We Shall Never Surrender: Wartime Diaries, 1939–1945* (London: Macmillan, 2011), 15.
6 Auxiliary Territorial Service entry, *National Army Museum*, https://www.nam.ac.uk/explore/auxiliary-territorial-service
7 Julie Summers, *Fashion on the Ration: Style in the Second World War* (London: Profile Books, 2015), 62.
8 David Wainwright, *The British Tradition*, 52–55.
9 *The Times*, 11 August 1939.
10 *Yorkshire Post*, 12 August 1939.
11 *Daily Mirror*, 11 August 1939.
12 *Liverpool Echo*, 11 August 1939.
13 *The Times*, 12 August 1939.
14 Chris Wild, 'To Hide From WWII Bombs, London Goes

Dark', *Mashable*, 13 October 2014, https://mashable.com/archive/to-hide-from-wwii-bombs-london-goes-dark
15 *ILN*, 30 September 1939.
16 Andrew Martin, *Underground, Overground*, 226.
17 Ibid.
18 *ILN*, 5 October 1940.
19 Andrew Martin, *Underground, Overground*, 228.
20 Midge Gillies, *Waiting for Hitler* (London: Hodder & Stoughton, 2006), 103.
21 Edward Burra, title unknown, 1940, Tate, https://www.tate.org.uk/art/artworks/burra-title-not-known-n05165
22 Rebecca Scragg, 'Hanging Hitler: Joseph Flatter's *Mein Kamp Illustrated* Series, 1938–1942', in Shulamith Behr and Marian Malet, *Arts in Exile in Britain 1933–1945: Politics and Cultural Identity*, Yearbook of the Research Centre for German and Austrian Exile Studies, vol. 6 (2004).
23 IWM Sound Archive, 4765, Reel 2, 1980.
24 6 April 1940.
25 *Middlesex Chronicle*, 5 January 1918.
26 *Advertiser* and *Gazette*, 15 January 1932.
27 Barbara Nixon, *Raiders Overhead* (London: Lindsay Drummond, 1943), 36.
28 Quoted in Midge Gillies, *Waiting for Hitler*, 75.

15. The Blitz-Proof Café de Paris

1 Joyce Grenfell & James Roose-Evans (eds), *Darling Ma: Letters to Her Mother, 1932–44* (London: Sceptre, 1997), 159.
2 *ODNB*.
3 See Catherine Tackley, 'Race, Identity and the Meaning

of Jazz in 1940s Britain', in Jon Stratton and Nabeel Zuberi (eds), *Black Popular Music in Britain since 1945* (London: Routledge, 2016), 11–26.

4 Quoted in *ODNB*.

5 His ashes still reside at the school.

6 *C&C*, 116.

7 Ibid., 118.

8 Ibid., 115.

9 Miles Edmund Whitelock, IWM 16499.

10 See 'Group Captain J Darwen, DFC' entry, IWM, https://www.iwm.org.uk/collections/item/object/10082

11 R.J. Minney, *The Two Pillars of Charing Cross: The Story of a Famous Hospital* (London: Cassell, 1967), 196, describes a couple who sound just like the Darwens.

12 Neil Belton, *The Good Listener: Helen Bamber, A Life against Cruelty* (London: Phoenix, 1999), 49.

13 IWM 29164.

14 Neil Belton, *The Good Listener*, 32.

15 Ibid., 47–8.

16 Commonwealth War Graves Commission, *Civilian War Dead in the United Kingdom, 1939–1945* (London: Peter Singlehurst, 7 vols, 1954–1957).

17 Charles Graves, *Off the Record* (London: unknown publisher, 1941), 109.

18 For more information on Boogie Barnes see Micky Barnes, *Ad – An Inside View of Advertising* (London: Bachman & Turner, 1973). I am indebted to Jonathan Kydd and Jill Weekes for further information and to Jo Turner for putting me in touch with Ian King, who increased my football knowledge and sent me a photo of Boogie and various press cuttings.

19 My thanks to Jenny Seeman, MSc, Manager, Archives,

Royal Roads University for further information about Kathleen ('Kat') Humphreys.

20 *People,* 8 June 1941.

21 Helen Stevens, IWM 2301.

22 *C&C*, 56.

23 IWM ('London Can Take It: The Blitz') 5340.

24 *Guardian* obituary, 27 November 2018.

25 IWM 29069.

26 John Mills, *Up in the Clouds, Gentlemen Please* (London: Weidenfeld & Nicolson, 1980), 170–1.

27 Pamela Margaret Jackes, IWM 10319.

28 Quoted in Christina L. Baade, *Victory through Harmony: The BBC and Popular Music in World War II* (Oxford: Oxford University Press, 2011), 2.

29 *C&C*, 120.

30 Ibid., 117.

31 Ibid., 121.

16. The Bomb Drops

1 The main official sources for the explosion at the Café de Paris are: Westminster City Archives (CD/2/5, 1213; CD/2/5; CD/2/17; CD/6/129; CD/22/142); TNA (HO 193/25; HO 202/3 City of Westminster District, 8/9 March 1941, entry number 5, HO 203/6, reports for 8/9 March 1941; HO 193/23 sheet 56/18 NW, HO 198/25, HO 193/68, CO 981/150); LMA (RM/22/61; LCC/FB/WAR/LFR/01/023; LCC/PH/WAR/03/017). See also Andrew James, 'The Bombing of the Café de Paris', TNA, 8 March 2013, https://blog.nationalarchives.gov.uk/the-bombing-of-the-cafe-de-paris. IWM oral history accounts, in addition to those already mentioned, are: Anon 10346;

Robert Beauchamp Duff 10344; Mrs Blair-Hickman 2301–2 [first name not available]; Richard Andrew Palethorpe Todd 29069; Trouncer 2303 [first name not available].

2 Mrs Blair-Hickman.

3 Ibid.

4 *C&C*, 118.

5 Trouncer 2303.

6 Mollie Panter-Downes, *London War Notes 1939–1945* (London: Persephone, 2014), 138–9.

7 Juliet Gardiner, *The Blitz: The British under Attack* (London: HarperPress, 2011), 274.

8 *C&C*, 119.

9 Private Papers of Miss B. L. Roose, IWM.

10 *C&C*, 122.

11 R.J. Minney, *The Two Pillars of Charing Cross*, 197.

12 Ibid.

13 Berkeley IWM.

14 Rob Baker, 'Murder, Fascists and Barbara Windsor – Five Strange Things That Happened in London Hotels', *Telegraph*, 10 December 2019, https://www.telegraph.co.uk/travel/destinations/europe/united-kingdom/england/london/articles/curious-tales-from-five-london-hotels

15 Neil Belton, *The Good Listener*, 52.

16 Diary of Anthony Heap, LMA, Acc/2243/15/1

17. Rainbow Corner

1 25,000, according to the *New York Times*, 17 March 1944.

2 See 'U.S. Servicemen Visit the American Red Cross Rainbow Corner Club in London During World War II' film clip, *Critical Past*, https://www.criticalpast.com/

video/65675034688_American-Red-Cross-Center_policeman-directing_soldiers-leaving-building

3 MO, Diarist 5349_105, 29 March 1944.

4 *Daily Journal* (Vineland, New Jersey), 10 September 1943.

5 Ralph C. Hammond, *My GI Aching Back* (New York: Hobson Book Press, 1946), 16.

6 *ILN*, 19 January 1946.

7 *The Times*, 27 January 1981.

8 Kathleen Riley, *The Astaires: Fred & Adele* (Oxford: Oxford University Press, 2012), 79.

9 P. G. Wodehouse and Guy Bolton, *Bring on the Girls: The Improbable Story of Our Life in Musical Comedy, With Pictures to Prove It* (London: Herbert Jenkins, 1954), 178.

10 Deborah Devonshire, *Wait For Me! Memoirs of the Youngest Mitford Sister* (London: John Murray, 2010), 169.

11 Kathleen Riley, *The Astaires*, 132.

12 Ibid., 152.

13 Deborah Devonshire, *Wait For Me!*, 169.

14 Ibid., 170.

15 Ibid.

16 *New York Times* obituary, 10 October 1971.

17 Vernon F. Gay, *The Story of Rainbow Corner* (no publisher given, 1944), 23–4.

18 Brian S. Gunderson, '"Slanguage", Part I: Letters A–C', *Air Power History*, vol. 47, no. 4 (Winter 2000), 54–9.

19 Vernon F. Gay, *The Story of Rainbow Corner*, 21.

20 *Sketch*, 9 February 1944.

21 John Costello, *Love, Sex and War: Changing Values, 1939–45* (London: Collins, 1985), 315.

22 *Sketch*, 9 February 1944.

23 M. Nava, 'Wider Horizons and Modern Desire: The Contradictions of America and Racial Difference in

London 1935–45', *New Formations: A Journal of Culture, Theory, Politics*, 37 (Spring 1999), 71–91.

24 Ibid.

25 Ibid.; *Picture Post*, 17 July 1943.

26 Ralph C. Hammond, *My GI Aching Back*, 20.

27 Telephone interview with author, 3 July 2020.

28 'Pin Ball' entry, Getty Images, https://www.gettyimages.co.uk/detail/news-photo/in-the-amusement-room-at-rainbow-corner-the-red-cross-club-news-photo/3314893?adppopup=true

29 *Daily Mirror*, 28 December 1942.

30 *Daily Tribune* (Wisconsin Rapids), 7 May 1945.

31 *Gazette*, 9 April 1945.

32 *Lincolnshire Echo*, 11 April 1944.

33 Ibid.

34 Don Lasseter, *Their Deeds of Honor* (Xlibris, US, 2002), 50.

35 Ibid., 68.

36 Kathleen Riley, *The Astaires*, 183; *New York Times*, 17 March 1944.

37 *St Louis Post-Dispatch*, 26 December 1944.

38 Ibid.

39 *Salt Lake Tribune*, 6 December 1943.

40 Wilfred Basil Mann, *Was There a Fifth Man?: Quintessential Recollections* (Oxford: Pergamon Press, 1982), 16.

41 *Evening Sun* (Baltimore, Maryland), 2 January 1943.

42 Vernon F. Gay, *The Story of Rainbow Corner*, 22; Ralph C. Hammond, *My GI Aching Back*, 21.

43 *Lubbock Morning Avalanche*, 15 May 1943.

44 Ralph C. Hammond, *My GI Aching Back*, 21.

45 *Star Press* (Muncie, Indiana), 19 March 1943.

46 Ralph C. Hammond, *My GI Aching Back*, 24.

47 *Morning Call* (Allentown, Pennsylvania), 7 March 1944.
48 Ralph C. Hammond, *My GI Aching Back*, 23.

18. 'Hello Yank, Looking for a Good Time?'

1 Rick Atkinson, 'The Road to D-Day: Behind the Battle That Won the War', *Foreign Affairs*, Council on Foreign Relations, vol. 92, no. 4 (July/August 2013), 57.
2 Rob Baker, 'Neon-lit Debauchery and the Wrong God'.
3 Matthew Sweet, *The West End Front*, 315–16.
4 John Costello, *Love, Sex and War*, 315.
5 Ibid.
6 Ralph C. Hammond, *My GI Aching Back*, 18; *St Louis Post-Dispatch*, 26 December 1944.
7 John Costello, *Love, Sex and War*, 328.
8 Matthew Sweet, *The West End Front*, 315.
9 Sonya O. Rose, 'The "Sex Question" in Anglo-American Relations in the Second World War', *The International History Review*, vol. 20. no. 4 (December 1998), 887–8.
10 Ibid.
11 MO, Topic Collection, 77_163.
12 Judith Walkowitz, *Nights Out*, 174; Mike Hutton, *Life in 1940s London* (Stroud: Amberley, 2014).
13 James Morton, *Gangland Soho* (London: Piatkus, 2008), 103.
14 *San Francisco Examiner*, 9 June 1944.
15 *Morristown Gazette and Mail*, 14 June 1944.
16 Matthew Sweet, *The West End Front*, 316; Judith Walkowitz, *Nights Out*, 284.

19. The Light Returns

1 MO Topic Collections, Victory Celebrations 1945–6, 49-1-B, The day before VE Day.
2 Steve Hardwick & Duane E. Hodgin, *WWII Duty, Honor, Country: The Memories of Those Who Were There* (iUniverse), 17.
3 Gerald D. Swick, 'V-E Day 1945: The Celebration Heard 'Round the World', *Military Times*, 8 May 2019, https://www.militarytimes.com/off-duty/military-culture/2019/05/08/v-e-day-1945-the-celebration-heard-round-the-world
4 MO Report into Victory in Europe.
5 Sally Sheard, *The Passionate Economist: How Brian Abel-Smith Shaped Global Health and Social Welfare* (Bristol: Bristol University Press, Policy Press, 2014), 26.
6 'Rare Colour Footage of London on VJ Day', IWM, https://www.iwm.org.uk/history/rare-colour-footage-of-london-on-vj-day
7 *Scotsman*, 11 August 1945.
8 'Sergeant I M Davison, Sergeant J Hinzall, Sergeant L A Colarossi: killed; Squadron . . .' entry, TNA, AIR 81/13754; 'Lucien 'Louis' Colarossi' entry, *Roll of Honour*, https://www.roll-of-honour.org.uk/c/html/colarossi-lucien.html
9 Midge Gillies, *Amy Johnson*, 382.
10 Information given to the author.
11 *Times* obituary, 22 January 1944; Brian Kingcome, *A Willingness to Die* (Stroud: Tempus, 1999), 154; 'Supplement to the London Gazette, 30 November, 1943', *Gazette*, https://www.thegazette.co.uk/London/issue/36267/supplement/5242/data.pdf
12 *C&C*, 123.
13 *Britannia & Eve*, 1 March 1942.

14 The nightclub appears, as the Café Madrid, in *The Soldier's Art*, the eighth novel of Anthony Powell's *A Dance to the Music of Time* series, and in Jill Paton Walsh's Lord Peter Wimsey novel *The Attenbury Emeralds* (2010). Snakehips Johnson and the Café de Paris play key roles in *Moon over Soho* (2011), Ben Aaronovitch's fantasy/crime novel. The venue also appears in *Dear Mrs Bird* (2018) by A.J. Pearce and *Transcription* (2018) by Kate Atkinson. The bombing of the Café de Paris is a main plot point in Matthew Bourne's production of *Cinderella*.
15 Quoted in *ODNB*.
16 *Detroit Tribune*, 25 August 1945.
17 *Halifax Daily Courier & Guardian*, 18 August 1945; James Morton, *Gangland Soho*, 155.
18 *The Times*, 9 January 1946.

Postscript: The Digital Screen

1 *Telegraph* obituary, Zoe Gail, 21 February 2020; *Sunday Post*, 3 April 1949.
2 *Sunday Pictorial*, 10 April 1949.
3 Dominic Sandbrook, *White Heat: A History of Britain in the Swinging Sixties* (London: Little, Brown, 2006), xiii.
4 *ODNB*.
5 *Daily Mirror*, 16 March 1954.
6 Peter Wildeblood, *Against the Law* (Kindle ed.; London: Victor Gollancz, 2012).
7 Jeremy Reed, *The Dilly*, 114. I am indebted to Lachlan Mackinnon for pointing me to this book.
8 Nicholas Tomalin, 'Twenty-four Hours in Piccadilly Circus', *Nicholas Tomalin Reporting* (London: Andre

Deutsch, 1975), 300–7. I am indebted to John Stokes for drawing my attention to the original article.

9 Craig Brown, *One, Two, Three, Four* (London: Fourth Estate, 2020), 234.

10 Ibid., 541–3.

11 See *London Picture Archive*, https://www.londonpicturearchive.org.uk

12 Naomi Rovnick, 'London's Historic Criterion Restaurant Falls into Administration', *Financial Times*, 24 June 2015, https://www.ft.com/content/ca573f2a-1a6e-11e5-a130-2e7db721f996

13 Oliver Wainwright, 'Eros in a Snow Globe – The Perfect Christmas Decoration for London', *Guardian*, 3 December 2013, https://www.theguardian.com/artanddesign/2013/dec/03/eros-worlds-biggest-snow-globe-london-christmas

Select bibliography

Ackroyd, Peter, *Alfred Hitchcock* (London: Chatto & Windus, 2015)

Ackroyd, Peter, *Biography of London* (London: Vintage, 2000)

Adair, Zakiya R., 'Respectable Vamp: A Black Feminist Analysis of Florence Mills' Career in Early Vaudeville Theater', *Journal of African American Studies* (New York), Vol. 17, No. 1, Special Issue: Black Girls' and Women's Resistance Strategies (March 2013), 7–21

Adburgham, Alison, *Shops and Shopping 1800–1914: Where, and in What Manner the Well-Dressed English Woman Bought Her Clothes* (London: George Allen & Unwin, 1981; first published 1964)

Allport, Alan, *Browned Off and Bloody-Minded: The British Soldier Goes to War 1939–1945* (New Haven: Yale University Press, 2015)

Atkinson, Rick, 'The Road to D-Day: Behind the Battle that Won the Way', *Foreign Affairs*, Vol. 92, No. 4 (July/August 2013), 55–75 [https://www.foreignaffairs.com/articles/europe/2013-06-11/road-d-day]

Baade, Christina, L., *Victory through Harmony: The BBC and Popular Music in World War II* (Oxford: Oxford University Press, 2011)

Baker, Rob, 'Neon-lit Debauchery and the Wrong God – The Fascinating History of Piccadilly Circus' [https://www.telegraph.co.uk/travel/destinations/europe/united-kingdom/

england/london/articles/the-fascinating-history-of-piccadilly-circus]

Barman, Christian, *The Man Who Built London Transport: A Biography of Frank Pick* (Newton Abbot: David & Charles, 1979)

Barnes, Micky, *Ad – An Inside View of Advertising* (London: Bachman & Turner, 1973)

Barrett, Duncan & Nuala Calvi, *GI Brides: The Wartime Girls Who Crossed the Atlantic for Love* (London: Harper, 2013)

Bell, Amy Helen, *Murder Capital: Suspicious Deaths in London, 1933–53* (Manchester: Manchester University Press, 2015)

Bell, Anne Olivier (ed.), *The Diary of Virginia Woolf, Volume I: 1915–1919* (London: Hogarth Press, 1977)

Bell, P. M. H., *Twelve Turning Points of the Second World War* (New Haven: Yale University Press, 2011)

Belton, Neil, *The Good Listener: Helen Bamber, A Life against Cruelty* (London: Weidenfeld & Nicolson,1998)

Bengry, Justin, 'Courting the Pink Pound: Men Only and the Queer Consumer, 1935–39', *History Workshop Journal* (Oxford), No. 68 (Autumn 2009), 122–48

Bennett, Arnold, *Piccadilly, The Story of the Film* (London: The Readers Library, 1929)

Bennett, Todd M., *One World, Big Screen: Hollywood, the Allies, and World War II* (Chapel Hill: University of North Carolina Press, 2012)

Biddle-Perry, Geraldine, 'The Rise of "The World's Largest Sport and Athletic Outfitter": A Study of Gamage's of Holborn, 1878–1913', *Sport in History* (Abingdon), Vol. 34, No. 2 (2014) 295–317

Bird, Peter, *The First Food Empire: A History of J. Lyons & Co.* (London: Phillimore, 2000)

Bloom, J., 'An Island within an Island: V. S. Pritchett during World War II', *The Sewanee Review*, Vol. 121, No. 1 (Winter 2013), 1 59–77

Boots Archives, *A History of Boots the Chemists* (Nottingham, 2007)

Bradley, Simon & Pevsner, Nikolaus, *London 6: Westminster* (Pevsner Architectural Guides: Buildings of England) (New Haven & London: Yale University Press, 2003)

Bradshaw, Kellie K., 'Reality, Expectations and Fears: Women Shop Assistants in London, 1890-1914' D. Phil. dissertation (George Mason University, 2019)

Brittain, Vera, *Testament of Youth* (London: Virago, 1978)

Brown, Craig, *Four, Three, Two, One* (London: Fourth Estate, 2020)

Brown, Helen, 'How It's a Long Way to Tipperary became the Hit of the First World War', *Financial Times*, 29 May 2017

Browne, Douglas G. & Tullett, E. V. *Bernard Spilsbury: His Life and Cases* (London: The Companion Book Club, 1952)

Brox, Jane, *Brilliant: The Evolution of Artificial Light* (London: Souvenir Press, 2011)

Buckley, Craig, 'Graphic Constructions: The Experimental Typography of Edward Wright', *October* (Cambridge, Massachusetts), Vol. 136, New Brutalism (Spring 2011), 156–81

Burke, Thomas, *London in My Time* (London: Rich & Cowan, 1934)

Bury, Adrian, *Shadow of Eros: A Biographical and Critical Study of the Life and Works of Sir Alfred Gilbert* (London: Macdonald & Evans, 1954)

Butcher, Geoffrey, *Next to a Letter from Home: Major Glenn Miller's Wartime Band* (Edinburgh: Mainstream Publishing, 1986)

Castle, Ian, *The First Blitz: Bombing London in the First World War* (Oxford: Osprey Publishing, 2015)

Chambers, Veronika & Fred & Higgins, Rob, *Hospitals of London* (Stroud: Amberley Publishing, 2014)

Child, Alison, *Tell Me I'm Forgiven: The Story of Forgotten Stars Gwen Farrar and Norah Blaney* (Machynlleth: Tollington Press, 2019)

Collis, Rosa, *Colonel Barker's Monstrous Regiment: A Tale of Female Husbandry* (London: Virago, 2001)

Compton, John, 'The Night Architecture of the Thirties', *The Journal of the Decorative Arts Society 1890–1940* (Brighton), No. 4 (1980), 40–7

Cook, Matt, '"A New City of Friends": London and Homosexuality in the 1890s', *History Workshop Journal* (Oxford), No. 56 (Autumn 2003), 33–58

Cook, Matt, *London and the Culture of Homosexuality, 1885–1914* (Cambridge: Cambridge University Press, 2003)

Costello, John, *Love, Sex and War: Changing Values, 1939–1945* (London: Collins, 1985)

Cottrell, Anna, *London Writing of the 1930s* (Edinburgh: Edinburgh University Press, 2017)

De Courcy, Anne, *Debs at War* (London: Weidenfeld & Nicolson, 2005)

Crawford, Elizabeth, *The Women's Suffrage Movement: A Reference Guide, 1866–1928* (London: UCL Press, 1999)

Crisp, Quentin, *The Naked Civil Servant* (London: Flamingo, 1985)

Cuthbertson, Guy, *Peace at Last: A Portrait of Armistice Day, 11 November 1918* (New Haven: Yale University Press, 2018)

Devonshire, Deborah, *Wait for Me! Memoirs of the Youngest Mitford Sister* (London: John Murray, 2010)

Dickenson, Tommy, *Curing Queers: Mental Nurses and Their Patients, 1935–74* (Manchester: Manchester University Press, 2015)

Dorment, Richard, with contributions from Timothy Bidwell, Charlotte Gere, Mark Girouard and Duncan James, *Alfred Gilbert: Sculptor and Goldsmith by Royal Academy of Arts* (London: Weidenfeld & Nicolson, 1986)

Dorment, Richard, *Alfred Gilbert* (New Haven and London: Yale University Press, 1985)

Dorment, Richard, 'Alfred Gilbert's Memorial to Queen Alexandra', *The Burlington Magazine* (London), Vol. 122, No. 922, Special Issue Devoted to Sculpture (January 1980), 47–54

Edwards, Bronwen, 'Making the West End Modern: Space, Architecture and Shopping 1930s London', PhD dissertation, (University of the Arts, London, November 2004)

Edwards, Elaine (ed.), *Scotland's Land Girls: Breeches, Bombers and Backaches* (Edinburgh: NMS, 2010)

Edwards, Jason, *Alfred Gilbert's Aestheticism: Gilbert amongst Whistler, Wilde, Leighton, Pater and Burne-Jones* (Aldershot: Ashgate, 2006)

Enroth, Clyde, 'Mysticism in Two of Aldous Huxley's Early Novels', *Twentieth Century Literature* (Durham, NC), Vol. 6, No. 3 (October 1960), 123–132

Ewing, Elizabeth & Mackrell, Alice, *History of 20th Century Fashion* (London: Batsford, 1992)

Fabian, Robert, *London after Dark: An Intimate Record of Night Life in London, and a Selection of Crime Stories from the Case Book of Ex-Superintendent Robert Fabian* (London: Naldrett Press, 1954)

Fabian, Robert, *Fabian of the Yard* (London: Naldrett Press, 1950)

Farson, Daniel, *Marie Lloyd and the Music Hall* (London: Tom Stacey, 1972)

Featherstone, Simon, 'The Mill Girl and the Cheeky Chappie: British Popular Comedy and Mass Culture in the Thirties', *Critical Survey* (New York), Vol. 15, No. 2, Literature of the Thirties (2003), 3–22

Feigel, Lara, *The Love-Charms of Bombs: Restless Lives in the Second World War* (London: Bloomsbury, 2014)

Field, Geoffrey, 'Nights Underground in Darkest London: The Blitz, 1940–1941', *International Labor and Working-Class History* (Cambridge), No. 62, Class and Catastrophe: September 11 and Other Working Class-Disasters (fall 2002), 11–49

Fox, James, '"Traitor Painters": Artists and Espionage in the First World War, 1914–1918', *The British Art Journal* (London), Vol. 9, No. 3 (Spring 2009), 62–8

Friedman, Melvin, 'The Two Traditions of Eros', *Yale French Studies* (New Haven), No. 11, Eros, Variations on an Old Theme (1953), 91–100

Gardiner, Juliet, *The Blitz: The British under Attack* (London: HarperPress, 2011)

Gardner, Viv & Atkinson, *Diane, Actor and Activist*, (Manchester: Manchester University Press, 2019)

Gay, Verbon F. *The Story of Rainbow Corner, the American Red Cross Club Near Piccadilly Circus London, November 1942 to December 1943* (publisher unknown, 1944)

Getsy, David J., 'John Chamberlain's Pliability: The New Monumental Aluminium Works', *Burlington Magazine* (London), Vol. 153, No. 1304 (November 2011), 738–44

Gilbert, Cecil (ed.), *The Studio Diaries of Alfred Gilbert between 1890 and 1897, Volume One, 1890–1894* (Newcastle upon Tyne: C. Gilbert, 1987)

Gillies, Midge, *Waiting for Hitler, Voices from Britain on the Britain of Invasion* (London: Hodder & Stoughton, 2006)

Gillies, Midge, *Amy Johnson: Queen of the Air* (London: Victor Gollancz, 2003)

Gillies, Midge, *Marie Lloyd: The One and Only* (London: Victor Gollancz, 1999)

Ginsburg, Madeleine, 'The Making and Distribution of Clothes', *Costume* (London: Costume Society by the Dept of Textiles, V&A Museum), Vol. 1, Supplement 1 (1967), 14–22

Graham, Wendy, 'Henry James's Subterranean Blues: A Rereading of "the Princess Casamassima"', *Modern Fiction Studies* (Baltimore), Vol. 40, No. 1 (Spring 1994), 51–84

Graves, Charles, *Champagne and Chandeliers: The Story of the Café de Paris* (London: Odhams Press, 1958)

Graves, Charles, *Off the Record* (London: unknown publisher, 1941)

Grenfell, Joyce & Roose-Evans, James (eds), *Darling M: Letters to Her Mother, 1932–44* (London: Sceptre, 1997)

Gunderson, Brian, S., '"Slanguage", Part I: Letters A–C', *Air Power History* (Virginia), Vol. 47, No. 4 (Winter 2000), 54–9

Gunston, Bill, *Chronicle of Aviation* (London: Chronicle Communications, 1992)

Gurney, Peter, *The Making of Consumer Culture in Modern Britain* (London: Bloomsbury Academic, 2019)

Gussenhoven, Carlos, 'The English Rhythm Rule as an Accent Deletion Rule', *Phonology* (Cambridge), Vol. 8, No. 1 (1991), 1–35

Hammond, Ralph C., *My GI Aching Back* (New York: Hobson Book Press, 1946)

Hampson, Robert, '"Chance" and the Secret Life: Conrad,

Thackeray, Stevenson', *The Conradian* (Joseph Conrad Society, UK), Vol. 17, No. 2, Conrad and Gender (Spring 1993), 105–22

Harding, Thomas, *Legacy: One Family, a Cup of Tea and the Company that Took on the World* (London: William Heinemann, 2019)

Hardwick, Steve & Hodgin, Duane E., *WW II, Duty, Honor, Country: The Memories of Those Who Were There* (iUniverse)

Hastings, Selina, *Nancy Mitford, A Biography* (London: Hamish Hamilton, 1985)

Haworth-Booth, Mark, *E. McKnight Kauffer: A Designer and His Public* (London: Gordon Fraser, 1979)

Hibbert, Christopher; Weinreb, Ben; Keay, John; Keay, Julia & Weinreb, Matthew, *The London Encyclopaedia* (London: Macmillan, 2003)

Hodges, Graham Russell Gao, *Anna May Wong: From Laundryman's Daughter to Hollywood Legend* (Hong Kong: Hong Kong University Press, 2012)

Holden, Philip, 'Castle, Coffin, Stomach: "Dracula" and the Banality of the Occult', *Victorian Literature and Culture* (Cambridge), Vol. 29, No. 2 (2001), 469–85

Houlbrook, Matt, *Queer London* (Chicago: University of Chicago Press, 2005)

Howard, Diana, *London Theatres and Music Halls, 1850–1950* (London: Library Association, 1970)

Huneault, Kristina, 'Flower-Girls and Fictions: Selling on the Streets, *RACAR: Revue d'Art Canadienne / Canadian Art Review*, Vol. 23, No. 1/2 (1996), 52–70

Humm, Maggie (ed.), *The Edinburgh Companion to Virginia Woolf and the Arts* (Edinburgh: Edinburgh University Press, 2010)

Hutton, Mike, *Life in 1940s London* (Stroud: Amberley, 2014)

Jones, Clara, *Virginia Woolf: Ambivalent Activist* (Edinburgh: Edinburgh University Press, 2016)

Kapsis, Robert E., *Hitchcock: The Making of a Reputation* (Chicago: University of Chicago Press, 1992)

Kauffer, E. McKnight, 'Advertising Art: The Designer and the Public', *Journal of the Royal Society of Arts* (Royal Society for the Encouragement of Arts, Manufactures and Commerce), Vol. 87, No. 4488 (25 November 1938), 51–70

Kingcome, Brian, *A Willingness to Die* (Stroud: Tempus, 1999)

Kohn, Marek, *Dope Girls: The Birth of the British Drug Underground* (London: Granta, 1992)

Konody, P. G., 'Garden Sculpture, with Special Reference to the Fountain', *The Artist: An Illustrated Monthly Record of Arts, Crafts and Industries* (American Edition), Vol. 31, No. 262 (November 1901), 83–9

Laite, Julia, *The Disappearance of Lydia Harvey: A True Story of Sex, Crime and the Meaning of Justice* (London: Profile Books, 2021)

Laite, Julia A. & Gordon, Mary, 'Taking Nellie Johnson's Fingerprints: Prostitutes and Legal Identity in Early Twentieth-Century London', *History Workshop Journal* (Oxford), No. 65 (Spring 2008), 96–116

Lancaster, Bill, *The Department Store: A Social History* (Leicester: Leicester University Press, 1995)

Langdon-Davies, John, *Westminster Hospital: Two Centuries of Voluntary Service, 1719–1948* (London: John Murray, 1952)

Levine, Joshua, *Forgotten Voices of the Blitz and the Battle for Britain* (London: Ebury Press, 2017)

Levine, Joshua, *The Secret History of the Blitz* (London: Simon & Schuster, 2015)

Liggins, Emma, 'Prostitution and Social Purity in the 1880s and 1890s', *Critical Survey* (New York), Vol. 15, No. 3, 'New' Female Sexualities 1870–1930 (2003), 39–55

London County Council, *Survey of London: Volumes 31 & 32, St James Westminster, Part 2* (London: London County Council, 1963)

Maclaran, Pauline, 'Marketing and Feminism in Historic Perspective', *Journal of Historical Research in Marketing* (Bingley), Vol. 4, No. 3 (2012), 462–9

Maclean, Caroline, *Circles and Squares: The Lives and Art of the Hampstead Modernists* (London: Bloomsbury, 2021)

MacQueen-Pope, W., *Goodbye Piccadilly* (Newton Abbot: David & Charles, 1960)

Martin, Andrew, *Underground Overground: A Passenger's History of the Tube* (London: Profile Books, 2012)

Mason, Bobby Ann, 'Underground', *The Virginia Quarterly Review* (Charlottesville), Vol. 58, No. 2 (Spring 1982), 91–299

McAllister, Isabel, *Alfred Gilbert* (London: A&C Black, 1929)

McGilligan, Patrick, *Alfred Hitchcock: A Life in Darkness and Light* (London: John Wiley, 2003)

McLaughlan, Robbie, *Re-imagining the 'Dark Continent' in fin de siècle Literature* (Edinburgh: Edinburgh University Press, 2012)

Mills, John, *Up in the Clouds, Gentlemen Please* (London: Weidenfeld & Nicolson, 1980)

Minney, R. J., *The Two Pillars of Charing Cross: The Story of a Famous Hospital* (London: Cassell, 1967)

Moholy-Nagy, Sibyl, *Moholy-Nagy: Experiment in Totality* (Cambridge, Massachusetts & London: MIT Press, 1969)

Monsarrat, Nicholas, *Life Is a Four Letter Word* (London: Pan Books, 1969–72)

Moore, Wendy, *Endell Street* (London: Atlantic, 2020)

Morton, H. V., *The Nights of London* (London: Methuen, 1948)

Morton, James, *Gangland Soho* (London: Piatkus, 2008)

Mosley, Charlotte (ed.), *Love from Nancy: The Letters of Nancy Mitford* (London: Sceptre, 1994)

Nava, M., 'Wider Horizons and Modern Desire: The Contradictions of America and Racial Difference in London 1935–45', *New Formations: A Journal of Culture, Theory, Politics* (London), Vol. 37 (Spring 1999), 71–91

Newbold, O., 'Regent Street: An Historical Retrospect [sic]', *The Town Planning Review* (Liverpool), Vol. 3, No. 2 (July 1912), 86–93

Nixon, Barbara, *Raiders Overhead* (London: Lindsay Drummond, 1943)

Olsen, Donald J., *The City as a Work of Art: London, Paris, Vienna* (New Haven: Yale University Press, 1986)

Oxford, David, *The Archive Photographs Series – Piccadilly Circus* (Stroud: Chalford Publishing Company, 1995)

Panter-Downes, Mollie, *London War Notes 1939–1945* (London: Persephone, 2014)

Paris, Barry, *Louise Brooks, A Biography* (Minneapolis: University of Minnesota Press, 2000)

Paxton, Naomi, *Stage Rights!: The Actresses' Franchise League, Activism and Politics 1908–58* (Manchester: Manchester University Press, 2018)

Petro, P. (ed.), *Idols of Modernity: Movie Stars of the 1920s* (New Brunswick: Rutgers University Press, 2010)

Pevsener, Nikolaus, *Studies in Art, Architecture and Design, Volume Two, Victorian and After* (London: Thames & Hudson, 1968)

Pooley, Colin G., 'Getting to Know the City: The Construction of Spatial Knowledge in London in the 1930s', *Urban History* (Cambridge), Vol. 31, No. 2 (August 2004), 210–28

Porter, Jeff, *Lost Sound: The Forgotten Art of Radio Storytelling* (Chapel Hill: University of North Carolina Press, 2016)

Potvin, John, 'Vapour and Steam: The Victorian Turkish Bath, Homosocial Health, and Male Bodies on Display', *Journal of Design History* (Oxford), Vol. 18, No. 4 (Winter 2005), 319–33

Rappaport, Erika, 'Art, Commerce, or Empire? The Rebuilding of Regent Street, 1880–1927', *History Workshop Journal* (Oxford), No. 53 (Spring 2002), 94–117

Rappaport, Erika Diane, *Shopping for Pleasure: Women in the Making of London's West End* (Princeton: Princeton University Press, 2001)

Reay, Barry, 'Writing the Modern Histories of Homosexual England', *The Historical Journal* (Cambridge), Vol. 52, No. 1 (March 2009), 213–33

Reed, Jeremy, *The Dilly: A Secret History of Piccadilly Rent Boys* (London: Peter Owen Publishers, 2014)

Ribbat, Christoph, *Flickering Light: A History of Neon* (London: Reaktion Books, 2011)

Richardson, A. E., 'London Architecture in 1916', *The Burlington Magazine for Connoisseurs* (London), Vol. 30, No. 167 (February 1917), 82–3

Riley, Kathleen, *The Astaires: Fred & Adele* (Oxford: Oxford University Press, 2012)

Rose, Douglas, *Tiles of the Unexpected Underground: A Study of Six miles of Geometric Tile patterns on the London underground* (London: Capital Transport Publishing, 2007)

Rose, June, *Marie Stopes and the Sexual Revolution* (London: Faber, 1992)

Rose, Peter, 'The Coloured Relief Decoration of Robert Anning Bell', *The Journal of the Decorative Arts Society 1850 – the Present* (Brighton), No. 14, Turn of the Century Design: Cross Currents in Europe (1990), 16–23

Rose, Sonya, O., 'The "Sex Question" in Anglo-American Relations in the Second World War', *The International History Review* (Abingdon), Vol. 20, No. 4 (December 1998), 884–903

St Pierre, Matthew, *E.A. Dupont and His Contribution to British Film* (Madison: Farleigh Dickinson University Press, 2010)

Saltzman, Rachelle Hope, *A Lark for the Sake of Their Country: The 1926 General Strike Volunteers in Folklore and Memory* (Manchester: Manchester University Press, 2012)

Sandbrook, Dominic, *White Heat: A History of Britain in the Swinging Sixties* (London: Little, Brown, 2006)

Sanders, Lise Shapiro, *Consuming Fantasies: Labor, Leisure and the London Shopgirl, 1880–1920* (Columbus: Ohio State University Press, 2006)

Schutt, Sita, A., 'Close Up from a Distance: London and Englishness in Ford, Bram Stoker and Conan Doyle', *International Ford Madox Ford Studies* (Leiden), Vol. 4, Ford Madox Ford and the City (2005), 55–65

Scragg, Rebecca, 'Hanging Hitler: Joseph Flatter's *Mein Kamp Illustrated* Series, 1938–1942', in Shulamith Behr and Marian Malet, *Arts in Exile in Britain 1933–1945: Politics and Cultural Identity,* Yearbook of the Research

Centre for German and Austrian Exile Studies Vol. 6 (2004)

Sheard, Sally, *The Passionate Economist: How Brian Abel-Smith Shaped Global Health and Social Welfare* (Bristol: Bristol University Press, 2014)

Shenton, Caroline, *National Treasures: Saving the Nation's Art in World War II* (London: John Murray, 2021)

Sheppard, Francis, *The Treasury of London's Past: An Historical Account of the Museum of London and Its Predecessors, the Guildhall Museum and the London Museum* (London: HMSO, 1991)

Sitton, Robert, *Lady in the Dark: Iris Barry and the Art of Film* (New York: Columbia University Press, 2014)

Slide, Anthony, *A Special Relationship: Britain Comes to Hollywood and Hollywood Comes to Britain* (Jackson: University Press of Mississippi, 2015)

Spalding, Frances, *The Tate: A History* (London: Tate Gallery Publishing, 1998)

Spotts, Frederic, *Cursed Legacy: The Tragic Life of Klaus Mann* (New Haven: Yale University Press, 2016)

Summers, Julie, *Fashion on the Ration* (London: Profile Books, 2015)

Sweet, Matthew, *The West End Front: The Wartime Secrets of London's Grand Hotels* (London: Faber & Faber, 2011)

Tackley, Catherine, 'Race, Identity and the Meaning of Jazz in 1940s Britain', in Jon Stratton and Nabeel Zuberi (eds), *Black Popular Music in Britain since 1945* (London: Routledge, 2016), 11–26

Tate, Trudi & Kennedy, Kate, *The Silent Morning: Culture and Memory after the Armistice* (Manchester: Manchester University Press, 2013)

Taylor, D. J., *Bright Young People: The Rise and Fall of a Generation: 1918–1940* (London: Chatto & Windus, 2007)

Taylor, John Russell, *Hitch: The Life and Work of Alfred Hitchcock* (London: Faber & Faber, 1978)

Tomalin, Nicholas, 'Twenty-four Hours at Piccadilly Circus', *Sunday Times* Magazine, 14 February 1971; reprinted in *Nicholas Tomalin Reporting* (London: André Deutsch, 1975)

Toynbee, Jason, 'Race, History, and Black British Jazz', *Black Music Research Journal*, Vol. 33, No. 1 (Spring 2013), 1–25

Turner, Alwyn W., *The Last Post: Music, Remembrance and the Great War* (London: Aurum, 2014)

Ugolini, Laura, 'The Illicit Consumption of Military Uniforms in Britain, 1914–1918', *Journal of Design History* (Oxford), Vol. 24, No. 2, Uniforms in Design History, edited by Artemis Yagou (2011), 125–38

Wainwright, David, *The British Tradition: Simpson – A World of Style* (London: Quiller Press, 1996)

Walkowitz, Judith R., *Nights Out: Life in Cosmopolitan London* (New Haven & London: Yale University Press, 2012)

Ward, Laurence, *The London County Council Bomb Damage Maps 1939–1945* (London: Thames & Hudson, 2015)

White, Jerry, *London in the 20th Century* (London: Bodley Head, 2016)

White, Jerry, *Zeppelin Nights: London in the First World War* (London: Vintage, 2015)

Wildeblood, Peter, *Against the Law* (London: Victor Gollancz, 2012)

Winston, Diane, *Red-Hot and Righteous: The Urban Religion of the Salvation Army* (Cambridge, Massachusetts: Harvard University Press, 1999)

Willoughby, Harold R., 'Art and Advertising, London Underground Railways' Publicity Service', *The American Magazine of Art* (New York), Vol. 14, No. 8 (August 1923), 441–7

Witchard, Anne, *Lao She in London* (Hong Kong: Hong Kong University Press, 2012)

Wodehouse P. G. & Bolton, Guy, *Bring on the girls: The Improbable Story of Our Life in Musical Comedy, with Pictures to Prove It* (London: Herbert Jenkins, 1954)

Woodworth, Christine, 'The Company She Kept: The Radical Activism of Actress Kitty Marion from Piccadilly Circus to Times Square', *Theatre History Studies* (Pleasant Hill, California), vol. 32 (2012), 80–92

York, Peter, *The Blue Riband* (London: Penguin Books, 2013)

Ziegler, Philip, *London at War, 1939–1945* (London: Sinclair-Stevenson, 1995)

Fiction

Green, Henry, *Caught* (London: Harvill Panther, 2001; originally published Hogarth Press, 1943)

Maugham, Somerset, *Collected Short Stories*, Volume 4 (London: Vintage, 2009)

Maugham, Somerset, *Of Human Bondage* (London: Vintage, 2000; originally published William Heinemann, 1915)

Selvon, Sam, *The Lonely Londoners* (London: Penguin Modern Classics, 2006)

Streatfeild, Noel, *I Ordered a Table for Six* (London: Bello, 2018)

Text Permissions

Thanks to the estate of Sam Selvon for permission to reproduce the extract from *The Lonely Londoners*.

The quotation from Vera Brittain's *Testament of Youth* is included by permission of Mark Bostridge and T. J. Brittain-Carlin, Literary Executors for the Estate of Vera Brittain 1970.

The extract from Mass-Observation is reproduced with permission of Curtis Brown, London on behalf of the Trustees of the Mass Observation Archive © The Trustees of the Mass Observation Archive.

The extract by Joyce Grenfell is from *Darling Ma: Letters to Her Mother* by Joyce Grenfell © The Joyce Grenfell Memorial Trust 1997. Reproduced by permission of Sheil Land Associates Ltd.

Image Permissions

Alamy Stock Photo: (2 above) John Frost Newspapers; (3 above and 9 above) Chronicle; (7) The Print Collector; (8) Everett Collection Inc; (9 below) Pictorial Press Ltd; (10 below and 12 above) PA Images • (6 below) 'London, Piccadilly Circus' by Renzo Picasso, 1929, © Archivio Renzo Picasso, Genoa • (3 below) Look and Learn / Peter Jackson Collection / Bridgeman Images • Getty Images: (4 above) Hulton Archive / Stringer; (5 below) Popperfoto / Contributor; (6 above) Mirrorpix / Contributor; (10 above and 12 below) Sasha / Stringer; (11 above) Fox Photos / Stringer; (11 below) Hulton Deutsch / Contributor; (13) George Dallison / Stringer; (14 below and 15 above) Reg Speller / Stringer • (1 below and 2 middle) © Imperial War Museum (FEQ 99, HU 21148) • (16) Lieut. Arthur L. Cole / Canada. Dept. of National Defence / Library and Archives Canada / PA-152103 • Mary Evans Picture Library: (4 below and 14 above) © Illustrated London News Ltd / Mary Evans; (5 above) Mary Evans / Jazz Age Club Collection; (15 below) Mary Evans / Grenville Collins Postcard Collection • (2 below) © National Portrait Gallery, London • (1 above) Punch Cartoon Library / TopFoto • (15 middle) ANL / Shutterstock.

Index

Index

About the Author

Midge Gillies is the author of seven non-fiction books, including biographies of the pioneering pilot Amy Johnson (Weidenfeld & Nicolson, 2003) and the Edwardian music hall star Marie Lloyd (Victor Gollancz, 1999).

Her book about the real lives of prisoners of war, *The Barbed-Wire University* (Aurum Press, 2011) was described by Nicholas Lezard of the *Guardian* as 'one of the best war books I have ever read'.

Midge studied History at Girton College and was Royal Literary Fund Fellow at Magdalene College, Cambridge for three years. She is Academic Director of Creative Writing at the University of Cambridge Institute of Continuing Education and has a PhD from the University of East Anglia.

She lives in Cambridgeshire with her husband, award-winning crime novelist Jim Kelly.